Psychological Aspects of Serious Illness:

Chronic Conditions, Fatal Diseases, and Clinical Care

Master Lectures in Psychology

Psychological Aspects of Serious Illness:
Chronic Conditions, Fatal Diseases, and Clinical Care

Master Lecturers

Gregory M. Herek

Sandra M. Levy

Salvatore R. Maddi

Shelley E. Taylor

Donald L. Wertlieb

Edited by
Paul T. Costa, Jr.
and Gary R. VandenBos

AMERICAN PSYCHOLOGICAL ASSOCIATION
WASHINGTON, DC 20036

Library of Congress Cataloging-in-Publication Data

Psychological aspects of serious illness: chronic conditions, fatal
　　diseases, and clinical care / master lecturers, Gregory M. Herek
　　. . . [et al.]; edited by Paul T. Costa, Jr. and Gary R. VandenBos.
　　　　p.　　cm.
　　Includes bibliographical references.
　　ISBN 1-55798-105-1: $18.00 ($24.00 nonmember)
　　1. Sick—Psychology. 2. Terminally ill—Psychology. 3. Health
behavior. I. Herek, Gregory M. II. Costa, Paul T. III. VandenBos,
Gary R.
　　[DNLM: 1. Attitude to Death. 2. Catastrophic Illness—psychology. 3. Chronic Disease—psychology. 4. Diabetes Mellitus,
Insulin-Dependent—psychology. 5. Health Behavior. WT 500
P974]
R726.5.P777　　　1990
616'.001'9—dc20
DNLM/DLC　　　　　　　　　　　　　　　　　　　　90-14494
for Library of Congress　　　　　　　　　　　　　　　CIP

Copies may be ordered from:
Order Department, P.O. Box 2710
Hyattsville, MD 20784

Published by the American Psychological Association, Inc.
1200 Seventeenth Street, N.W., Washington, DC 20036

Printed in the United States of America on acid-free paper
First edition

CONTENTS

PREFACE

The link between health and behavior is of great national concern. It is the subject of federal policy debates. It is the focus of a vast array of clinical research. It is an issue of increasing attention in training programs. It is the subject of major public information campaigns.

At this point, it is well known that the National Academy of Sciences has documented that as much as 50% of all of the mortality from the 10 leading causes of death in the United States can be traced to life-style—that is, specific individual decisions about behavior, whether it relates to excessive consumption of high caloric fatty foods; noncon-sumption of fruits, vegetables, and high-fiber products; wearing seatbelts while driving or riding in a car; the decision to smoke or not; engaging in regular physical exercise; the excessive consumption of alcoholic beverages; going for regular medical examinations and dental check-ups; abusing addictive drugs, including intravenous needle sharing; high-risk sexual behavior; or many other discrete health-related behaviors and decisions.

Now it is fairly well accepted that physical health problems have complex etiologies. Rarely is there a single cause—or a single treatment. Health psychologists, both as researchers and practitioners, are examin-ing a broader and broader array of issues related to psychological aspects of physical health and physical illness. They are developing and evaluating educational and information strategies geared to individuals within every segment of the age continuum designed for facilitating health enhancement and disease prevention. Psychologists are studying how individuals perceive (or fail to perceive) emerging symptoms of physical functioning and physical illness—and the decision-making process about how and when to respond to them. The psychological and behavioral responses to illness, particularly to serious or chronic conditions, is increasingly becoming a topic of research concern—including why some individuals are disabled by a condition when others are not, how personal and situational factors contribute to relapse and prevention, and how different individuals manage chronic illness and pain. In this regard, there is a growing consensus about the importance of enduring individual differences in effecting all of the above processes.

As this brief listing of issues in health psychology reveals or suggests, there is a rich diversity of issues that are being addressed by health psychologists. We would need to have an handbook of health psychology to cover all of these. The present volume is a sampler of some of the current interests in the field, although all of the chapters here relate to the psychological aspects of serious illness. Even so, many issues have not been addressed, such as national health policy issues, systematic issues in the organization and delivery of health researchers and health practitioners, and the intervention and treatment strategies in relation to specific diseases.

The chapters in this volume highlight some of the major issues in the psychological aspects of serious illness. Shelley Taylor and Lisa Aspinwall deal with the psychosocial factors associated with chronic diseases, such as cancer, hypertension, diabetes, and rheumatoid arthritis and speak of health attitudes and behaviors as well as cognitive and behavioral interventions. Donald Wertlieb and colleagues present an overview of childhood diabetes and argue the usefulness of a stress and coping perspective in recent and future research. Gregory Herek tackles one of the most pressing issues that developed in the 1980s and will occupy a good deal of attention in the decade ahead: acquired immune deficiency syndrome (AIDS) and the social stigma that has been and remains associated with it. Salvatore Maddi offers an existential perspective on the options and dilemmas presented to individuals and society by the technological advances that allow for extraordinary attempts to prolong life. Finally, Sandra Levy discusses some of the bioethical issues involved in dealing with dying patients and their families, such as levels of medical care, withdrawing life support, "hastening" death, appropriate types of and places for treatment at both the preterminal and terminal stages, follow-up care for survivors of the deceased patient, and implications for therapists.

Paul T. Costa, Jr.
Gary R. VandenBos

PSYCHOSOCIAL ASPECTS OF CHRONIC ILLNESS

S helley E. Taylor is a professor of social psychology and health psychology at the University of California at Los Angeles. She is also the director of the Health Psychology Training Program. Taylor received her PhD from Yale University in social psychology in 1972. Following a one-year appointment in the Department of Administrative Sciences at Yale, she was an assistant and associate professor of psychology at Harvard University from 1972 to 1979. In 1980, she joined the faculty at UCLA, where she helped develop the Health Psychology Program, which she currently co-directs with Bertram Raven and Christine Dunkel-Schetter.

Taylor's publications have spanned a wide range of problems in adjustment to chronic disease and disability. Her early work concerned psychological adjustment to breast cancer and the psychological consequences of treatment, such as mastectomy (versus lumpectomy), chemotherapy, and radiotherapy. Other of her investigations have included the psychological impact of hospitalization, the relationship of attributions and beliefs in control to adjustment to chronic disease, the impact of cancer on family members, social comparison processes as methods of coping with stressful events, sources of satisfaction and dissatisfaction among cancer support group members, psychological consequences of CPR training for family members and high-risk cardiac patients, determinants of reactions to successful and failed kidney transplants, and the exploration of reactions to multiple episodes of a chronic disease. She is perhaps best known for her work that explores the interface of social cognition and health psychology, especially the "illusions" that help people cope with illness.

Taylor is the author or coauthor of six books and over 100 articles. She is the author of *Health Psychology*, one of the few textbooks in the field (Random House, 1986, currently under revision). She has contributed to numerous volumes on health research, writing on her work concerning adjustment to chronic disease.

Taylor is the recipient of a number of awards, including the Distinguished Scientific Award for an Early Career Contribution to Psychology, presented by the American Psychological Association (APA) in 1980. She has also been the recipient of a Research Scientist Development Award from the National Institute of Mental Health from 1981 to 1986 and from 1986 to 1991. She is a Fellow of the APA, the Society of Behavioral Medicine, and the Academy of Behavioral Medicine Research. In 1988, she was a Science Weekend lecturer at the APA annual convention, presenting her research on illusions. She has been the recipient of many research grants from the National Science Foundation, the National Institute of Mental Health, the National Heart, Lung, and Blood Institute, and the National Cancer Institute, and currently holds grants to study (a) social comparison as coping processes, (b) psychosocial processes as cofactors in the development of AIDS, (c) adjustment to life-threatening illnesses and treatments, and (d) consequences of CPR training for families of cardiac patients.

PSYCHOSOCIAL ASPECTS OF CHRONIC ILLNESS

Introduction

Chronic disease is the major health problem facing the nation. Its prevalence is substantial. For example, arthritis in its various forms afflicts 37 million Americans, with more than 2 million suffering from rheumatoid arthritis (R. C. Lawrence et al., 1989). In addition, 5 million people have or have had cancer (American Cancer Society, 1989); diabetes afflicts 11 million people (American Diabetes Association, 1986); more than 2 million people have sustained a stroke (American Heart Association, 1988); almost 5 million people have a history of heart attack or angina pectoris (American Heart Association, 1988), nearly 29 million people have hypertension (U.S. Bureau of the Census, 1989), and estimates of the prevalence of high blood pressure run as high as 60 million people (American Heart Association, 1988). These statistics represent a major change from patterns of illness at the turn of the century, when acute infectious disorders, such as influenza, tuberculosis, measles, and polio were both the most prevalent disorders and the major causes of death. Because chronic diseases are ones with which people often live for many years, their active management contributes substantially to the more than $500 billion that is spent annually on health care.

The role of behavioral factors in the development of chronic disease is increasingly clear. For example, the risk factors for coronary artery disease, which is the major cause of death in the United States, include a diet high in calories, fat, and salt; a high serum cholesterol level; a sedentary life-style; being overweight; cigarette smoking; hypertension; and Type A behavior (Kannel & Eaker, 1986). Hypertension, the most prevalent chronic disease and a precursor for coronary artery disease, has been related to low socioeconomic status, poor dietary habits, poor exercise habits, exposure to environments that require sustained vigilance and coping, such as demanding work settings, and certain personality predispositions involving dominance/submission and difficulties in the expression of anger (Krantz et al., 1987). Cancer has been related to a diet high in fat and low in fiber, to smoking, and to exposure to specific carcinogens, among other causes (American Cancer Society, 1989).

We begin this chapter with a consideration of the psychosocial factors in the development of chronic disease, the nature of the models that have examined these possible links, and the state of the evidence at present. We next turn to the modification of risk factors and adherence to treatment regimens in chronic disease. We then address the psychosocial sequelae of chronic disease including emotional responses, such as depression and anxiety, and the role of premorbid psychological reactions in exacerbating these reactions. In this context, we examine the pharmacologic and psychologic interventions that have been employed to reduce distress and improve quality of life. We then consider the spontaneous coping efforts and use of social support that patients enlist in response to the specific problems and emotional distress posed by chronic illness. Finally, we consider quality of life among the chronically ill and directions for future research and intervention.

A word about the nature of the evidence is warranted. Many hundreds of empirical studies were reviewed for this chapter. We are including only those that address the issues noted above and that, in our judgment, meet minimum criteria of competent research. This means that many studies have been jettisoned in the process. Because of space limitations, it is not possible to evaluate the methods and data collection of individual investigations. We note specific studies that have been especially well designed to make a particular point and note as well careful reviews of the literature that promote the ability to draw broad conclusions. This review does not provide methodological detail and

Preparation of this manuscript was supported by National Institute of Mental Health grant MH 34167, National Institute of Mental Health grant MH 42258, and National Institute of Mental Health grant MH 42152. Taylor was supported by a Research Scientist Development Award from the National Institute of Mental Health (MH 00311), and Aspinwall was supported by a National Science Foundation Fellowship.

evaluation; it does not supplant individual consideration of specific studies, but rather attempts to review the best literature and to point to the most appropriate directions for further inquiry.

Psychosocial Factors in the Development of Chronic Diseases

Philosophers and scientists have long speculated about the roles that personality and stress may play in the development of illness. In the 1930s and 1940s, Flanders Dunbar (1943), Franz Alexander (1950), and their associates developed personality profiles of those prone to several chronic diseases, including hypertension, coronary artery disease, cancer, ulcers, and rheumatoid arthritis (RA). Convincing evidence regarding these relationships, however, was lacking, in part because testable models were largely absent. Over the past few decades, the research picture has improved. Investigators have elucidated both general models that relate psychosocial factors to an array of disorders and more specific models that examine psychosocial factors that may be particularly implicated in a specific order.

General Models

In terms of general models, recent research using meta-analysis suggests that a negative affective style marked by depression, anxiety, and hostility may be associated with the development of several chronic diseases, including coronary artery disease, asthma, proneness to headaches, ulcers, and arthritis (Friedman & Booth-Kewley, 1987; see also Peterson, Seligman, & Vaillant, 1988). These findings suggest the possibility of a disease-prone personality, although at present the exact nature of the relationship is uncertain. Negative emotional states clearly result from illness, but longitudinal studies also suggest the reverse direction of causality. The biopsychosocial pathways whereby such relationships might occur are an obvious direction for future research: A negative emotional state may produce pathogenic physiologic changes; it may lead people to practice faulty health behaviors; it may produce illness behavior but no underlying pathology; or it may be associated with illness via other factors in a presently undetermined manner.

Complementing the research on negative affectivity and disease is the increasing focus on the potentially protective role of positive emotional states. Chief among these are optimism and perceived control. Optimists appear to experience fewer physical symptoms (Scheier & Carver, 1985), and they may show faster or better recoveries from certain illnesses (Scheier, Weintraub, & Carver, 1986). Beliefs in personal control or self-efficacy appear to affect the likelihood of developing illness both by directly influencing the practice of health behaviors (Allred & Smith, 1989; Bandura, 1986; Wiebe & McCallum, 1986) and by buffering individuals against the adverse effects of stress (Cohen & Edwards, 1989). The relation of these positive states to negative affectivity also merits consideration (Smith, Pope, Rhodewalt, & Poulton, 1989).

Type A Behavior Syndrome

Researchers have also focused on specificity models of the psychosocial factor–illness relationship, that is, the relation of particular personality predispositions to specific diseases. Chief among these has been the continued exploration of the Type A behavior syndrome in coronary artery disease, characterized by competitive drive, impatience, hostility, and rapid speech and motor movements. Research demonstrates that Type A behavior as measured by the structured interview, although not by questionnaire measures, predicts both the physiological changes that have been associated with the development of coronary heart disease (CHD), and the development of CHD itself (see Booth-Kewley & Friedman, 1987; Contrada, Wright, & Glass, 1985; Friedman & Booth-Kewley, 1987; Matthews, 1988). Recent work analyzing the components of Type A behavior suggests that hostility, rather than competitiveness and time urgency, is strongly related to CHD (Dembroski & Costa, 1987; Friedman & Booth-Kewley, 1987; Hecker, Chesney, Black, & Frautschi, 1988). Other negative emotional states may also be implicated (Friedman & Booth-Kewley, 1987).

The Type A behavior pattern is associated with enhanced physiological reactivity to stress, which may be the mechanism that initiates and hastens the development of CHD (Contrada et al. 1985; Krantz & Manuck, 1984). Type As may be genetically predisposed to enhanced sympathetic nervous system activity, suggesting that Type A behavior may be, at least in part, a result as well as a cause of excessive neuroendocrine reactions to environmental stressors (Krantz & Deckel, 1983). Type As may not simply react to stress with enhanced neuroendocrine responses, they may also create physiologically more taxing situations. In responding psychologically to their enhanced physiological reactivity, Type As may take situations that others would experience as less stressful and make them more so. Thus, the Type A behavior pattern may represent an ongoing process of creating challenge and responding with demand-engendering behavior that produces pathogenic physiological results (Smith, 1989).

The propensity for Type As to get themselves into stressful situations has been regarded as a potential general risk factor for physical disorder (Suls & Sanders, 1988). While Type A behavior does not appear to be associated with illness in general, Type As are more likely to have accidents, to die from accidents or violence, or to have cerebrovascular and peripheral atherosclerosis. Type As may be more prone to migraine and muscle contraction headaches as well (Woods, Morgan, Day, Jefferson, & Harris, 1984). Type As may also exhibit higher levels of other risk factors for cardiovascular disease, such as smoking and serum cholesterol. Type As appear to have a slightly increased risk of dying from cancer (Fox, Ragland, Brand, & Rosenman, 1987). The Type A behavior, then, appears to be a risk factor not only for CHD, but for a selected array of other disorders as well.

Psychosocial Factors and Cancer

For many years, researchers have suspected that there may be links between a passive, acquiescent, or repressed personality style and the development or progression of cancer (e.g., Bahnson, 1981; Temoshok, 1987). Convincing research relating personality variables to cancer onset is generally lacking in a large part because such studies are difficult to design (Fox, 1978). However, longitudinal studies of individual predispositions avoid some of these methodological problems by looking at personality inventory scores collected some years earlier and relating them to subsequent development of cancer (e.g., Dattore, Shontz, & Coyne, 1980).

Generally, research has focused on two potential psychosocial factors in the development of cancer: depression and distressed interpersonal relationships. Evidence attempting to relate early depression to later onset of cancer has been inconsistent (e.g., Fox, 1978). Some studies have found a positive association between depression and cancer (e.g., Fox, 1978), whereas others have found a negative relation (e.g., Zonderman, Costa, & McCrea, 1989). Lack or loss of social support has also been proposed to affect the onset and course of cancer (Sklar & Anisman, 1981). Again, the results have been inconsistent, with some studies finding social isolation to be associated with a higher risk of cancer, and others finding no relation at all (Fox, 1988; Joffrees, Reed, & Nomura, 1985; Kaplan & Reynolds, 1988; Keehn, 1980; Reynolds & Kaplan, 1986; Thomas & Duszynski, 1974).

Researchers have also attempted to relate personality factors to the course of cancer—that is, to whether the cancer progresses rapidly or slowly (Levy, 1983). The data are not consistent regarding this relation either. Some research has suggested that a rapid course of illness terminating in an early death is characteristic of polite, unaggressive, acquiescent individuals, whereas a longer course of illness and better immune functioning is associated with a more combative, angry stance toward illness and toward medical practitioners (e.g., Derogatis, Abeloff, & Melasaratos, 1979; Levy, Herberman, Maluish, Schlien, & Lippman, 1985; Pettingale, Greer, & Tee, 1977; Rogentine et al., 1979). However, the evidence remains equivocal and may depend in part upon the stage of the disease (e.g., Cassileth et al., 1985; Cassileth, Walsh, & Lusk, 1988). Psychosocial factors may also interact with other risk factors to enhance overall risk. For example, Linkins and Comstock (1988) found that a depressive mood had no general effect on cancer risk alone, but substantially elevated cancer risk in conjunction with smoking.

Psychosocial Factors and Hypertension

Stress has been suspected to be a contributor to hypertension for many years (Henry & Cassel, 1969), and a large body of literature indicates that stressful events evoke rises in blood pressure. These responses appear to be augmented in individuals diagnosed with or at risk for hypertension (Fredrikson & Matthews, in press). Chronically hypertensive individuals show stronger blood pressure responses than do normotensives to a wide variety of stressors and take longer to return to baseline following the termination of the stressful event. Stressful events that require active adaptation may have a greater role in the development of hypertension among borderline hypertensives than do stressful events that require only passive acceptance. However, in those already diagnosed with hypertension, all stressful events appear to produce elevated blood pressure responses.

The idea of a hypertensive personality has been in the literature for decades. Evidence sustaining such a concept, however, is weak (Krantz & Glass, 1984; Krantz et al., 1987). Although personality factors do not appear to be sufficient for the development of hypertension, they may be important when combined with other risk factors. A large amount of research has focused on suppressed rage or hostility as a predictor of hypertension (e.g., Dimsdale et al., 1986; Harburg et al., 1973; James, 1987; Sommers-Flanagan & Greenberg, 1989). Blacks have a particularly high risk for hypertension. James and his colleagues (e.g., James, Hartnett, & Kalsbeek, 1983, 1984) have developed the concept of "John Henryism," which refers to a personality predisposition to cope actively with social stressors. The concept is based on the story of John Henry, the "steel-driving" man, an uneducated black laborer who allegedly defeated a mechanical steam drill in a contest to see which could complete the most work in the shortest period of time. After winning the battle, John Henry reportedly dropped dead from exhaustion. James used this story as a metaphor for the physiological impact of unsuccessful efforts to achieve among Black men with low levels of education. John Henryism is assumed to become lethal when active coping efforts are likely to be unsuccessful, as may be the case among the disadvantaged, especially lower-income and poorly educated Blacks.

Psychosocial Factors and Rheumatoid Arthritis

The possibility of an RA personality has been a prominent idea for nearly 100 years. The personality type has been characterized as perfectionistic, depressed, and restricted in emotional expression, especially the expression of anger. Although a number of studies have investigated these possibilities, most have failed to control for appropriate sociodemographic and disease factors or failed to include appropriate control groups, thus rendering conclusions questionable. Findings from studies that have correlated negative personality characteristics with arthritis are more reasonably explained as reactions to rather than causes of the disease (Anderson, Bradley, Young, McDaniel, & Wise, 1985).

Efforts to relate stress to the onset or course of RA have also been problematic. The literature has consistently identified disturbed interpersonal relationships as major stressful events among RA patients, and it is possible that these events bear a relation to the etiology of RA (Anderson et al., 1985). In an extensive and careful review of the literature, Anderson et al. (1985) concluded that the role of psychological factors in the etiology of RA remains unclear, although psychological factors appear to play an important role in its course. More so than other patients with chronic medical disorders, RA patients appear to maintain higher electromyograph (EMG) levels near their affected joints, show greater increases and slower returns to base EMG levels in response to stress, and show greater increases in electrodermal activity in response to stress. A likely focus for future research will be the potential of psychoimmunologic mediation of these effects.

Psychosocial Factors and Diabetes

No convincing research evidence suggests the existence of a diabetes-prone personality or of distinctive individual differences that are associated with the development of diabetes. There is also little research to suggest that particular coping methods or ways of dealing with stress are associated with the onset or exacerbation of diabetes. However, among Type II diabetics, stress *may* be implicated as a causal factor, and it clearly aggravates the course of diabetes (Surwit & Feinglos, 1988). At least 14 studies have reported direct links between stress and poor diabetic control (see Brand, Johnson, & Johnson, 1986; Hanson & Pichert, 1986), and this relationship appears to be unmediated by adherence (Hanson, Henggeler, & Burghen, 1987); coping efforts (Frenzel, McCaul, Glasgow, & Schafer, 1988); or insulin regimen, diet, or exercise (Hanson & Pichert, 1986). The role of stress in the onset and aggravation of Type I diabetes has yet to be conclusively demonstrated.

In summary, research relating psychosocial variables to the development and progression of chronic diseases continues to focus on general relationships between personality predispositions and illness out-comes, as well as on relationships between specific personality factors and specific illnesses. In terms of etiology, negative emotional states have been related to several chronic disorders, and research suggests the usefulness of examining positive emotional states as possible protec-tive factors against these disorders. Type A behavior, particularly the hostility component, has been related to the etiology of CHD, and the etiology of cancer and RA may be marked by disturbances in emotional expression or interpersonal relationships. In terms of the course of illness, stress appears to exacerbate several chronic disorders, most notably Type II diabetes, hypertension, and RA. Negative emotions may be related to a rapid course of cancer. More complex interactive models relating specific stressors or coping mechanisms to other risk factors to predict the onset or exacerbation of disease have yet to be fully developed, but appear to be promising in understanding several chronic diseases, including hypertension and cancer. The research evidence clearly points to a need for models relating psychosocial variables to disease onset and progression more carefully and to a need to detail more clearly the biologic pathways by which such linkages may occur.

Health Behaviors and Chronic Illness

The prevalence of chronic disease is influenced by the practice of health-compromising behaviors and the nonpractice of health-enhancing behaviors. For example, 25% of all cancer deaths and approximately 350,000 premature deaths from heart attack could be avoided each year by eliminating just one risk factor: smoking (American Heart Association, 1988). A 10% weight reduction through dietary modification and exercise in men aged 35 to 55 years would produce an estimated 20% decrease in coronary artery disease (American Heart Association, 1984; Ashley & Kannel, 1974) and would lower the prevalence of degenerative arthritis, gastrointestinal cancer, diabetes, strokes, and heart attacks. Accordingly, psychologists have been heavily involved in efforts to modify health behaviors.

Changing Health Attitudes

Changing health habits is in part a process of changing attitudes. Al-though a number of conceptual models have been developed to explain attitudes toward health practices, there is now theoretical convergence on the relevant beliefs. Specifically, we know that people are most likely to practice a good health measure or to change a faulty one when the threat to health is severe; personal vulnerability or the likelihood of developing the disorder is high; the person believes that he or she is able to perform the response that will reduce the threat (self-efficacy); the response is effective in overcoming the threat (response efficacy); and the person intends to engage in the behavior (behavioral intention). These five elements borrow from distinct theoretical models, specifically Bandura's (1986) self-efficacy framework, Rogers' (1984) protection motivation theory, Rosenstock's (1974) health belief model, and Ajzen & Fishbein's (1977) theory of reasoned action.

These principles have proven useful in identifying not only who practices which health behaviors, but in targeting particular beliefs for change (e.g., Becker & Janz, 1987; Wilson et al., 1986, regarding diabetes care). For example, by altering perceptions of response efficacy of a particular health measure or by providing communications that enhance perceptions of personal vulnerability, attitudes and, to a lesser extent, behavior can be changed. Such interventions have been used to enhance participation in particular health-oriented screening programs, such as X-rays, physical exams, and breast cancer screening programs (e.g., Becker, Maiman, Kirscht, Haefner, & Drachman, 1977; Haefner & Kirscht, 1970; Kirscht, Becker, Haefner, & Maiman, 1978). Similarly, enhancing expectations of self-efficacy for changing a health habit, such as stopping smoking, produces a greater likelihood of success (Maddux & Rogers, 1983; Rippetoe & Rogers, 1987). However, attitude change procedures are not sufficient to alter health habits. These techniques may instill the motivation to change a health habit and the knowledge base for doing so, but they do not provide the skills necessary to actually alter behavior and maintain behavior change.

Cognitive–Behavioral Interventions

Accordingly, psychologists have turned to the principles of learning theory and to cognitive–behavioral therapy in an effort to modify health habits. These approaches focus on the target behavior itself: The conditions that elicit and maintain it, and the factors that reinforce it. Such interventions also recognize the significance of people's cognitions about their behavior. That is, people generate internal monologues about their health habits that can interfere with their ability to change a behavior (Meichenbaum & Cameron, 1974). For example, self-generated doubts about giving up smoking may interfere with the quitting process ("I'll never be able to give up smoking"). Thus, the cognitive–behavioral change perspective adopts the principles of cognitive–behavioral change to attack both cognitions and behaviors related to health habits. The most effective approach to health habit modification often comes from combining multiple cognitive–behavioral change techniques. Such interventions have been termed *broad-spectrum* behavior therapy or *multimodal* behavior therapy.

Most programs of cognitive–behavioral modification use self-observation and self-monitoring as first steps toward behavior change. These techniques involve pinpointing the target behavior (e.g., identifying the urge to smoke) and recording and charting the behavior. Sometimes, self-monitoring itself produces behavior change. Interventions are then initiated to modify the focal behavior itself. Classical conditioning is often used in the modification of health habits. For example, drinking alcohol may be paired with Antabuse to induce vomiting. Principles of operant conditioning are often included, with patients instructed to make use of principles of positive reinforcement, negative reinforcement, and punishment to control target behaviors, such as overeating, smoking, or alcohol abuse. Stimulus control involves manipulating stimuli in the environment to control the occurrence of the behavior. The client may be trained to rid the environment of discriminative stimuli that elicit the problem behavior (such as having one's favorite ashtray on the breakfast table, thus inducing the desire to smoke) and to create new discriminative stimuli that signal the new target behavior to be reinforced. Eating, for example, is heavily under the control of discriminative stimuli, such as the presence of desirable foods, and so those attempting to lose weight are urged to rid their homes of tempting stimuli.

An important feature of most cognitive–behavioral interventions for health habits is enlisting the client as a comanager in the behavior change process. The client acts at least partly as his or her own therapist; with outside guidance, he or she learns to control the antecedents and consequents of the target behavior to be modified. The client may be trained in the techniques of positive self-reward, which involve reinforcing oneself with something desirable following successful modification of the target behavior. For example, after meeting target weight loss for a week, the person might reward himself or herself with a movie or remove an aversive stimulus from the environment, such as taking the Miss Piggy poster off the refrigerator.

Another principle that is widely used in behavior modification is contingency contracting, in which the client forms a contract with another person, such as the therapist, detailing what rewards and punishments will be contingent upon the performance or nonperformance of some behavior. For example, Thoresen and Mahoney (1974) reported the case of a Black woman who was attempting to control her abuse of amphetamines. She deposited a large sum of money with her therapist and authorized the therapist to give $50 to the Ku Klux Klan every time she abused amphetamines. This contract was effective in inducing her to change her behavior.

As noted earlier, covert self-control involves the manipulation and alteration of private events. Clients may be trained to respond to smoking urges by thinking antismoking thoughts ("Smoking causes cancer") and thoughts that favor nonsmoking ("My food will taste better if I stop smoking"). Behavioral assignments are commonly employed in health-behavior change programs and may ease the transition from a therapist-controlled to a client-controlled intervention. Behavioral assignments are home-practice activities that are integrated into a therapeutic intervention. For example, if an early therapy session with an obese client involved training in self-monitoring, the client would be encouraged to practice systematic recording at home.

Many faulty health habits are believed to arise at least partly in response to anxiety, especially social anxiety, and over time they come to be evoked by this emotional experience. The anxious obese person at a dinner party, for example, may overeat in response to his or her social anxiety. As a consequence, a number of programs designed to alter health habits include social skills training, relaxation training, or assertiveness training as part of the intervention package. The goals of these programs are to reduce the anxiety that occurs in target settings, to introduce new skills for dealing with situations that previously aroused anxiety, and to provide an alternative behavior for the faulty health habit that arose in response to the situation.

Relapse Prevention

The fact that many patients relapse after initially changing their behavior successfully is a great concern. Relapse is a particular problem with the addictive disorder of alcoholism, smoking, and overeating (Brownell, Marlatt, Lichtenstein, & Wilson, 1986), where relapse rates range from 50% to 90% (Marlatt & Gordon, 1985). Relapse has been tied to a variety of factors, both internal and external to the individual. These include negative emotional states such as stress, depression, or anxiety; a decline in motivation; the absence of proximal goals toward maintaining behavior change; lack of social support for the behavior change; or current involvement in an interpersonal situation involving conflict. Relapse is also highly likely to occur when there is a reinstatement of environmental cues that were previously associated with the behavior (e.g., being in a bar and resuming drinking or smoking) (see Brownell et al., 1986, for a review).

Traditionally, behavioral interventions to control relapse have centered on three techniques. Booster sessions following the termination of the initial treatment phase have been introduced for the addictive disorders, but are generally unsuccessful (Brownell et al., 1986). Some programs have added additional components such as relaxation therapy or assertiveness training, but the addition of such components does not appear reliably to increase adherence rates. In fact, the opposite may be the case, inasmuch as complex treatment regimens are more difficult to adhere to than simple ones (Turk & Meichenbaum, 1989). The third approach is to consider abstinence a lifelong treatment process, as in Alcoholics Anonymous and other well-established lay treatment programs. Although this approach has been successful in many cases, it has the disadvantages of leaving people with the perception that they are constantly vulnerable to relapse and that they are not in control of their habit (Brownell et al., 1986). Expectations of self-efficacy are important in the practice of certain health behaviors and adherence to treatment (e.g., Bandura, 1986; Rosenbaum & Smira, 1986).

Marlatt and Gordon (1985) and their associates (e.g., Brownell et al., 1986) argued that relapse prevention must be integrated into treatment programs from the outset. They pointed out that people are less likely to relapse if they are initially highly committed and motivated to engage in behavior change. Consequently, methods of increasing initial motivation and the use of screening techniques to weed out those people who are not truly committed to behavior change are ways of reducing relapse. Brownell et al. (1986) pointed out the ethical dilemmas involved in screening criteria, which remains a highly controversial area.

Relapse preventions skills can also be incorporated in the initial behavior change period. Typically, each individual is urged to identify his or her likely high-risk-for-relapse situations, to develop coping skills, and to learn how to reappraise events in ways that will render relapse in such situations less likely. For example, high-risk situations for diabetics include eating out in restaurants and receiving inappropriate food offers from others. Cue elimination or restructuring one's environment in order to avoid those situations that are most likely to cue the target behavior is a technique for avoiding relapses.

Long-term maintenance of behavior change may be enhanced by life-style balancing. This refers to modifying one's life-style in a healthy direction, for example, by increasing social support and adding relaxation or exercise to one's daily life (Marlatt & Gordon, 1985). Long-term monitoring of the target behavior also reduces the likelihood of relapse. Although most of the research testing that Marlatt and Gordon's (1985) relapse prevention model has examined involves health behaviors such as smoking and weight control (see Ginter, 1988), this model has also been employed in studies of chronically ill patients' adherence to medication. Examining the determinants of relapse to dietary treatment of diabetes, Kirkley and Fisher (1988) found that, as the model predicted, most nonadherence episodes occurred in specific high-risk situations.

Health Habit Change: An Evaluation

Multimodal cognitive–behavioral therapeutic interventions have been employed on a wide variety of health habits with at least modest degrees of success. For example, a review of alcohol abuse programs suggests several factors that favor successful treatment outcomes: An active orientation that takes account of all the factors in the environment that might control drinking, a moderate length of participation in a formal program (six to eight weeks), use of aversion therapy, outpatient after-care, and an active involvement of relatives and employers in the treatment process (Costello, 1975a, 1975b). Similar programs with heavy-drinking college students that incorporate relapse prevention techniques have also shown some success in reducing drinking (e.g., Baer, Kivlahan, Fromme, & Marlatt, 1989; Lang & Marlatt, 1983; Marlatt & Gordon, 1985). Researchers are increasingly finding that lengthy in-patient programs may not be required for the treatment of alcoholism and that brief hospitalization, partial hospitalization, or outpatient programs oriented around behavioral principles may also be successful (Holden, 1987).

Cognitive–behavioral interventions have also been used success-fully to help people stop smoking. Typically such programs show high initial rates of success, but they often suffer from high rates of relapse. Some of the best short-term and long-term abstinence rates are achieved by combining aversive or focused smoking as an initial quitting tech-nique, with relapse prevention training to aid long-term maintenance (Curry, Marlatt, Gordon, & Baer, 1988; Leventhal, Baker, Brandon, & Fleming, 1989). Cognitive–behavioral techniques coupled with relapse-prevention methods have also been successful in helping people adhere to exercise programs (Belisle, Roskies, & Levesque, 1987). Research on exercise adherence indicates that adherence is higher when exercise is made convenient (such as being performed in one's own home), when it is enjoyable, and when it is ties into one's social system (e.g., if one's spouse is also involved in the program). The techniques of contingency contracting, social reinforcement, self-monitoring, and goal setting also appear to promote exercise adherence (e.g., Dishman, 1982). Evaluations of cognitive–behavioral programs for obesity suggest that patients can lose nearly two pounds a week for up to 20 weeks. This weight loss can be maintained for up to two years among participants who have been trained in self-monitoring and other relapse-prevention strategies (Brownell, 1982, 1990). Responses to such programs are quite variable, however.

Considerable research has focused on the most appropriate venue for changing health behaviors. One-on-one therapy with a client can be highly effective but extremely expensive. Consequently, health behavior change experts have sought more cost-effective interventions. Group efforts to change health problems (such as smoking or obesity) are often highly successful, and at least 400,000 Americans are involved weekly in such programs. Work site interventions have been successful in modi-fying certain health problems, such as smoking and obesity, particularly when work groups compete against each other to see who can improve the most (Brownell, Cohen, Stunkard, Felix, & Cooley, 1984). The schools are effective intervention sites for preventing poor health habits from developing. Programs designed to keep elementary-school students and junior-high-school students from starting to smoke or use drugs are the most widely studied and show at least some success (e.g., Flay, 1985; Murray, Davis-Hearn, Goldman, Pirie, & Luepker, 1988).

Because much health habit modification is undertaken in conjunction with a physician's recommendation, psychologists have a role in educating physicians concerning how best to make effective use of their power in inducing behavior change (Rodin & Janis, 1979). Recommendation by a physician is one of the strongest predictors of successful behavior change. Providing physicians with the names of services that a patient can be referred to for training in behavior change would also strengthen the link between the recommendation to change behavior and the actual process of changing behavior.

In order to reach the largest numbers of people possible, researchers are increasingly turning to community-based intervention programs. These programs typically include media messages alerting people to the risks of particular health habits, and they make use of existing community resources for training people identified as at risk in behavior change principles. For example, the Multiple Risk Factor Intervention Trial (MRFIT) was designed to modify cardiovascular risk factors, such as smoking, dietary cholesterol, and high blood pressure, through a combination of media interventions and behavior change efforts targeted to those with multiple risk factors. Community programs may be an especially good way to modify health behavior because: They reach more people than individually based interventions; they have the potential to build on community social support in reinforcing compliance with recommendations; they provide built-in vehicles for implementing the intervention; and they may facilitate the maintenance of behavior change by altering the environment to provide new cues to get people to maintain their behavior change.

Why Is Health Behavior Change Important?

There are several reasons for considering cognitive–behavioral change methods in changing health habits. First, since health habits such as smoking, diet, and alcoholism are heavily implicated in the onset of chronic diseases, effective programs to modify these target behaviors are essential in making progress against chronic diseases. Second, these health habits are important not only in producing disease initially, but also in increasing secondary risk once a disease has been diagnosed. Many chronically ill patients, such as those suffering from hypertension, heart disease, cancer, or RA, are told to modify aspects of their life-style, such as the degree of stress to which they expose themselves, the amount of exercise they get, or the nature of their diet. Yet they are rarely given effective training in how to enact this life-style change. Adherence to life-style change programs is consequently low. It is estimated that 20% to 80% of participants drop out of life-style change programs (Dunbar & Agras, 1980; Turk & Meichenbaum, 1989), and that those who do complete the programs are often unable to maintain the behavior change over time. Cognitive–behavioral interventions coupled with relapse prevention skills can potentially improve these figures.

Cognitive–behavioral techniques can also be used to change several health habits simultaneously. Treatment regimens for chronic illness often involve a number of difficult and complex activities carried out on a daily basis over the long term that require extensive time commitments and may bear unknown relationships to treatment outcomes. For example, patients diagnosed with coronary artery disease must often stop smoking, lose weight, engage in an exercise program, lower their cholesterol levels, and modify their volume of food intake. Effective change techniques targeted to multiple health habits can be pulled from the arsenal of cognitive–behavioral methods.

Another reason for concentrating heavily on cognitive–behavioral principles in the modification of health habits stems from the fact that premorbid personality factors do not appear to explain much of the variance in adherence. Extensive reviews of the literature (DiMatteo & DiNicola, 1982; Kirscht & Rosenstock, 1979) found that patient factors account for relatively little of the variance in nonadherence. Typically, lack of knowledge of the treatment regimen, lack of knowledge about the disease, disorder-specific anxiety, and the presence of competing activities are more important predictors of nonadherence than are individual differences or personality factors. Cognitive–behavioral techniques can reduce some of these barriers.

Finally, these cognitive–behavioral interventions are important because they have the potential to reduce the dependence of the chronically ill on medical treatments. For example, it is possible that hypertension patients trained in cognitive–behavioral techniques designed to reduce their blood pressure may require lower drug dosages than untrained patients (Richter-Heinrich et al., 1988). Drugs to treat hypertension have many side effects that adversely affect quality of life, thus promoting nonadherence to medication. Thus, the potential for cognitive–behavioral therapy not only to reduce drug dosages, but also to ameliorate the adverse side effects that promote nonadherence, is very high.

In short, the past five years have seen fairly substantial changes in the modification of health behaviors, particularly those involving addiction. Previously these problems were thought to be best solved by adding additional treatment sessions or components to the treatment program; however, it is now believed that relapse prevention involves particular skills that must be concretely addressed from the outset of a behavioral intervention problem.

Psychological Sequelae of Chronic Illness

The diagnosis of a chronic disease not only produces the need for behavior change, it also evokes many emotional changes that may require attention. The impact of chronic illness on the individual can be pervasive, affecting physical and emotional well-being, work, sex, and family life (see Burish & Bradley, 1983, for a review). Chronic disease can produce a variety of adverse outcomes, including pain and discomfort, fear and uncertainty about the future, and a variety of adverse emotional effects (see Burish, Meyerowitz, & Carey, for cancer), such as anxiety and depression. When left untreated, the emotional distress associated with chronic illness represents a substantial reduction in patients' quality of life and may further interfere with physical rehabilitation and return to work, leisure, and social activities. Researchers are documenting the high prevalence of emotional distress in chronically ill patients and are designing interventions to prevent or reduce this distress.

Of particular concern in this regard is the patient's premorbid personality and any history of depression or anxiety disorders prior to the onset of chronic illness. Those with prior histories of such disorders have a higher risk for exacerbated emotional responses to chronic illness, because chronic illness becomes an additional stressful event for them. Their psychological resources may leave them unprepared, and their coping skills may be insufficient to deal with these adverse effects.

Anxiety

Chronically ill patients often experience anxiety (Derogatis et al., 1983; Hughes, 1987; Popkin, Callies, Lentz, Cohen, & Sutherland, 1988), and heightened levels of anxiety can interfere with physical and psychosocial functioning. For example, anxiety is associated with poor functioning following radiotherapy (Graydon, 1988), poor glucose control and increased symptom reporting in diabetics (Lustman, 1988), and less return to work in myocardial infarction (MI) patients (Maeland & Havik, 1987a).

Although much of the documented anxiety among the chronically ill may be a manifestation of a premorbid propensity for anxiety, there are also clear specific sources of anxiety during rehabilitation and treatment. Welch-McCaffrey (1985) found that the following sources produced high levels of anxiety: Waiting for test results, a diagnosis of cancer, invasive procedures, the side effects of treatments, life-style alterations, dependency on health professionals, and fear of recurrence. In fact, one study (Scott, 1983) found levels of anxiety among women waiting for breast biopsy results to be comparable to norms for patients with acute anxiety reactions. Among cancer patients and their families, anxiety appears to peak at the time of cancer surgery (Welch-McCaffrey, 1985). Certain forms of surgery create additional sources of anxiety, such as the fear of loss of femininity among mastectomy patients (Meyerowitz, 1980). The challenges posed by rehabilitation may also produce anxiety. Thompson, Webster, Cordle, and Sutton (1987) found that, while anxiety about an MI declined steadily over a one-year period, anxiety about possible complications, the future, returning to work, leisure activities, relations with others, and sexual relations increased at six weeks postdischarge, and then declined at one year. Christman et al. (1988) suggested that uncertainty among MI patients remains high because patients realize that the risk-reducing actions they undertake cannot guarantee that they will not have another infarct. Waltz, Badura, Pfaff, and Schott (1988) found that primary appraisals of threat, harm, and loss were the most important predictors of subsequent anxiety and depression in a sample of 1,000 cardiac patients.

Depression

Depression is a common and often disabling reaction to chronic illness. In their (1986) review, Rodin and Voshart concluded that one third of medical inpatients reported moderate symptoms of depression, and up to one quarter suffered from severe depression (see Bukberg, Penman, & Holland, 1984; Derogatis et al., 1983; Massie & Holland, 1987, for cancer; Popkin et al., 1988, for diabetes; Primeau, 1988, for stroke). This high rate of depression may be partially accounted for by either a premorbid propensity for depression or neurological damage (see Whitlock, 1982, for a review), whereas other instances of depression may represent reactions to the stressors associated with chronic illness.

Some theorists have suggested that depression is a reliable stage of reaction to chronic illness, but this notion has little empirical support (Silver & Wortman, 1980). Unfortunately, very little work has been done to document the course of depression over time in large samples of chronically ill patients to determine common, normal reactions. An exception is the work of Silver and Wortman (Silver, Boon, & Stones, 1983; Wortman & Silver, 1987, 1989) that examined reactions to negative life events such as bereavement, incest, and spinal cord injury.

Depression is important not only because of the distress that it produces, but also because it may have an impact on long-term rehabilitation and recovery (Primeau, 1988). Depressed stroke patients have longer hospital stays and are more often discharged to nursing homes than other patients (Cushman, 1986), they show less motivation to undergo rehabilitation (Thompson, Sobolew-Shubin, Graham, & Janigian, 1989), they are less likely to maintain gains made during rehabilitation (Sinyor et al., 1986), and they are less likely to restore their quality of life to prestroke levels (Niemi, Laaksonen, Kotila, & Waltimo, 1988).

Myocardial infarction patients who were depressed while in the hospital were less likely to have returned to work one year later and were more likely to have been rehospitalized (Stern, Pascale, & Ackerman, 1977). Depression has also been linked to suicide among the chronically ill.[1]

Assessment of depression in the chronically ill can be problematic. First, many of the physical signs of depression, such as fatigue, sleeplessness, or weight loss, may also be symptoms of the disease or a side effect of its treatment. If depressive symptoms are attributed to the illness itself, depression may be masked and infrequently diagnosed (Hughes, 1987; Massie & Holland, 1987; Rodin & Voshart, 1986). Sinyor et al. (1986) found that only one third of the depressed stroke victims in their sample had been referred for treatment, and Lustman and Harper (1987) reported similar findings for diabetics. These problems are exacerbated in illnesses that can affect brain function like cancer, stroke, diabetes, AIDS, and epilepsy (House, 1987, and Primeau, 1988, for stroke; Levin, Banks, & Berg, 1988, for epilepsy; Massie & Holland, 1987, for cancer; Popkin et al., 1988, for diabetes).

Few studies have tried to adjust standard measures of depression to eliminate overlap with somatic symptoms. Some investigators have applied greater weights to items tapping nonsomatic symptoms to correct this problem (Koenig, Meador, Cohen, & Blazer, 1988). Another approach has been to validate standardized instruments of depression on chronically ill patients. In their latent trait analysis of the Beck Depression Inventory in medical inpatients, Clark, Cavanaugh, and Gibbons (1983) found seven items that discriminate severe depression in a medical sample: sense of failure, loss of social interest, sense of punishment, suicidal thoughts, dissatisfaction, indecision, and crying. Most of the vegetative symptoms did not discriminate well between depressed and nondepressed chronically ill subjects.

Another barrier to assessment is that there are no standards for diagnosing depression in the medically ill (Rodin & Voshart, 1986). Depression in the chronically ill often goes untreated because many people believe that one is supposed to be depressed after a diagnosis of chronic illness (Goldberg, 1981; Greer, 1987; Robinson, 1986). Koenig et al. (1988) wrote, "It is often argued that older persons with serious medical illnesses and disability have a right to be depressed, given their conditions" (p. 1943). Popkin et al. (1988) added, "If physicians caring for diabetic patients view depression as an understandable concomitant

[1]Several of the chronic diseases include components of treatment regimens that may be used as methods for suicide. Kaminer and Robbins (1989), for example, documented insulin misuse as a form of suicidal behavior, and Abram, Moore, and Westervelt (1971) reported that patients undergoing dialysis were easily able to use the procedure to end their lives. In particular, the suicide rate among dialysis patients is reported to be 400 times that of the general population, through the use of exsanguination, overdose, and food or drink binges.

(in a psychological, reactive sense) condition. . . , patients may be denied meaningful psychiatric intervention" (pp. 66–67). Clearly, guidelines must be developed concerning how much depression can be expected after diagnosis of a life-threatening illness and the point at which depression becomes severe enough to warrant intervention.

Causes and Correlates of Depression

In their excellent review, Morris and Raphael (1987) noted that factors such as family history of affective disorders, personal history of psychiatric disorder, and premorbid personality have yet to be fully addressed in studying the link between physical illness and depression. Some evidence supports the intuitive notion that premorbid depression is associated with postmorbid depression. For example, Stern et al. (1977) noted that half of the depressed patients in their sample were depressed or anxious before their infarction. In cancer patients, a past history of depression was correlated with greater emotional distress during treatment (Weisman, 1976).

Clarifying the role of premorbid factors in depression should facilitate early intervention for patients who are at high risk for emotional distress. Physicians and clinicians should ask about family history of depression and prior episodes of depression in their patients (Goldberg, 1981). Screening instruments have been developed and can be used to identify vulnerable patients (Weisman, 1976; Weisman, Worden, & Sobel, 1980; Worden, 1984; Worden & Weisman, 1984). Future research in this area could also profitably address the match between the illness and its consequences to specific sources of vulnerability in individual patients. For example, to a person whose self-esteem is based on physical achievement or on body image, a stroke may be a potent precipitant of depression (Morris & Raphael, 1987).

Disease severity. In general, the likelihood of depression increases with the severity of illness (Bukberg et al., 1984; Cassileth et al., 1985; Koenig et al., 1988; Rodin & Voshart, 1986). There is disagreement about the point in the disease course when depression is at its worst. Some authors present evidence for the most severe depression occurring shortly after diagnosis (Cassileth et al., 1984); others suggest that depression reaches its peak after patients realize the full extent of their disability (see Baum, 1982, for arthritis) and experience long periods of forced inactivity (Hughes & Lee, 1987). It is also possible that the relationship between physical impairment and depression is reciprocally sustaining (Parikh, Lipsey, Robinson, & Price, 1988).

The contribution of disease severity to depression appears to increase over time. Depressions that last more than one year have been found to be highly associated with physical impairment (Morris & Raphael, 1987). Level of disability contributed to higher levels of pessimism, decreased leisure activities, and deterioration of personal relationships in stroke patients over a three-year follow-up (Lawrence & Christie, 1979). In the case of stroke, problems in communication may also enhance isolation and compound frustration stemming from physical handicaps, sexual difficulties, and dependency (Primeau, 1988).

Psychosocial factors in depression. Although disease severity reliably accounts for part of the variance, it does not fully account for depression in chronically ill patients. Hawley and Wolfe (1988) found that pain and disability (and lower age) explained only 25% of the variance in depression in arthritis patients. Studies that control for disease severity have found that other negative life events, social stress, and lack of social support are associated with depression in chronically ill patients (Bukberg et al., 1984, for cancer; Murphy, Creed, & Jayson, 1988, for arthritis). Thompson et al. (1989) found that poststroke depression was predicted by lower ratings of the meaningfulness of life and overprotectiveness on the part of care givers. As noted above, the premorbid history of depression also accounts for some of the depression seen following the development of a chronic illness. The contributing role of premorbid personality factors may be underrepresented in studies of chronic disease, largely because premorbid assessments of a propensity for depression (or for other emotional reactions such as anxiety) are rarely available. Consequently, depression that may be a chronic element in a patient's personality may be falsely attributed to the chronic disease.

Morris and Raphael (1987) proposed a framework that takes both physical and psychosocial factors into account in predicting depression. In the specific case of stroke, they suggest that these factors change in relative importance over time. Within the first six months, the location of central nervous system (CNS) damage predicts depression (see Robinson, 1986). Later, factors like cognitive impairment, physical disability, social support, changes in body image and self-esteem, and the mood-altering effects of therapeutic drugs may influence depression. It is also possible that depression, in turn, reduces the quality of social support during a prolonged illness (Morris & Raphael, 1987).

Long-Term or Chronic Depression

Unlike anxiety, which appears to be episodic, depression can be a long-term reaction to chronic illness. For many illnesses, depression lasts a year or more following surgery or the onset of the illness (Meyerowitz, 1980, for breast cancer; Robinson & Price, 1982, for stroke; Stern et al., 1977, for MI). Lustman, Griffith, and Clouse (1988) followed diabetic adults suffering from major depression over a five-year period and found that two thirds had recurrent major depression and that an additional

14% met the criteria for dysthymic disorder, compared with 10% in a comparison group of diabetics who were not depressed during the first evaluation. The occurrence of depressive episodes was independent of diabetic complications and diagnosis (patients were interviewed five years after onset of diabetes). Lustman et al. (1988) found that the depressed group had worse glucose control than the comparison group.

Psychological Assessment and Intervention

The clear conclusion to be drawn from the review of depression and anxiety among chronically ill patients is that evaluation for these potential problems should be part of chronic care. Recognition that patients' early reactions to and perceptions of their illness play a role in their recovery suggests that researchers and clinicians should identify patients who are at high risk for emotional distress (Maeland & Havik, 1987a; Marks, Richardson, Graham, & Levine, 1987; Waltz et al., 1988). Patients who have a premorbid history of depression or other mental illness are prime candidates for early intervention. Given the evidence for the long-term nature of depression, researchers and clinicians should attend to emotional distress and to declines in mental status over time (see Ell, Nishimoto, Morvay, Mantell, & Hamovitch, 1989).

A variety of interventions—ranging from informal communication with a health care professional to antidepressant drugs—has been proposed to alleviate emotional distress in chronically ill patients.

Improving Staff–Patient Communication

Informal interventions can be accomplished within the medical setting by improving staff–patient communication. Telling patients and their families what to expect may substantially alleviate anxiety. Maguire (1975) found that women who were warned ahead of time about physical discomfort following surgery were less disturbed by their symptoms (see also Egbert, Battit, Welch, & Bartlett, 1964). By simply telling patients that anxiety is a normal response to the stress of diagnosis and treatment (Welch-McCaffrey, 1985) or that depression is a physiologic sequela of stroke (Goodstein, 1983; Robinson, 1986), medical staff may alleviate patients' and family members' concerns that the patient is reacting inappropriately to his or her illness. Over the course of treatment, continuity of care may reduce anxiety, especially among elderly patients (Holland & Massie, 1987).

Increasing Patient Involvement in Treatment

Increasing patient involvement in treatment can also ameliorate adverse psychological responses. Such interventions are often simple to implement, such as one intervention that was designed to increase diabetics' involvement in their health care (Greenfield, Kaplan, Ware, Yano, & Frank, 1988). In this study, the patient and a research assistant reviewed the patient's medical record to identify issues that were likely to arise during an upcoming doctor's appointment and to rehearse the negotiation skills that the patient might use in querying the doctor about his or her case. Compared with those with standard patient education, the intervention group had the same knowledge of diabetes, but had better blood sugar control 12 weeks later, lost fewer days from work, and had more success in obtaining information from their physicians. These findings suggest that involvement in the medical process may have improved adherence, resulting in better blood sugar control. Considerable variability in the number of questions asked by patients in the intervention group suggests that some patients may have found it difficult to take an active role in their care.

A more complex intervention developed by Follick et al. (1988) for MI patients also illustrates the value of patient involvement. Compared with control patients who received standard medical care, patients who were equipped to phone in their electrocardiograph readings to the hospital showed fewer concerns about physical functioning and symptoms and were less than half as likely to be clinically depressed. Patients' perceptions of their ability to manage a recurrence of cardiac symptoms were inversely related to depressive affect. In addition, intervention patients were more likely to have returned to work at the nine-month follow-up. This system differs significantly from interventions that train family members in CPR, because it restores control to the patient instead of a family member.

Pharmacological Treatment

Pharmacological treatments of depression in chronically ill patients have yet to be extensively researched, but their clinical use suggests that antidepressants may be appropriate for patients suffering from major depression (Massie & Holland, 1987, for cancer; Primeau, 1988, and Robinson, 1986, for stroke; Rodin & Voshart, 1986), although these authors note potential counterindications of the use of antidepressants in elderly patients). In what has been reported to be the first study of its kind, Evans et al. (1988) presented preliminary findings showing improvement in depression and in psychosocial adjustment to cancer in depressed patients receiving antidepressant treatment. Although antidepressant treatment holds promise, a concomitant risk of such treatment is that patients may not take the drugs as prescribed. Evans et al. (1988) noted that several patients in their study had used the medications inappropriately or had abandoned them because of side effects. Pharmacological treatment of depression in medical populations represents a promising area for future research.

Nonpharmacological interventions to reduce emotional distress and to control symptoms have also been undertaken, including psychotherapy, coping skills training, patient education programs, relaxation training, and exercise programs.

Psychotherapy

Psychotherapeutic interventions, such as crisis intervention, brief psychotherapy, family therapy, and group therapy, have been shown to reduce emotional distress in patients. However, it has been difficult to compare the effectiveness of these treatments because psychotherapy is typically tailored to individual cases, and because investigators have not fully described their treatments (Greer, 1987; Linn, 1988).

Psychosocial Interventions

Patient education programs—many of which include coping skills training—can increase knowledge about the disease, reduce anxiety, increase patients' feelings of purpose and meaning in life (Johnson, 1982, for cancer), reduce pain and depression (Lorig, Chastain, Ung, Shoor, & Holman, 1989, for arthritis), improve coping (Maeland & Havik, 1987b), and increase confidence in the ability to manage pain (Parker et al., 1988, for arthritis) relative to control patients who are on a waiting list or who will get no treatment at all. Welch–McCaffrey (1985) cautioned that patient education must take into account individual differences in desire for information and be timed so that it does not coincide with elevated levels of anxiety (e.g., at time of diagnosis) that might interfere with learning. Additionally, Telch and Telch (1985) suggested that the beneficial effects of patient education may depend on whether the prognosis for the particular disease is favorable. If the prognosis is unfavorable, such information may reduce expectancies about recovery.

In a well controlled study, Telch and Telch (1986) compared group coping skills training to supportive group therapy for highly distressed cancer patients. After six weeks, the coping skills patients showed less emotional distress and more vigor than did the support group or no-treatment patients. Coping skills patients also reported heightened self-efficacy and fewer problems. The success of the coping skills instruction was attributed to enhanced perceptions of control.

In their (1985) review of the handful of experimental studies of psychosocial interventions with cancer patients, Telch and Telch identified several methodological problems. Many of the measures used to evaluate such interventions have not been validated in patient populations. Moreover, most studies have failed to control for patients' initial level of difficulties. This shortcoming has limited the ability to detect treatment effects, because some patients may not have needed the intervention and thus appeared unresponsive to treatment. Knowledge of pretreatment efficacy in a variety of domains would have allowed for the design of individually tailored interventions and would have facilitated assessment of the impact of the intervention on coping with specific problem areas. Another limitation of studies in this area is that follow-ups longer than a few months are rare.

Relaxation Training

Relaxation training is a widely used, promising nonpharmacological intervention with the chronically ill. Relaxation training decreases anxiety and nausea from chemotherapy and decreases pain (Bridge, Benson, Pietroni, & Priest, 1986; Sims, 1987; see Carey & Burish, 1988, for a comprehensive review of the treatment of psychological side effects associated with chemotherapy). Various combinations of relaxation training and stress management (Patel & Marmot, 1987), thermal biofeedback (Wittrock, Blanchard, & McCoy, 1988), and blood pressure monitoring (Chesney, Black, Swan, & Ward, 1987) have proved beneficial in the treatment of essential hypertension, even for patients whose blood pressures were not well controlled by antihypertensive medication (Agras, Taylor, Kraemer, Southam, & Schneider, 1987).

Cardiac Rehabilitation Programs

There have been mixed results of interventions to improve cardiac functioning after MI. Taylor, Houston-Miller, Ahn, Haskell, and DeBusk (1986) reported that supervised exercise reduced depression and anxiety relative to control groups. In their (1988) review, Greenland and Chu found substantial spontaneous improvement among untreated controls, but only small additional gains for exercise interventions (an extra 15% to 25% in maximal exercise capacity). The biggest gains were for patients whose initial physical fitness was lowest. Greenland and Chu (1988) concluded that exercise alone has not been demonstrated to improve psychological well-being or to reduce mortality, although exercise programs of 12 months or more do produce gains in myocardial performance.

Nonexercise interventions have been shown to be effective with cardiac patients, but may be more so for patients with less severe infarcts. Dennis et al. (1988) found that administering a treadmill test to low-risk patients three to four weeks after the MI and making a formal recommendation to the patient and physician that the patient return to work in two weeks cut the convalescence period by 32% compared to patients receiving usual care. Powell and Thoresen (1988) found that Type A behavioral counseling to reduce the frequency and intensity of daily emotional arousal (in conjunction with a regular cardiac education program) predicted longer survival in patients with mild prior MIs, but not in patients with serious prior infarcts in a 4½-year follow-up. In a review of cardiac rehabilitation programs that includes exercise therapy, Type A modification, and nonspecific psychological therapeutic interventions, Blumenthal and Emery (1988) concluded that such programs do improve quality of life among post-MI patients; at least some of these programs may also prolong life or significantly reduce morbidity in post-MI patients, when compared with routine medical care (Friedman et al., 1986).

Coping with Chronic Disease

Despite the fact that the majority of patients with chronic disease suffer at least some adverse psychological sequelae as a result of the disease, most do not seek formal or informal treatment for these symptoms. Instead, they draw upon internal and social resources for solving problems and alleviating psychological distress. In the next two sections, we examine the process of coping and the role of social support in adjustment to chronic disease.

The appraisal of a chronic disease as threatening or challenging leads to the initiation of coping efforts (cf. Lazarus & Folkman, 1984). Like most major stressful events, chronic disease poses a variety of specific challenges, including the practical problems of obtaining and following through on treatment, dealing with adverse emotional reactions such as depression or anxiety, managing the impact that the disease has on one's social network (cf. Wortman & Dunkel-Schetter, 1979), coping with any work-related or leisure-related losses or limitations (such as those produced by fatigue or disability), and managing threats to self-esteem or sense of self that may result (see Foltz, 1987, for a review for cancer patients).

Coping Strategies: An Overview

Coping consists of "efforts, both action-oriented and intrapsychic, to manage (i.e., master, tolerate, reduce, minimize) environmental and internal demands and conflicts among them" (Lazarus & Launier, 1978,

p. 311). Generally, two types of coping efforts have been distinguished: problem-solving efforts and efforts at emotional regulation (Folkman, Schaefer, & Lazarus, 1979; Lazarus & Folkman, 1984; Leventhal & Nerenz, 1982; Pearlin & Schooler, 1978). Problem-solving efforts are attempts to do something constructive about the stressful condition, whereas emotion-focused coping involves efforts to regulate its emotional consequences. Generally, however, researchers have found it more useful to go beyond this simple dichotomy to identify the more specific coping strategies adopted for managing stressful events.

Relatively few investigations have looked systematically at coping strategies among chronically ill patient groups. In a study by Dunkel-Schetter, Feinstein, Taylor, and Falke (1990), the coping strategies adopted by cancer patients in managing problems associated with cancer were identified through factor analyses of the Ways of Coping instrument (Folkman & Lazarus, 1980). The five identified strategies were: *social support/direct problem-solving*, which included items indicating the seeking-out and use of social support, as well as other direct problem-solving actions (e.g., "I talked to someone to find out more about the situation"); *distancing*, which involved efforts to detach oneself from the stressful situation (e.g., "I didn't let it get to me. I refused to think about it too much"); *positive focus*, characterized by efforts to find meaning in the experience by focusing on personal growth (e.g., "I came out of the experience better than I went in"); *cognitive escape/avoidance*, which involved such efforts as wishful thinking (e.g., "I wished that the situation would go away"), and *behavioral escape/avoidance*, which involved efforts to avoid the situation by eating, drinking, smoking, using drugs, or taking medications.

The ways that people cope with chronic disease are not confined to these five strategies, nor would factor analyses of strategies employed by victims of chronic illnesses other than cancer necessarily find the same structure (cf. Felton & Revenson, 1984; Felton, Revenson, & Hinrichsen, 1984). One caveat is the fact that the cancer patients in the Dunkel-Schetter et al. (1988) study rated their coping efforts based on which aspects of cancer they had found to be the most stressful: Fear and uncertainty about the future (41%); limitations in physical abilities, appearance, and life-style (24%); and pain management (12%). It is likely that the preponderance of uncontrollable concerns that patients expressed produced a factor structure deemphasizing such factors as planning and problem-solving or confrontational coping, which involves direct action (cf. Lazarus & Folkman, 1984). For example, among those coping with the aftermath of MI, confrontational coping and planning and problem-solving might emerge, as people actively modify their health habits and life-style with the hopes of reducing subsequent risk. Indeed, in many studies, problem-solving activities and the use of social support emerge as separate factors that are only modestly correlated (e.g., Marshall & Dunkel-Schetter, 1987).

Felton et al. (1984) found that terminally ill cancer patients were less likely than patients with hypertension, diabetes, or RA to cognitively restructure their disease by concentrating on something good that could come out of it. These results may have been a function of prognosis, however. Because of the limited number of studies that have addressed coping styles and specific chronic diseases, a full analysis of the types of coping strategies employed is currently precluded and constitutes an important direction for future research.

Coping and Adjustment

A logical next step in the analysis of coping strategies used by patients coping with the stresses of chronic disease is to identify which strategies facilitate psychological adjustment. That question has yet to be answered definitively. There is some evidence from coping with stressors other than chronic disease that the use of avoidant coping is associated with increased psychological distress and may therefore constitute a psychological risk factor for adverse responses to stress (Cronkite & Moos, 1984; see also Quinn, Fontana, & Reznikoff, 1987; Holahan & Moos, 1986, 1987). Consistent with this argument, Felton et al. (1984) found in a study of patients with cancer, hypertension, diabetes, or RA that cognitive restructuring was associated with good emotional adjustment, whereas coping by fantasizing, expressing emotion, or blaming the self was associated with poor adjustment. Information seeking and threat minimization were not related to adjustment. Similarly, Weisman and Worden (1976–1977) found poor adjustment to be associated with efforts to forget the cancer, fatalistic views of cancer, passive acceptance, withdrawal from others, blaming of others, and self-blame. At least one study has also found avoidant coping to be associated with poor glycemic control among insulin-dependent diabetics (Frenzel et al., 1988).

Research has also found lower psychosocial morbidity to be associated with positive active responses to stress, to high internal locus of control (Burgess, Morris, & Pettingale, 1988), and to beliefs that one can personally exert direct control over an illness (e.g., Affleck, Tennen, Pfeiffer, & Fifield, 1987; Jenkins & Pargament, 1988; Taylor, Lichtman, & Wood, 1984). Similarly, low levels of helplessness have been associated with superior psychological and behavioral functioning and reduced symptom severity in a group of RA patients (Stein, Wallston, Nicassio, & Castner, 1988). External health locus of control beliefs appear to be consistently associated with poor diabetes control, a finding now found in both children and adults (Burns, Green, & Chase, 1986), although Burns et al. (1986) have suggested that poor diabetes control may lead to external health beliefs, rather than the reverse. An exception to this pattern is the study by Affleck et al. (1987) which found that perceptions of personal control among arthritic patients with severe disease were associated with poor adjustment.

Some research suggests that hardiness (Kobasa, 1979) is associated with physiologic and psychosocial adaptation to diabetes, but not necessarily to hypertension or RA (Pollard, 1985). Implications of these findings and generalizations to other diseases, however, are complicated by the multidimensional nature of this construct, by the fact that low hardiness may simply reflect a propensity for negative affect (Allred & Smith, 1989), and by questions concerning whether hardiness actually enables people to combat stressors better or simply leads to better health practices (Allred & Smith, 1989; see also Funk & House, 1987; Wiebe & McCallum, 1986).

Denial

Denial has been a particularly controversial factor in the exploration of coping strategies among the chronically ill. Researchers have known for decades that intermittent denial may be useful in enabling people to come to terms gradually with the threatening aspects of stressful events, including the diagnosis of a chronic illness (e.g., Lazarus, 1983; Meyerowitz, 1980). In fact, Hackett and Weisman (1969) argued that denial is an appropriate and adaptive way to deal with stress in the face of a life-threatening illness (see also Meyerowitz, 1983). The confusion over the adaptiveness of denial has been reflected in the cancer literature, with Wool and Goldberg (1986) noting that cancer researchers interpret denial as either a positive or negative influence on adjustment to the disease (see also Matt, Sementilli, & Burish, 1988).

Denial may be more adaptive at some points in the adjustment to chronic disease than it is at others (Meyerowitz, 1983). For example, among MI patients, Levine and his colleagues (Levine et al., 1988) found that high denial was associated with fewer days in intensive care and fewer signs of cardiac dysfunction relative to low deniers, but, in the year following discharge, high deniers showed poorer adaptation to disease. High deniers were less adherent and required more days of rehospitalization, suggesting that denial was interfering with their effective monitoring of the long-term nature of their condition.

The findings concerning denial imply that coping strategies may be most effective when they are matched to the particular problems or points in time when they may be most useful (i.e., a matching hypothesis). There is evidence that people spontaneously match coping strategies to aspects of a stressful event. For example, people are more likely to use problem-solving strategies for aspects of a stressor that are amenable to direct control and to use emotion-focused coping for aspects of a stressful event that remain uncontrollable (e.g., Folkman & Lazarus, 1980; McCrae, 1984). Also consistent with a matching hypothesis, research suggests that multiple coping strategies may be most effective in managing some stressful events (see Collins, Taylor, & Skokan, in press, in the context of cancer; Pearlin & Schooler, 1978, in the context of general stress). Collins et al. (in press) found that people who used multiple coping strategies were better able to find some sort of benefit from the cancer experience than patients who used a predominant coping style, regardless of what that style was and controlling for the total amount of coping.

An answer to the question, "Which coping strategies work best?," then, is likely to be complex (Manuel, Roth, Keefe, & Brantley, 1987). The answer is dependent upon which aspects of a stressful event an individual is coping with at a particular point in the adjustment process (Meyerowitz, 1983). Despite this caveat, a general conclusion that can be drawn at present is that active coping efforts seem to be more consistently associated with good adjustment than avoidant strategies, so long as there are aspects of the disease amenable to active coping efforts.

Social Support from Family, Friends, and Care Givers

Social support appears to be an important resource for those suffering from chronic disease. It may lower the likelihood of illness initially, although research results are mixed on this point (e.g., Wallston et al., 1983). Social support does reliably speed recovery from illness, and it reduces risk of mortality (House, Landis, & Umberson, 1988; Neal, Tilley, & Vernon, 1986). Self-reports of good social relationships and positive adjustment to chronic disease are consistently found in the literature for cancer (Fitzpatrick, Newman, Lamb, & Shipley, 1988; Neuling & Winefield, 1988; Siegal, Calsyn, & Cuddihee, 1987; Taylor et al., 1984), arthritis (Fitzpatrick et al., 1988), and end-stage renal disease (Siegal et al., 1987), although it is unclear whether both positive assessments result from a common response bias, such as a tendency toward optimism or positivity. Social support has been associated with better recoveries from congestive heart failure (Chambers & Reiser, 1953), kidney disease (Dimond, 1979), childhood leukemia (Magni, Silvestro, Tamiello, Zanesco, & Carl, 1988), and stroke (Robertson & Suinn, 1968). Social support has also been linked to a reduced likelihood of mortality from MI (Wiklund et al., 1988), better diabetes control (Marteau, Bloch, & Baum, 1987; Schwartz, Springer, Flaherty, & Kiani, 1986; but see Kaplan & Hartwell, 1987), and less pain among arthritis patients (DeVellis, DeVellis, Sauter, & Cohen, 1986).

Social support may also reduce the distress that accompanies chronic illness (e.g., Zich & Temoshok, 1987). Fewer illness-related problems among chronically ill or elderly populations have been documented for those with high levels of social support (Wallston et al., 1983). Social support also appears to affect health habits and, in particular, promotes adherence to medical regimen. People with high levels of social support are usually more compliant with their medication requirements (e.g., Wallston et al., 1983) and are more likely to use health services (e.g., Wallston et al., 1983).

Generally, when researchers have measured social support in social integration terms, such as the number of people one identifies as friends or the number of organizations one belongs to, direct effects of social support on health have been found. That is, social support is associated with good physical and psychological health regardless of whether an individual is under stress or not. When social support has been assessed more qualitatively, such as the degree to which a person feels that there are others available to him or her in the environment to help him or her if needed, buffering effects of social support have been found (Cohen & Wills, 1985; House, Umberson, & Landis, 1988; Kessler & McLeod, 1985; Wortman & Dunkel-Schetter, 1987); that is, social support is associated with good physical and psychological health primarily when an individual is under stress. Research on social support and chronic disease implicitly focuses on buffering effects because chronic disease is typically a state producing chronic stress. Social support may then be particularly effective under such circumstances (e.g., Chrvala & Weiner, 1989).

There may be certain barriers to receiving the kind of social support that a patient with a chronic disease needs. A study of disabled people found that disabled women were subject to deficits in social support because they were less likely to be married or to get married than disabled men (Kutner, 1987; see also Bramwell, 1986). Another study suggesting social support gaps for chronically ill women found that marriage protected men but not women from institutionalization following stroke (Kelly-Hayes et al., 1988). Stern et al. (1977) found that post-MI women were less likely to be married, and if they were unmarried, they were more likely to die shortly after the MI. Sex differences in the availability and effects of social support among the chronically ill clearly merit additional study.

Individual differences may predict the use of social support. Some people may be less effective in extracting social support from others, and this may be especially true with respect to emotional support (Dunkel-Schetter, Folkman, & Lazarus, 1987). Stressful events can also interfere with the ability to use social support effectively. People who are under extreme stress may express their distress to others in a manner that drives them away, instead of enlisting them in making the situation better. Chronic disease can itself adversely affect potential social support resources. For example, Wortman and Dunkel-Schetter (1979) suggested that the stressful event of cancer creates fear and aversion in family and friends, but also creates a simultaneous awareness of the need to provide support. These tensions may produce a variety of adverse outcomes, such as physically avoiding the patient, avoiding open communication about the disease, minimizing its impact, or demonstrating forced cheerfulness. Under such conditions, the availability of effective social support may be reduced (e.g., Chrvala & Weiner, 1989; Stephens, Kinney, Norris, & Ritchie, 1987).

Distant relationships with friends and acquaintances appear to be more adversely affected in these ways than intimate relations (Dakof & Taylor, 1990; Fitzpatrick et al., 1988). However, intimate others may themselves be highly distressed by the loved one's condition and be ineffective in providing support, because their own support needs are unmet (e.g., Cassileth et al., 1985; Ell, Nishimoto, Mantell, & Hamovitch, 1988; Wellisch, Jamison, & Pasnau, 1978; Zarski, West, DePompei, & Hall 1988). Additional research identifying the kinds of social support that are generally available to victims of chronic disease and the factors that may interfere with its availability or use is clearly needed (Bramwell, 1986; Kutner, 1987).

Recently, researchers have suggested that social support may be most effective when it provides coping assistance (Thoits, 1987). Different stressors create different needs that elicit different coping efforts. Social support efforts may be effectively viewed as assisting these coping efforts and should be most effective when they match the person's needs. The benefits of social support have generally been grouped into three categories: tangible assistance, information, and emotional support (House, 1981; Schaefer, Coyne, & Lazarus, 1981). Thus, at particular times during the course of an illness, an individual may be best served by tangible aid, such as being driven to and from medical appointments or having errands and housekeeping done during times of infirmity. At other times, however, emotional support may be more valuable. Consistent with this view that social support represents coping assistance, Dunkel-Schetter, Folkman, and Lazarus (1987) found that individuals' ways of coping were strongly associated with the types of support that they received.

Studies with cancer patients suggest a further qualification to this matching hypothesis (Dakof & Taylor, 1990; Dunkel-Schetter, 1984; Neuling & Winefield, 1988). These studies found that different kinds of support may be valued from different members of the social support network, in that each member may have unique abilities to be helpful along particular dimensions. Emotional support is most important from intimate others, whereas information and advice may be more valuable from experts and may actually be experienced as aversive when received from intimate others (see also Cohen & McKay, 1984).

Social Support Groups

Social support groups represent another social support resource for the chronically ill. Potentially, such groups can satisfy needs for social support that have been unmet by family members and care givers. Alternatively, such support groups may be viewed as an additional source of support provided by those going through the event. In some cases, such socially supportive ties may evolve from rehabilitation programs, as for MI, and in other cases, linkages between the primary health care setting and established groups (such as "I Can Cope" for cancer patients) may facilitate entry into such programs. Chronically ill patients report a variety of positive as well as negative experiences from such contacts. On the positive side, among cancer patients, fellow patients were reported to be especially helpful when they acted as good role models on whom patients could pattern their own coping efforts or when they functioned as role models by surviving over the long term (e.g., Taylor, Falke, Shoptaw, & Lichtman, 1986). Patients who practiced faulty health behaviors or who expressed substantial psychological distress were reported to be unhelpful.

Generally, studies that have evaluated the efficacy of social support group interventions compared with wait list or untreated control groups have found beneficial effects. Such research has involved programs with RA patients (e.g., Bradley et al., 1987), cancer patients (e.g., Telch & Telch, 1986), and MI patients (e.g., Dracup, 1985; Waltz, 1986), among others. Self-help groups may help victims cope with the stigma associated with certain disorders, such as cancer or epilepsy (Droge, Arntson, & Norton, 1986), and they may help patients develop the motivation and techniques to adhere to hypertension regimen (Storer, Frate, Johnson, & Greenberg, 1987). However, Telch and Telch (1985) noted that research on support groups has generally failed to identify the therapeutic ingredient underlying reported improvements.

Although widely heralded as a low-cost convenient treatment option for people to deal with a wide variety of personal problems, self-help groups in fact reach a relatively small proportion of chronically ill patients (e.g., Andersen, 1988, in the context of stroke; see Taylor et al., 1986, in the context of cancer). Moreover, self-help groups appear to appeal disproportionately to well-educated, middle-class White females. Not only is this the segment of the population that is also served by more traditional treatment services, but the population served by self-help groups may actually be the same individuals who are using the more traditional services (Taylor et al., 1986). In their study of cancer patients, Taylor et al. (1986) found that those who participated in self-help groups were significantly more likely to have used helping services of all kinds. The potential, then, for self-help groups to be a general resource for the chronically ill has yet to be realized.

Social Support: Research and Intervention Implications

Research on social support has been hampered somewhat by methodological problems concerning both the definition and the measurement of social support (Wortman, 1984). The amount of support that is available, desired, and actually received, for example, may be very different. In addition, outcome measures assessed in studies of social support for the chronically ill have included psychological distress, illness behavior, and various health parameters, without considering the fact that each outcome variable may be affected by different factors. Moreover, relatively few studies have collected the best kind of evidence regarding the efficacy of social support, namely longitudinal investigations relating availability and use of support to psychological and health outcomes at later points in time.

Perhaps the most important task currently facing social support researchers is the need to identify the psychological and biological pathways by which different aspects of social support may exert their effects on health (Cohen, 1988; House, Umberson, & Landis, 1988). For example, the propensity of available social support to enhance adherence to treatment regimens is of particular importance in chronic disease. Knowledge of these pathways may be particularly helpful in identifying ways in which social support may be used to retard the progression of chronic disease and to improve the patient's ability to cope with the disease.

Social support interventions should figure strongly into secondary prevention efforts with chronically ill patients. Finding ways to increase the effectiveness of existing or potentially naturally occurring support from patients' families and friends should be a high research and intervention priority. People need to recognize the potential sources of support in their environment and be taught how to draw on these resources effectively. Patients might also be trained in how to develop social support resources, for example, by joining community groups, interest groups, informal social groups, and self-help groups.

In addition, family members and significant others who are going through stressful events with the patient could receive guidance in the most effective ways to provide social support and in the well-intended actions that they should avoid because these actually make a stressful situation worse (e.g., Dakof & Taylor, 1990). In some cases, even the simple provision of information may be supportive. For example, in a study of wives of MI patients, the majority felt poorly informed about MI, reported few opportunities to ask experts questions, and consequently experienced a high degree of physical and emotional stress (Thompson & Cordle, 1988). Presumably, a short intervention designed to acquaint them with MI could have ameliorated this situation.

Enlisting the cooperation of community linking individuals such as teachers or clergy who can communicate helpful information to kin-based, care-giving networks is another potential intervention (Bramwell, 1986; Kutner, 1987). Psychologists can contribute to the development of social support resources by exploring ways of creating social ties, designing interventions that can be implemented in primary health care settings (Gates, 1988), and developing means of identifying and aiding socially marginal individuals who have not availed themselves of this valuable resource.

Quality of Life

The research covered in the previous section of this chapter points in a single direction: The need to understand the impact of chronic disease and its treatment on a patient's quality of life and to develop interventions that may improve quality of life. Oddly enough, this seemingly self-evident insight did not appear until recently in the literature on chronic illness. Prior to 1979, quality of life was assessed almost entirely by the medical indicators of whether or not any signs of disease were present and whether or not the patient was still living (Fayers & Jones, 1983; Hollandsworth, 1988; Kaplan, 1985)! Even from 1977 to 1989, medical citations on quality of life continued to outnumber psychological ones by 10 to 1.

Yet physician ratings of patient quality of life are known to be only weakly correlated with patient ratings (Presant, 1984; Slevin, Plant, Lynch, Drinkwater, & Gregory, 1988). In one classic study, Jachuck, Brierley, Jachuck, and Willcox (1982) asked physicians, patients, and family members to rate the patient's quality of life after the initiation of antihypertensive drug treatments. Physicians estimated that quality of life had improved in 100% of the patients, only 49% of the patients perceived any improvement in the quality of their lives, and 96% of the relatives perceived no change or a deterioration in the patient's quality of life.

Unfortunately, this insight has not led to any uniformity as to what constitutes quality of life or convergence in measures of quality of life (de Haes & van Knippenberg, 1985; van Dam, Somers, & van Beek-Couzijn, 1981). Research instruments have moved from assessing the mere presence or absence of the disease to assessing functional status, including the ability of people to conduct their daily personal and role-related activities.[2] Examples of these are the Sickness Impact Profile

---

[2]Currently, there is an international effort to establish a comprehensive, standardized method of quality of life assessment in cancer clinical trials. Aaronson, Bullinger, and Ahmedzai's (1988) Quality of Life Questionnaire (QLQ) includes 36 core questions that assess functional status, disease- and treatment-related symptoms reported frequently by cancer patients, psychological distress, social interaction, the financial aspect of illness, and global health and quality of life items. To this core they add a supplement of nine items specific to the illness in question (lung cancer in their validation research). The QLQ represents a potential improvement over other measures in this area because the supplemental questions provide clinical sensitivity to the specific type of cancer while the core questions provide comparability to other forms of cancer; furthermore, repeated measures are taken to assess changes in quality of life over the disease course, as well as changes in the relative importance of specific quality of life dimensions over time. Validation of the QLQ is now being conducted in the 15 member countries of the European Organization for the Research and Treatment of Cancer. This modular approach is likely to yield valuable results.

(SIPS; Bergner, Bobbitt, Carter, & Gilson, 1981), the Index of Daily Activities (ADL; Katz, Ford, Moskowitz, Jackson, & Jaffee, 1983), the Cancer Inventory of Problem Situations (CIPS; Schag, Heinrich, & Ganz, 1983), and the Karnofsky Performance Status measure for use with cancer patients (KPS; Grieco & Long, 1984). However, functional status measures miss much that is important in quality of life, because less than one third of patients who have a serious chronic illness have measurable limitations in personal or role functioning (Ware, 1984). Moreover, functional status measures do not adequately assess mental health (Ware, 1984).

Despite the fact that the medical literature has generally ignored psychosocial aspects of quality of life, psychologists have been concerned with this issue for some time. Generally, quality of life has been evaluated according to a variety of outcomes. One primary criterion has included measures of biochemical and physiological functioning. People are generally judged to be coping successfully with a stressful event if they can reduce their arousal and its indicators, such as heart rate, pulse, and skin conductivity. When blood or urine levels of catecholamines and corticosteroids are reduced, adjustment is judged to be better.

A second criterion of successful adjustment has been the length of time it takes people to return to their prestress activities. Often a chronic illness interferes with the conduct of daily life activities. To the extent that a person is able to resume those activities, adjustment is said to be better. However, there is an implicit bias in this criterion to the effect that the person's prior living situation was in some sense an ideal one. This is not always true. In fact, substantial life change may follow a stressful event, and this may be a sign of successful rather than unsuccessful adjustment (Collins et al., in press; Taylor, 1983). Most frequently, researchers have measured adjustment in terms of psychological distress. When a person's anxiety or depression is low, adjustment is judged to be successful. In summation, then, there have been several criteria of successful adjustment, which are now being incorporated more formally into quality of life measures.

Despite the fact that there has been little agreement about how to define or measure quality of life, a number of factors have been identified that consistently predict low quality of life. Patients with a poorer prognosis have reduced life satisfaction (Taylor et al., 1985). Unpleasant and debilitating treatments, such as chemotherapy and radiotherapy, also reduce quality of life, although these effects appear to be reversed once the treatments end (Lichtman, Taylor, & Wood, 1987; Taylor et al., 1985). However, for some patients who take medications on a regular basis, quality of life can be substantially and chronically diminished by the treatment side effects. Treatment side effects are a particular problem for patients suffering from hypertension, cancer, and arthritis (Nail, King, & Johnson, 1986; see also Love, Leventhal, Easterling, & Nerenz, 1989, for cancer; and Anderson et al., 1985, for arthritis; Zachariah, 1987). Pain has also been associated with diminished quality of life (Davis, Hess, Van Harrison, & Hiss, 1987), especially for arthritis and cancer patients (Laborde & Powers, 1985), and functional impairment has been associated with low quality of life (Anderson et al., 1985; Baum, 1982; Hughes & Lee, 1987; Lawrence & Christie, 1979; Parikh et al., 1988).

There are several important reasons for being able to assess quality of life in a detailed manner that enables researchers to understand not only the functional problems of people with advanced disease, but also the somewhat milder though still problematic adverse emotional responses or role disruptions. First, and perhaps foremost, effective assessment of quality of life can identify problems that may be particular to certain disorders so that more focused assessments of individual patients can occur, and appropriate interventions can be initiated early. For example, the knowledge that interpersonal relations and sexual disturbances are common difficulties among gynecologic patients (Anderson et al., 1985) should provoke a more detailed assessment of these problems in that particular population, leading to psychotherapeutic or intervention efforts to help ameliorate these problems. The knowledge that depression is a potential concomitant of beta-blocker therapy for hypertension or MI recovery can lead to interventions designed to avoid these complications or offset them if they occur.

Quality of life information can also be useful in making medical treatment decisions, and it is a widely used outcome measure in clinical trials. For example, among cancer patients, it is important to demonstrate that palliative treatment is not more harmful than the disease itself (Burns, Chase, Goodwin, & Jarrard, 1987; Greer, 1984), especially when there are disappointing survival rates and increasingly toxic treatments (e.g. Aaronson, Calais de Silva et al., 1986; Buccheri, Ferrigno, Curcio, Vola, & Rosso, 1989). Finally, from a health policy standpoint, policymakers need standard units to compare the impact of different chronic diseases and to assess the cost-effectiveness of interventions. Capable assessment of quality of life can greatly help in calculating both the direct and indirect costs of illness (Kaplan, 1985; Lubeck & Yelin, 1988).

Positive Change and Chronic Disease

As the previous discussion has implied, the meager research that has focused on psychosocial determinants of quality of life has heavily addressed the problems and stressors created by chronic disease. A more complete assessment of quality of life reveals an important point, namely that chronic disease can produce positive outcomes as well as negative ones. In one study of cancer patients (Collins et al., in press), over 90% of the respondents found at least some beneficial changes in their lives as the result of the cancer. These patients reported an increased ability to appreciate each day and the inspiration to do things now instead of postponing them. In terms of relationships, respondents reported that they were putting more effort into their relationships and believed they had acquired more awareness of others' feelings and more sympathy and compassion for others. They reported feeling stronger, more self-assured, and more compassionate toward the unfortunate (see also Taylor, 1983).

Similarly, a study of MI patients found that 46% reported that their lives were unchanged by the disease, 21% reported that it had worsened, but a third felt that their lives had improved overall (Laerum, Johnsen, Smith, & Larsen, 1987). Moreover, half of the patients reported increased joy in life and found increased value in hobbies, family, and good health. Positive changes in family relationships following MI have also been reported (Laerum et al. 1987; Waltz, 1986). Two studies have compared the quality of life experienced by cancer patients with that of a normal sample free of chronic disease, and both have found the quality of life experienced by the cancer patients to be higher in certain respects than that of the non-ill sample (Danoff, Kramer, Irwin, & Gottlieb, 1983; Tempelaar et al., in press). Less research has examined adjustment to other chronic diseases, and so it is difficult to reach definitive conclusions regarding the existence and frequency of benefits resulting from other chronic illnesses.

When researchers have uncovered these positive changes in response to chronic disease, they have sometimes viewed them with suspicion. Some have regarded these processes as defensive ones, as transparently compensatory efforts to restore some sense of personal dignity and self-esteem following a devastating event. Others have implied that these effects may result from response biases, such as a need to say something positive to a research investigator. Moreover, psychological and psychiatric models of mental health and adjustment have historically left relatively little room for understanding the kinds of positive changes that can be observed in response to chronic illness.

This approach may be quite shortsighted. There exists now, among some psychoanalytic theorists, an effort to reexamine some of the assumptions underlying the imputation of defensiveness to these kinds of processes. For example, Sackheim and his associates (Sackeim, 1983; Sackeim & Gur, 1979) have written persuasive papers and assembled evidence to suggest that the creative reconstructions and distortions that one sometimes sees of negative events are actually associated with mental health and should be thought of as offensive rather than defensive processes. Daniel Weinberger at Stanford has reached similar conclusions (Weinberger, 1990).

Our own framework for thinking about these changes, which we have termed *cognitive adaptation theory* (Taylor, 1983; Taylor & Brown, 1988), emphasizes the continuity in the strategies that people use for dealing with everyday stressful events as well as major life-threatening events such as a chronic illness. We argue that people deal with the world generally—and with negative events in particular—through a set of illusions or biases that represent themselves and the world more positively than may actually be the case. When people encounter damaging information and circumstances, they sometimes distort them to reduce the negative implications for themselves or their worldview, or they represent them in as unthreatening a manner as possible. In the case of events with negative consequences that are difficult to deny, a person may attempt to offset them with perceived gains incurred from the event, such as finding meaning through the experience or believing that the self is a better person for having withstood the event.

In making these claims, we are not suggesting that a chronic illness is a generally positive experience and that patients should be grateful for their illness because it can bring meaning into their lives. Clearly, people experiencing a chronic illness report both positive and negative changes. However, what does seem evident is that people actively struggle with chronic illness, attempting, often successfully, to derive benefits and value from the event while simultaneously seeking to accommodate their perspectives realistically to the adverse changes in their lives.

We believe that these adaptive offensive processes and the factors that enable people to make effective use of them merit additional study. In making this point, we hope to divert at least some of the research on adjustment to chronic illness to understanding the paradoxical but very important positive effects that can occur in response to these events. Hopefully, with a broad base of understanding of these effects, we can draw psychotherapeutic implications that will enable those who work with the chronically ill not only to help them solve the problems and stressors that disease brings about, but also to benefit and grow from these otherwise adverse experiences.

References

Aaronson, N. K., Bullinger, M., & Ahmedzai, S. (1988). A modular approach to quality-of-life assessment in cancer clinical trials. In H. Scheurlen, R. Kay, & M. Baum (Eds.), *Cancer clinical trials: A critical appraisal* (Vol. 111, pp. 231–249). Heidelberg, Germany: Springer-Verlag.

Aaronson, N. K., Calais de Silva, F., Yoshida, O., van Dam F. S. A. M., Fossa, S. D., Miyakawa, M., Raghavan, D., Riedl, H., Robinson, M. R. G., & Worden, J. W. (1986). Quality of life assessment in bladder cancer clinical trials: Conceptual, methodological and practical issues. *Progress in Clinical and Biological Research, 22*, 149–170.

Abram, H. S., Moore, G. L., & Westervelt, F. B. (1971). Suicidal behavior in chronic dialysis patients. *American Journal of Psychiatry, 127*, 119–124.

Affleck, G., Tennen, H., Pfeiffer, C., & Fifield, J. (1987). Appraisals of control and predictability in adapting to a chronic disease. *Journal of Personality and Social Psychology, 53*, 273–279.

Agras, W. S., Taylor, C. B., Kraemer, H. C., Southam, M. A., & Schneider, J. A. (1987). Relaxation training for essential hypertension at the worksite: II. The poorly controlled hypertensive. *Psychosomatic Medicine, 49*, 264–273.

Ajzen, I., & Fishbein, M. (1977). Attitude-behavior relations: A theoretical analysis and review of empirical research. *Psychological Bulletin, 84*, 888–918.

Alexander, F. (1950). *Psychosomatic medicine*. New York: Norton.

Allred, K. D., & Smith, T. W. (1989). The hardy personality: Cognitive and physiological responses to evaluate threat. *Journal of Personality and Social Psychology, 56*, 257–266.

American Cancer Society. (1989). *Cancer facts and figures–1989*. Atlanta, GA: American Cancer Society, Inc.

American Diabetes Association. (1986). *Diabetes: Facts you need to know*. Alexandria, VA: American Diabetes Association.

American Heart Association. (1984). *Heart facts, 1984*. Dallas, TX: American Heart Association.

American Heart Association. (1988). *1989 heart facts*. Dallas, TX: American Heart Association.

Andersen, R. (1988). The contribution of informal care to the management of stroke. *International Disability Studies, 10*, 107–112.

Anderson, K. O., Bradley, L. A., Young, L. D., McDaniel, L. K., & Wise, C. M. (1985). Rheumatoid arthritis: Review of psychological factors related to etiology, effects and treatment. *Psychological Bulletin, 98*, 358–387.

Ashley, F., Jr., & Kannel, W. (1974). Relation of weight change to changes in atherogenic traits: The Framingham Study. *Journal of Chronic Diseases, 27*, 103–114.

Baer, J. D., Kivlahan, D. R., Fromme, K., & Marlatt, G. A. (1989). Secondary prevention of alcohol abuse with college student populations: A skills-training approach. In G. Howard (Ed.), *Issues in alcohol use and misuse by young adults*. Notre Dame, IN: Notre Dame University.

Bahnson, C. B. (1981). Stress and cancer: The state of the art. *Psychosomatics, 22*, 207–220.

Bandura, A. (1986). *Social foundations of thought and action: A social cognitive theory*. Englewood Cliffs, NJ: Prentice Hall.

Baum, J. (1982). A review of the psychological aspects of neumatic diseases. *Seminars in Arthritis and Rheumatism, 11*, 352–361.

Becker, M. H., & Janz, N. K. (1987). On the effectiveness and utility of health hazard/health risk appraisal in clinical and nonclinical settings. *Health Services Research, 22*, 537–551.

Becker, M. H., Maiman, L., Kirscht, J., Haefner, D., & Drachman, R. (1977). The health belief model and dietary compliance: A field experiment. *Journal of Health and Social Behavior, 18*, 348–366.

Belisle, M., Roskies, E., & Levesque, J.-M. (1987). Improving adherence to physical activity. *Health Psychology, 6*, 159–172.

Bergner, M., Bobbitt, R. A., Carter, W. B., & Gilson, B. S. (1981). The sickness impact profile: Development and final revision of a health status measure. *Medical Care, 19*, 787–805.

Blumenthal, J. A., & Emery, C. F. (1988). Rehabilitation of patients following myocardial infarction. *Journal of Consulting and Clinical Psychology, 56*, 374–381.

Booth-Kewley, S., & Friedman, H. S. (1987). Psychological predictors of heart disease: A quantitative review. *Psychological Bulletin, 101*, 343–362.

Bradley, L. A., Young, L. D., Anderson, K. O., Turner, R. A., Agudelo, C. A., McDaniel, L. K., Pisko, E. J., Semble, E. L., & Morgan, T. M. (1987). Effects of psychological therapy on pain behavior of rheumatoid arthritis patients: Treatment outcome and six-month followup. *Arthritis and Rheumatism, 30*, 1105–1114.

Bramwell, L. (1986). Wives' experiences in the support role after husbands' first myocardial infarction. *Heart and Lung, 15*, 578–584.

Brand, A. H., Johnson, J. H., & Johnson, S. B. (1986). Life stress and diabetic control in children and adolescents with insulin-dependent diabetes. *Journal of Pediatric Psychology, 11*, 481–495.

Bridge, L. R., Benson, P., Pietroni, P. C., & Priest, R. G. (1986). Relaxation and imagery in the treatment of breast cancer. *British Medical Journal, 297*, 1169–1172.

Brownwell, K. D. (1982). Obesity: Understanding and treating a serious, prevalent and refractory disorder. *Journal of Consulting and Clinical Psychology, 50*, 820–840.

Brownell, K. D. (1990). *The Learn Program for weight control.* Dallas, TX: Brownell & Hager.

Brownell, K. D., Cohen, R. Y., Stunkard, A. J., Felix, M. R., & Cooley, N. B. (1984). Weight loss competitions at the worksite: Impact on weight, morale, and cost effectiveness. *American Journal of Public Health, 74*, 1283–1285.

Brownell, K. D., Marlatt, G. A., Lichtenstein, E., & Wilson, G. T. (1986). Understanding and preventing relapse. *American Psychologist, 41*, 765–782.

Buccheri, G. F., Ferrigno, D., Curcio, A., Vola, F., & Rosso, A. (1989). Continuation of chemotherapy versus supportive care alone in patients with inoperable non-small cell lung cancer and stable disease after two or three cycles of MACC: Results of a randomized prospective study. *Cancer, 63*, 428–432.

Bukberg, J., Penman, D., & Holland, J. C. (1984). Depression in hospitalized cancer patients. *Psychosomatic Medicine, 46*, 199–212.

Burgess, C., Morris, T., & Pettingale, K. W. (1988). Psychological response to cancer diagnosis—II. Evidence for coping styles (coping styles and cancer diagnosis). *Journal of Psychosomatic Research, 32*, 263–272.

Burish, T. C., & Bradley, L. A. (1983). *Coping with chronic disease: Research and applications.* New York: Academic Press.

Burish, T. G., Meyerowitz, B. E., & Carey, M. P. (1987). The stressful effects of cancer in adults. In A. Baum & J. Singer (Eds.), *Handbook of psychology and health* (Vol. 5, pp. 137–173). Hillsdale, NJ: Erlbaum.

Burns, K. L., Green, P., & Chase, H. P. (1986). Psychosocial correlates of glycemic control as a function of age in youth with insulin-dependent diabetes. *Journal of Adolescent Health Care, 7*, 311–319.

Burns, L., Chase, D., & Goodwin, W. J. (1987). Treatment of patients with Stage IV cancer: Do the ends justify the means? *Otolaryngology: Head and Neck Surgery, 97*, 8–14.

Carey, M. P., & Burish, T. G. (1988). Etiology and treatment of the psychological side effects associated with cancer chemotherapy: A critical review and discussion. *Psychological Bulletin, 104*, 307–325.

Cassileth, B. R., Lusk, E. J., Strouse, T. B., Miller, D. S., Brown, L. L., Cross, P. A. (1985). A psychological analysis of cancer patients and their next-of-kin. *Cancer, 55*, 72–76.

Cassileth, B. R., Lusk, E. J., Strouse, T. B., Miller, D. S., Brown, L. L., Cross, P. A., & Tenaglia, A. N. (1984). Psychosocial status in chronic illness: A comparative analysis of six diagnostic groups. *New England Journal of Medicine, 311*, 506–511.

Cassileth, B. R., Walsh, W. P., & Lusk, E. J. (1988). Psychosocial correlates of cancer survival: A subsequent report 3 to 8 years after cancer diagnosis. *Journal of Clinical Oncology, 6*, 1753–1759.

Chambers, W. N., & Reiser, M. F. (1953). Emotional stress in the precipitation of congestive heart failure. *Medicine, 15*, 38–60.

Chesney, M. A., Black, G. W., Swan, G. E., & Ward, M. M. (1987). Relaxation training for essential hypertension at the worksite: I. The untreated mild hypertensive. *Psychosomatic Medicine, 49*, 250–263.

Christman, N. J., McConnell, E. A., Pfeiffer, C., Webster, K. K., Schmitt, M., & Ries, J. (1988). Uncertainty, coping, and distress following myocardial infarction: Transition from hospital to home. *Research in Nursing and Health, 11*, 71–82.

Chrvala, C. A., & Weiner, A. W. (1989, April). *Need and availability of social support for the cancer patient.* Paper presented at the Western Psychological Association annual meetings, Reno, NV.

Clark, D. C., Cavanaugh, S., & Gibbons, R. D. (1983). The core symptoms of depression in medical and psychiatric patients. *Journal of Nervous and Mental Disease, 171*, 705–713.

Cohen, S. (1988). Psychosocial models of the role of social support in the etiology of physical disease. *Health Psychology, 7*, 269–297.

Cohen, S., & Edwards, J. R. (1989). Personality characteristics as moderators of the relationship between stress and disorder. In R. W. J. Neufeld (Ed.), *Advances in the investigation of psychological stress* (pp. 235–283). New York: Wiley.

Cohen, S., & McKay, G. (1984). Social support, stress and the buffering hypothesis: A theoretical analysis. In A. Baum, J. E. Singer, & S. E. Taylor (Eds.), *Handbook of psychology and health* (pp. 253–267). Hillsdale, NJ: Erlbaum.

Cohen, S., & Wills, T. A. (1985). Stress, social support, and the buffering hypothesis. *Psychological Bulletin, 98*, 310–357.

Collins, R. L., Taylor, S. E., & Skokan, L. A. (in press). A better world or a shattered vision? Changes in perspectives following victimization. *Social Cognition.*

Contrada, R. J., Wright, R. A., & Glass, D. C. (1985). Psychophysiological correlates of Type A behavior: Comments on Houston (1983) and Holmes (1983). *Journal of Research in Personality, 19*, 12–30.

Costello, R. M. (1975a). Alcoholism treatment and evaluation: In search of methods. *International Journal of the Addictions, 10*, 251–275.

Costello, R. M. (1975b). Alcoholism treatment and evaluation: Collation of two-year followup studies. *International Journal of the Addictions, 10*, 275–293.

Cronkite, R. C., & Moos, R. H. (1984). The role of predisposing and moderating factors in the stress–illness relationship. *Journal of Health and Social Behavior, 25*, 372–393.

Curry, S. J., Marlatt, G. A., Gordon, J., & Baer, J. S. (1988). A comparison to alternative theoretical approaches to smoking cessation and relapse. *Health Psychology, 7*, 545–556.

Cushman, L. A. (1986). Secondary neuropsychiatric complications in stroke: Implications for acute care. *Archives of Physical Medicine Rehabilitation, 69*, 877–879.

Dakof, G. A., & Taylor, S. E. (1990). Victims' perceptions of social support: What is helpful from whom? *Journal of Personality and Social Psychology, 58*, 80–89.

Danoff, B., Kramer, S., Irwin, P., & Gottlieb, A. (1983). Assessment of the quality of life in long-term survivors after definitive radiotherapy. *American Journal of Clinical Oncology, 6*, 339–345.

Dattore, R. I., Shontz, F. C., & Coyne, L. (1980). Premorbid personality differentiation of cancer and noncancer groups: A test of the hypothesis of cancer proneness. *Journal of Consulting and Clinical Psychology, 48*, 388–394.

Davis, W. K., Hess, G. E., Van Harrison, R., & Hiss, R. G. (1987). Psychosocial adjustment to and control of diabetes mellitus: Differences by disease type and treatment. *Health Psychology, 6*, 1–14.

de Haes, J. C. J. M., & van Knippenberg, F. C. E. (1985). The quality of life of cancer patients: A review of the literature. *Social Science and Medicine, 20*, 808–817.

Dembroski, T. M., & Costa, P. R., Jr. (1987). Coronary prone behavior: Components of the Type A pattern and hostility. *Journal of Personality, 55*, 211–235.

Dennis, C., Houston-Miller, N., Schwartz, R. G., Ahn, D. K., Kraemer, H. C., Gossard, D., Juneau, M., Taylor, C. B., & DeBusk, R. F. (1988). Early return to work after uncomplicated myocardial infarction: Results of a randomized trial. *Journal of The American Medical Association, 260*, 214–220.

Derogatis, L. R., Abeloff, M., & Melasaratos, N. (1979). Psychological coping mechanisms and survival time in metastatic breast cancer. *Journal of the American Medical Association, 242*, 1504–1508.

Derogatis, L. R., Morrow, G. R., Fetting, J., Penman, D., Piasetsky, S., Schmale, A. M., Henrichs, M., & Carnicke, C. L. M., Jr. (1983). The prevalence of psychiatric disorders among cancer patients. *Journal of the American Medical Association, 249*, 751–757.

DeVellis, R. F., DeVellis, B. M., Sauter, S. V. H., & Cohen, J. L. (1986). Predictors of pain and functioning in arthritis. *Health Education Research, 1*, 61–67.

DiMatteo, M. R., & DiNicola, D. D. (1982). *Achieving patient compliance*. New York: Pergamon Press.

Dimond, M. (1979). Social support and adaptation to chronic illness: The case of maintenance hemodialysis. *Research in Nursing and Health, 2*, 101–108.

Dimsdale, J. E., Pierce, C., Schoenfeld, D., Brown, A., Zusman, R., & Graham, R. (1986). Suppressed anger and blood pressure: The effects of race, sex, social class, obesity, and age. *Psychometric Medicine, 48*, 430–436.

Dishman, R. K. (1982). Compliance/adherence in health-related exercise. *Health Psychology, 1*, 237–267.

Dracup, K. (1985). A controlled trial of couples group counseling in cardiac rehabilitation. *Journal of Cardiopulmonary Rehabilitation, 5*, 436–442.

Droge, D., Arntson, P., & Norton, R. (1986). The social support function in epilepsy self-help groups. *Small Group Behavior, 17*, 139–163.

Dunbar, F. (1943). *Psychosomatic diagnosis*. New York: Hoeber.

Dunbar, J. M., & Agras, W. S. (1980). Compliance with medical instructions. In J. M. Ferguson & C. B. Taylor (Eds.), *Comprehensive handbook of behavioral medicine* (Vol. 3, pp. 115–145). New York: Spectrum.

Dunkel-Schetter, C. (1984). Social support and cancer: Findings based on patient interviews and their implications. *Journal of Social Issues, 40*, 77–98.

Dunkel-Schetter, C., Feinstein, L., Taylor, S. E., & Falke, R. (1990). *Patterns of coping with cancer and their correlates*. Manuscript submitted for publication.

Dunkel-Schetter, C., Folkman, S., & Lazarus, R. S. (1987). Correlates of social support receipt. *Journal of Personality and Social Psychology, 53*, 71–80.

Egbert, L. D., Battit, G. E., Welch, C. E., & Bartlett, M. K. (1964). Reduction of postoperative pain by encouragement and instruction of patients: A study of doctor-patient rapport. *New England Journal of Medicine, 270*, 825–827.

Ell, K. O., Nishimoto, R. H., Mantell, J. E., & Hamovitch, M. B. (1988). Psychological adaptation to cancer: A comparison among patients, spouses and non-spouses. *Family System Medicine, 6*, 335–348.

Ell, K. O., Nishimoto, R. H., Morvay, T., Mantell, J. E., & Hamovitch, M. B. (1989). A longitudinal analysis of psychological adaptation among survivors of cancer. *Cancer, 63*, 406–413.

Evans, D. L., McCartney, C. F., Haggerty, J. J., Nemeroff, C. B., Golden, R. N., Simon, J. B., Quade, D., Holmes, V., Droba, M., Mason, G. A., Fowler, W. C., & Raft, D. (1988). Treatment of depression in cancer patients is associated with better life adaptation: A pilot study. *Psychosomatic Medicine, 50*, 71–76.

Fayers, P. M., & Jones, D. R. (1983). Measuring and analyzing quality of life in cancer clinical trials: A review. *Statistics in Medicine, 2*, 429–446.

Felton, B. J., & Revenson, T. A. (1984). Coping with chronic illness: A study of illness controllability and the influence of coping strategies on psychological adjustment. *Journal of Consulting and Clinical Psychology, 52*, 343–353.

Felton, B. J., Revenson, T. A., & Hinrichsen, G. A. (1984). Coping and adjustment in chronically ill adults. *Social Science and Medicine, 18*, 889–898.

Fitzpatrick, R., Newman, S., Lamb, R., & Shipley, M. (1988). Social relationships and psychological well-being in rheumatoid arthritis. *Social Science and Medicine, 27*, 399–403.

Flay, B. R. (1985). Psychosocial approaches to smoking prevention: A review of findings. *Health Psychology, 4*, 448–488.

Folkman, S., & Lazarus, R. S. (1980). An analysis of coping in a middle-aged community sample. *Journal of Health and Social Behavior, 21*, 219–239.

Folkman, S., Schaefer, C., & Lazarus, R. S. (1979). Cognitive processes as mediators of stress and coping, In V. Hamilton & D. M. Warburton (Eds.), *Human stress and cognition: An information processing approach*. London: Wiley.

Follick, M. J., Gorkin, L., Smith, T. W., Capone, R. J., Visco, J., & Stablein, D. (1988). Quality of life post-myocardial infarction: Effects of a transtelephonic coronary intervention system. *Health Psychology, 7*, 169–182.

Foltz, A. T. (1987). The influence of cancer on self-concept and life quality. *Seminars in Oncology Nursing, 3*, 303–312.

Fox, B. H. (1978). Premorbid psychological factors as related to cancer incidence. *Journal of Behavioral Medicine, 1*, 45–134.

Fox, B. H. (1988). Psychogenic factors in cancer, especially its incidence. In S. Maes, D. Spielberger, P. B. Defares, & I. G. Sarason (Eds.), *Topics in health psychology* (pp. 37–55). New York: Wiley.

Fox, B. H., Ragland, D. R., Brand, R. J., & Rosenman, R. H. (1987). Type A behavior and cancer mortality. *Annals of the New York Academy of Science, 496*, 620–627.

Fredrikson, M., & Matthews, K. A. (in press). Cardiovascular responses to behavior stress and hypertension: A meta-analytic review. *Annals of Behavioral Medicine.*

Frenzel, M. P., McCaul, K. D., Glasgow, R. E., & Schafer, L. C. (1988). The relationship of stress and coping to regimen adherence and glycemic control of diabetes. *Journal of Social and Clinical Psychology, 6*, 77–87.

Friedman, H. S., & Booth-Kewley, S. (1987). The "disease-prone" personality: A meta-analytic view of the construct. *American Psychologist, 42*, 539–555.

Friedman, M., Thoresen, C. E., Gill, J. J., Powell, L. H., Ulmer, D., Thompson, L., Price, V. A., Rabin, D. D., Breall, W. S., Dixon, T., Levy, R., & Bourg, E. (1986). Alteration of Type A behavior and its effect on cardiac recurrences in post myocardial infarction patients: Summary results of the recurrent coronary prevention project. *American Heart Journal, 112*, 653–665.

Funk, S. C., & House, B. K. (1987). A critical analysis of the hardiness scale's validity and utility. *Journal of Personality and Social Psychology, 53*, 572–578.

Gates, C. C. (1988). The "most-significant-other" in the care of the breast cancer patient. *CA—A Cancer Journal for Clinicians, 38*, 146–153.

Ginter, G. G. (1988). Relapse prevention in health promotion: Strategies and long-term outcome. *Journal of Mental Health Counseling, 10*, 123–135.

Goldberg, R. J. (1981). Management of depression in the patient with advanced cancer. *Journal of the American Medical Association, 246*, 373–376.

Goodstein, R. K. (1983). Overview: Cerebrovascular accident and the hospitalized elderly—A multidimensional clinical problem. *American Journal of Psychiatry, 140*, 141–147.

Graydon, J. E. (1988). Factors that predict patients' functioning following treatment for cancer. *International Journal of Nursing Studies, 25*, 117–124.

Greenfield, S., Kaplan, S. H., Ware, J. E., Yano, E. M., & Frank, H. J. L. (1988). Patients' participation in medical care: Effects on blood sugar control and quality of life in diabetes. *Journal of General Internal Medicine, 3*, 448–457.

Greenland, P., & Chu, J. S. (1988). Efficacy of cardiac rehabilitation services with emphasis on patients after myocardial infarction. *Annals of Internal Medicine, 109*, 650–663.

Greer, S. (1984). The psychological dimension in cancer treatment. *Social Science and Medicine, 18*, 345–349.

Greer, S. (1987). Psychotherapy for the cancer patient. *Psychiatric Medicine, 5*, 267–279.

Grieco, A., & Long, C. J. (1984). Investigation of the Karnofsky Performance Status as a measure of quality of life. *Health Psychology, 3*, 129–142.

Hackett, T. P., & Weisman, A. D. (1969). Denial as a factor in patients with heart disease and cancer. *Annals of the New York Academy of Sciences: Care of Patients with Fatal Illness, 164*, 802–817.

Haefner, D., & Kirscht, J. (1970). Motivational and behavioral effects of modifying health beliefs. *Public Health Reports, 85*, 478–484.

Hanson, C. L., Henggeler, S. W., & Burghen, G. A. (1987). Models of associations between psychosocial variables and health-outcome measures of adolescents with IDDM. *Diabetes Care, 10*, 752–758.

Hanson, S. L., & Pichert, J. W. (1986). Perceived stress and diabetes control in adolescents. *Health Psychology, 5*, 439–452.

Harburg, E., Erfurt, J., Hauenstein, L., Chape, C., Schull, W., & Schork, M. (1973). Socioecological stress, suppressed hostility, skin color, and Black-White blood pressure: Detroit. *Journal of Chronic Diseases, 26*, 595–611.

Hawley, D. J., & Wolfe, F. (1988). Anxiety and depression in patients with rheumatoid arthritis: A prospective study of 400 patients. *Journal of Rheumatology, 15,* 932–941.

Hecker, M. H. L., Chesney, M. A., Black, G. W., & Frautschi, N. (1988). Coronary-prone behaviors in the Western collaborative group study. *Psychosomatic Medicine, 50,* 153–164.

Henry, J. P., & Cassel, J. C. (1969). Psychosocial factors in essential hypertension: Recent epidemiologic and animal experimental evidence. *American Journal of Epidemiology, 90,* 171–200.

Holahan, C. J., & Moos, R. H. (1986). Personality, coping, and family resources in stress resistance: A longitudinal analysis. *Journal of Personality and Social Psychology, 51,* 389–395.

Holahan, C. J., & Moos, R. H. (1987). Personal and contextual determinants of coping strategies. *Journal of Personality and Social Psychology, 52,* 946–955.

Holden, C. (1987). Is alcoholism treatment effective? *Science, 236,* 20–22.

Holland, J. C., & Massie, M. J. (1987). Psychosocial aspects of cancer in the elderly. *Clinics in Geriatric Medicine, 3,* 533–539.

Hollandsworth, J. G., Jr. (1988). Evaluation the impact of medical treatment on the quality of life: A 5-year update. *Social Science and Medicine, 26,* 425–434.

House, A. (1987). Depression after stroke. *British Medical Journal, 294,* 76–78.

House, J. A. (1981). *Work stress and social support.* Reading, MA: Addison-Wesley.

House, J. S., Landis, K. R., & Umberson, D. (1988). Social relationships and health *Science, 241,* 540–545.

House, J. S., Umberson, D., & Landis, K. R. (1988). Structures and processes of social support. *American Review of Sociology, 14,* 293–318.

Hughes, J. E. (1987). Psychological and social consequences of cancer. *Cancer Surveys, 6,* 455–475.

Hughes, J. E., & Lee, D. (1987). Depressive symptoms in patients with terminal cancer. In M. Watson & S. Greer (Eds.) *Psychosocial issues in malignant disease.* Oxford, England: Pergamon Press.

Jachuck, S. J., Brierley, H., Jachuck, S., & Willcox, P. M. (1982). The effect of hypotensive drugs on the quality of life. *Journal of the Royal College of General Practitioners, 32,* 103–105.

James, S. A. (1987). Psychosocial precursors of hypertension: A review of the epidemiologic evidence. *Circulation* (Suppl. I), *76,* I60–I66.

James, S. A., Hartnett, S., & Kalsbeek, W. (1983). John Henryism and blood pressure differences among Black men. *Journal of Behavior Medicine, 6,* 259–278.

James, S. A., Hartnett, S. A., & Kalsbeek, W. D. (1984). John Henryism and blood pressure differences among Black men. I. The role of occupational stressors. *Journal of Behavioral Medicine, 7,* 259–276.

Jenkins, R. A., & Pargament, K. I. (1988). Cognitive appraisals in cancer patients. *Social Science and Medicine, 26,* 625–633.

Joffres, M., Reed, D. M., & Nomura, A. M. Y. (1985). Psychosocial processes and cancer incidence among Japanese men in Hawaii. *American Journal of Epidemiology, 121,* 488–500.

Johnson, J. (1982). The effects of a patient education course on persons with a chronic illness. *Cancer Nursing,* 117–123.

Kaminer, Y., & Robbins, D. R. (1989). Insulin misuse: A review of an overlooked psychiatric problem. *Psychosomatics, 30,* 19–24.

Kannel, W. B., & Eaker, E. D. (1986). Psychosocial and other features of coronary heart disease: Insights from the Framingham Study. *American Heart Journal, 112*, 1066–1073.

Kaplan, G. A., & Reynolds, P. (1988). Depression and cancer mortality and morbidity: Prospective evidence from the Alameda County study. *Journal of Behavioral Medicine, 11*, 1–13.

Kaplan, R. M. (1985). Quality of life measurement. In P. Karoly (Ed.), *Measurement strategies in health psychology* (pp. 115–146). New York: Wiley.

Kaplan, R. M., & Hartwell, S. L. (1987). Differential effects of social support and social network on physiological and social outcomes in men and women with Type II diabetes mellitus. *Health Psychology, 6*, 387–398.

Katz, S. T., Ford, A. B., Moskowitz, R. W., Jackson, B. A., & Jaffee, M. W. (1983). Studies of illness in the aged: The index of ADL. *Journal of the American Medical Association, 185*, 914–919.

Keehn, R. J. (1980). Follow-up studies of World War II and Korean conflict prisoners. *American Journal of Epidemiology, 111*, 194–200.

Kelly-Hayes, M., Wolf, P. A., Kannel, W. B., Sytkowski, D., D'Agostino, R. B., & Gresham, G. E. (1988). Factors influencing survival and need for institutionalization following stroke: The Framingham Study. *Archives of Physical Medical Rehabilitation, 69*, 415–418.

Kessler, R. C., & McLeod, J. D. (1985). Social support and mental health in community samples. In S. Cohen & S. L. Syme (Eds.), *Social support and health* (pp. 219–240). Orlando, FL: Academic Press.

Kirkley, B. G., & Fisher, E. B., Jr. (1988). Relapse as a model of nonadherence to dietary treatment for diabetes. *Health Psychology, 7*, 221–230.

Kirscht, J. P., Becker, M., Haefner, D., & Maiman, L. (1978). Effects of threatening communications and mothers' beliefs on weight change in obese children. *Journal of Behavioral Medicine, 1*, 147–157.

Kirscht, J. P., & Rosenstock, I. M. (1979). Patients' problems in following recommendation of health experts. In G. C. Stone, F. Cohen, & N. E. Adler (Eds.), *Health psychology—A handbook*. San Francisco: Jossey-Bass.

Kobasa, S. C. (1979). Stressful life events and health: An inquiry into hardiness. *Journal of Personality and Social Psychology, 37*, 1–11.

Koenig, H. G., Meador, K. G., Cohen, H. J., & Blazer, D. G. (1988). Depression in elderly hospitalized patients with medical illness. *Archives of Internal Medicine, 148*, 1929–1936.

Krantz, D. S., & Deckel, A. W. (1983). Coping with coronary heart disease and stroke. In T. G. Burish & L. A. Bradley (Eds.), *Coping with chronic disease: Research and applications*. New York: Academic Press.

Krantz, D. S., DeQuattro, V., Blackburn, H. W., Eaker, E., Haynes, S., James, S. A., Manuck, S. B., Myers, H., Shekelle, R. B., Syme, S. L., Tyroler, H. A., & Wolf, S. (1987). Task Force 1: Psychosocial factors in hypertension. *Circulation, 76* (Suppl. 1), I84–I88.

Krantz, D. S., & Glass, D. C. (1984). Personality, behavior patterns, and physical illness: Conceptual and methodological issues. In W. D. Gentry (Ed.), *Handbook of behavioral medicine* (pp. 38–86). New York: Guilford Press.

Krantz, D. S., & Manuck, S. B. (1984). Acute psychophysiologic reactivity and risk of cardiovascular disease: A review and methodological critique. *Psychological Bulletin, 96*, 435–464.

Kutner, N. G. (1987). Social ties, social support, and perceived health status among chronically disabled people. *Social Science and Medicine, 25,* 29–34.

Laborde, J. M., & Powers, M. J. (1985). Life satisfaction, health control orientation, and illness-related factors in persons with osteoarthritis. *Research in Nursing and Health, 8,* 183–190.

Laerum, E., Johnsen, N., Smith, P., & Larsen, S. (1987). Can myocardial infarction induce positive changes in family relationships? *Family Practice, 4,* 302–305.

Lang, A. R., & Marlatt, G. A. (1983). Problem drinking: A social learning perspective. In R. J. Gatchel, A. Baum, & J. E. Singer (Eds.), *Handbook of psychology and health: Vol. 1. Clinical psychology and behavioral medicine: Overlapping disciplines* (pp. 121–169). Hillsdale, NJ: Erlbaum.

Lawrence, L., & Christie, D. (1979). Quality of life after stroke: A three-year follow-up. *Age and Ageing, 8,* 167–172.

Lawrence, R. C., Hochberg, M. C., Kelsey, J. L., McDuffie, F. C., Medsger, T-A., Felts, W. R., & Shulman, L. E. (1989). Estimates of the prevalence of selected arthritis and musculo-skeleto diseases in the U.S. *Journal of Rheumatology, 16,* 427–441.

Lazarus, R. S. (1983). The costs and benefits of denial. In S. Brenitz (Ed.), *Denial of stress* (pp. 1–30). New York: International Universities Press.

Lazarus, R. S., & Folkman, S. (1984). *Stress, appraisal, and coping.* New York: Springer.

Lazarus, R. S., & Launier, R. (1978). Stress-related transactions between person and environment. In L. A. Pervin & M. Lewis (Eds.), *Internal and external determinants of behavior.* New York: Plenum.

Leventhal, H., Baker, T. B., Brandon, T., & Fleming, R. (1989). Intervening and preventing cigarette smoking. In T. Ney & A. Gale (Eds.), *Smoking and human behavior* (pp. 313–336). New York: Wiley.

Leventhal, H., & Nerenz, D. (1982). A model for stress research and some implications for the control of stress disorders. In D. Meichenbaum & M. Jaremko (Eds.), *Stress prevention and management: A cognitive behavioral approach* (pp. 5–38). New York: Plenum.

Levin, R., Banks, S., & Berg, B. (1988). Psychosocial dimensions of epilepsy: A review of the literature. *Epilepsia, 29,* 805–816.

Levine, M. N., Guyatt, G. H., Gent, M., De Pauw, S., Goodyear, M. D., Hryniuk, W. M., Arnold, A., Findlay, B., Skillings, J. R., Bramwell, V. H., Levin, L., Bush, H., Abu-Zahra, H., & Kotalik, J. (1988). Quality of life in Stage II breast cancer: An instrument for clinical trials. *Journal of Clinical Oncology, 6,* 1798–1810.

Levy, S. M. (1983). Host differences in neoplastic risk: Behavioral and social contributors to disease. *Health Psychology, 2,* 21–44.

Levy, S. M., Herberman, R., Maluish, A., Schlien, B., & Lippman, M. (1985). Prognostic risk assessment in primary breast cancer by behavioral and immunological parameters. *Health Psychology, 4,* 99–113.

Lichtman, R. R., Taylor, S. E., & Wood, J. V. (1987). Responses to treatment and quality of life after radiation therapy for breast cancer. In H. P. Withers & L. Peters (Eds.), *Innovations in radiation oncology research.* New York: Springer-Verlag.

Linkins, R. W., & Comstock, G. W. (1988). Depressed mood and development of cancer. *American Journal of Epidemiology, 128,* (Abstract), 1266–1270.

Linn, M. W. (1988). Psychotherapy with cancer patients. *Advances in Psychosomatic Medicine, 18*, 54–65.

Lorig, K., Chastain, R. L., Ung, E., Shoor, S., & Holman, H. (1989). Development and evaluation of a scale to measure perceived self-efficacy in people with arthritis. *Arthritis and Rheumatism, 32*, 37–44.

Love, R. R., Leventhal, H., Easterling, D. V., & Nerenz, D. R. (1989). Side effects and emotional distress during cancer chemotherapy. *Cancer, 63*, 604–612.

Lubeck, D. P., & Yelin, E. H. (1988). A question of value: Measuring the impact of chronic disease. *The Millbank Quarterly, 66*, 444–464.

Lustman, P. J. (1988). Anxiety disorders in adults with diabetes mellitus. *Psychiatric Clinics of North America, 11*, 419–432.

Lustman, P. J., Griffith, L. S., & Clouse, R. E. (1988). Depression in adults with diabetes: Results of a 5-year follow-up study. *Diabetes Care, 11*, 605–612.

Lustman, P. J., & Harper, G. W. (1987). Nonpsychiatric physicians' identification and treatment of depression in patients with diabetes. *Comprehensive Psychiatry, 28*, 22–27.

Maddux, J. E., & Rogers, R. W. (1983). Protection motivation and self-efficacy: A revised theory of fear appeals and attitude change. *Journal of Experimental Social Psychology, 19*, 469–479.

Maeland, J. G., & Havik, O. E. (1987a). Psychological predictors for return to work after a myocardial infarction. *Journal of Psychosomatic Research, 31*, 471–481.

Maeland, J. G., & Havik, O. E. (1987b). The effects of an in-hospital education programme for myocardial infarction patients. *Scandinavian Journal of Rehabilitation Medicine, 19*, 57–65.

Magni, G., Silvestro, A., Tamiello, M., Zanesco, L., & Carl, M. (1988). An integrated approach to the assessment of family adjustment to acute lymphocytic leukemia in children. *Acta Psychiatrica Scandinavia, 78*, 639–642.

Maguire, P. (1975). The psychological and social consequences of breast cancer. *Nursing Minor, 140*, 54–57.

Manuel, G. M., Roth, S., Keefe, F. J., & Brantley, B. A. (1987). Coping with cancer. *Journal of Human Stress, 13*, 149–158.

Marks, G., Richardson, J. L., Graham, J. W., & Levine, A. (1986). Role of health locus of control beliefs and expectations of treatment efficacy in adjustment to cancer. *Journal of Personality and Social Psychology, 51*, 443–450.

Marlatt, G. A., & Gordon, J. R. (Eds.). (1985). *Relapse prevention: Maintenance strategies in addictive behavior change*. New York: Guilford.

Marshall, G., & Dunkel-Schetter, C. (1987, August). *Conceptual and methodological issues in the study of coping: The dimensionality of coping*. Paper presented at the American Psychological Association annual meetings, New York.

Marteau, T. M., Bloch, S., & Baum, J. D. (1987). Family life and diabetic control. *Journal of Child Psychology and Psychiatry, 28*, 823–833.

Massie, M. J., & Holland, J. C. (1987). Consultation and liaison issues in cancer care. *Psychiatric Medicine, 5*, 343–359.

Matt, D. A., Sementilli, M. E., & Burish, T. G. (1988). Denial as a strategy for coping with cancer. *Journal of Mental Health Counseling, 10*, 136–144.

Matthews, K. A. (1988). Coronary heart disease and Type A behavior: Update on and alternative to the Booth-Kewley and Friedman (1987) quantitative review. *Psychological Bulletin, 104*, 373–380.

McCrae, R. R. (1984). Situational determinants of coping responses: Loss, threat and challenge. *Journal of Personality and Social Psychology, 46*, 919–928.

Meichenbaum, D. H., & Cameron, R. (1974). The clinical potential and pitfalls of modifying what clients say to themselves. In M. J. Mahoney & C. E. Thoresen (Eds.), *Self-control: Power to the person.* Monterey, CA: Brooks-Cole.

Meyerowitz, B. E. (1980). Psychosocial correlates of breast cancer and its treatments. *Psychological Bulletin, 87*, 108–131.

Meyerowitz, B. E. (1983). Postmastectomy coping strategies and quality of life. *Health Psychology, 2*, 117–132.

Morris, P. L. P., & Raphael, B. (1987). Depressive disorder associated with physical illness: The impact of stroke. *General Hospital Psychiatry, 9*, 324–330.

Murphy, S., Creed, F., & Jayson, M. I. (1988). Psychiatric disorder and illness behaviour in rheumatoid arthritis. *British Journal of Rheumatology, 27*, 357–363.

Murray, D. M., Davis-Hearn, M., Goldman, A. I., Pirie, P., & Luepker, R. V. (1988) Four- and five-year follow-up results from four seventh-grade smoking prevention strategies. *Journal of Behavioral Medicine, 11*, 395–406.

Nail, L. M., King, K. B., & Johnson, J. E. (1986). Coping with radiation treatment for gynecologic cancer: Mood and disruption in usual function. *Journal of Psychosomatic Obstetrics and Gynaecology, 5*, 271–281.

Neale, A. V., Tilley, B. C., & Vernon, S. W. (1986). Marital status, delay in seeking treatment and survival from breast cancer. *Social Science and Medicine, 23*, 305–312.

Neuling, S. J., & Winefield, H. R. (1988). Social support and recovery after surgery for breast cancer: Frequency and correlates of supportive behaviours by family, friends and surgeon. *Social Science and Medicine, 4*, 385–392.

Niemi, M. L., Laaksonen, R., Kotila, M., & Waltimo, O. (1988). Quality of life 4 years after stroke. *Stroke, 19*, 1101–1107.

Parikh, R. M., Lipsey, J. R., Robinson, R. G., & Price, T. R. (1988). A two year longitudinal study of poststroke mood disorders: Prognostic factors related to one and two year outcome. *International Journal of Psychiatry in Medicine, 18*, 45–56.

Parker, J. C., Frank, R. G., Beck, N. C., Smarr, K. L., Buescher, K. L., Phillips, L. R., Smith, E. I., Anderson, S. K., & Walker, S. E. (1988). Pain management in rheumatoid arthritis patients: A cognitive–behavioral approach. *Arthritis and Rheumatism, 31*, 593–601.

Patel, C., & Marmot, M. G. (1987). Stress management, blood pressure and quality of life. *Journal of Hypertension, 5* (Suppl. 1), S21–S28.

Pearlin, L. I., & Schooler, C. (1978). The structure of coping. *Journal of Health and Social Behavior, 19*, 2–21.

Peterson, C., Seligman, M. E. P., & Vaillant, G. E. (1988). Pessimistic explanatory style is a risk factor for physical illness: A thirty-five year longitudinal study. *Journal of Personality and Social Psychology, 55*, 23–27.

Pettingale, K., Greer, S., & Tee, D. (1977). Serum IgA and emotional expression in breast cancer patients. *Journal of Psychosomatic Research, 21*, 395–399.

Pollock, S. E. (1985). Human responses to chronic illness: Physiologic and psychosocial adaptation. *Nursing Research, 35*, 90–95.

Popkin, M. K., Callies, A. L., Lentz, R. D., Colon, E. A., & Sutherland, D. E. (1988). Prevalence of major depression, simple phobia, and other psychiatric disorders in patients with long-standing Type I diabetes mellitus. *Archives of General Psychiatry, 45*, 64–68.

Powell, L. H., & Thoresen, C. E. (1988). Effects of Type A behavioral counseling and severity of prior acute myocardial infarction on survival. *The American Journal of Cardiology, 62*, 1159–1163.

Presant, C. A. (1984).Quality of life in cancer patients: Who measures what? *American Journal Of Clinical Oncology, 7*, 571–573.

Primeau, F. (1988). Post-stroke depression: A critical review of the literature. *Canadian Journal of Psychiatry 33*, 757–765.

Quinn, M. E., Fontana, A. F., & Reznikoff, M. (1987). Psychological distress in reaction to lung cancer as a function of spousal support and coping strategy, *Journal of Psychosocial Oncology, 4*, 79–90.

Reynolds, P., & Kaplan, G. (1986, March). *Social connections and cancer: A prospective study of Alameda County residents.* Paper presented at the Society of Behavioral Medicine annual meetings, San Francisco, CA.

Richter-Heinrich, E., Homuth, B., Heinrich, B, Knust, U., Schmidt, K. H., Wiedemann, R., & Gohlke, H. R. (1988). Behavioral therapies in essential hypertensives: A controlled study. In T. Elbert, W. Langosch, A. Steptoe, & D. Vaitl (Eds.), *Behavioral medicine in cardiovascular disorders* (pp. 113–127). London: John Wiley.

Rippetoe, P. A., & Rogers, R. W. (1987). Effects of components of protection–motivation theory on adaptive and maladaptive coping with a health threat. *Journal of Personality and Social Psychology, 52*, 596–604.

Robertson, E. K., & Suinn, R. M. (1968). The determination of rate of progress of stroke patients through empathy measures of patient and family. *Journal of Psychosomatic Research, 12*, 189–191.

Robinson, R. G. (1986). Post-stroke mood disorder. *Hospital Practice, 21*, 83–89.

Robinson, R. G., & Price, T. R. (1982). Post-stroke depressive disorders: A follow-up study of 103 patients. *Stroke, 13*, 635–640.

Rodin, G., & Voshart, K. (1986). Depression in the medically ill: An overview. *American Journal of Psychiatry, 143*, 696–705.

Rodin, J., & Janis, I. L. (1979). The social power of health-care practitioners as agents of change. *Journal of Social Issues, 35*, 60–81.

Rogentine, G. N., Van Kammen, D., Fox, B., Docherty, J., Rosenblatt, J., Boyd, S., & Bunney, W. (1979). Psychological factors in the prognosis of malignant melanoma: A prospective study. *Psychosomatic Medicine, 41*, 647–655.

Rogers, W. (1984). Changing health-related attitudes and behavior: The role of preventive health psychology. In J. H. Harvey, J. E. Maddux, R. P. McGlynn, & C. D. Stoltenberg (Eds.), *Social perception in clinical and counseling psychology* (Vol. 2, pp. 91–112). Lubbock, TX: Texas Tech University Press.

Rosenbaum, M, & Smira, K. B-A. (1986). Cognitive and personality factors in the delay of gratification of hemodialysis patients. *Journal of Personality and Social Psychology, 51*, 357–364.

Rosenstock, I. M. (1974). The health belief model and preventive health behavior. *Health Education Monographs, 2*, 354–386.

Sackeim, H. A. (1983). Self-deception, self-esteem and depression: The adaptive value of lying to oneself. In J. Masling (Ed.), *Empirical studies of psychoanalytic theories* (Vol. 1, pp. 101–157). Hillsdale, NJ: Analytic Press.

Sackeim, H. A., & Gur, R. C. (1979). Self-deception, other-deception, and self-reported psychopathology. *Journal of Consulting and Clinical Psychology, 47*, 213–215.

Schag, C. C., Heinrich, R. L., & Ganz, P. A. (1983). Cancer Inventory of Problem Situations: An instrument for assessing cancer patients' rehabilitation needs. *Journal of Psychosocial Oncology 1*, 11–24.

Schaefer, C., Coyne, J. C., & Lazarus, R. S. (1981). The health-related functions of social support. *Journal of Behavioral Medicine, 4*, 381–406.

Scheier, M. F., & Carver, C. S. (1985). Optimism, coping, and health: Assessment and implications of generalized outcome expectancies. *Health Psychology, 4*, 219–247.

Scheier, M. F., Weintraub, J. K., & Carver, C. S. (1986). Coping with stress: Divergent strategies of optimists and pessimists. *Journal of Personality and Social Psychology*, 51, 1257–1264.

Schwartz, L. S., Springer, J., Flaherty, J. A., & Kiani, R. (1986). The role of recent life events and social support in the control of diabetes mellitus. *General Hospital Psychiatry, 8*, 212–216.

Scott, D. W. (1983). Anxiety, critical thinking, and information processing during and after breast biopsy. *Nursing Research, 32*, 24–28.

Siegal, B. R., Calsyn, R. J., & Cuddihee, R. M. (1987). The relationship of social support to psychological adjustment in end-stage renal disease patients. *Journal of Chronic Disease, 40*, 337–344.

Silver, R. L., Boon, C., & Stones, M. (1983). Searching for meaning in misfortune: Making sense of incest. *Journal of Social Issues, 39*, 81–102.

Silver, R. L., & Wortman, C. B. (1980). Coping with undesirable life events. In J. Garber & M. E. P. Seligman (Eds.), *Human helplessness: Theory and applications* (pp. 279–340). New York: Academic Press.

Sims, S. E. R. (1987). Relaxation training as a technique for helping patients cope with the experience of cancer: A selective review of the literature. *Journal of Advanced Nursing 12*, 583–591.

Sinyor, D., Amato, P., Kaloupek, D. G., Becker, R., Goldenberg, M., & Coopersmith, H. (1986). Post-stroke depression: Relationships to functional impairment, coping strategies, and rehabilitation outcomes. *Stroke, 17*, 1102–1107.

Sklar, L. W., & Anisman, H. (1981). Stress and cancer. *Psychological Bulletin, 89*, 369–406.

Slevin, M. L., Plant, H., Lynch, D., Drinkwater, J., & Gregory, W. M. (1988). Who should measure quality of life, the doctor or the patient? *British Journal of Cancer, 57*, 109–112.

Smith, T. W. (1989). Interactions, transactions, and the Type A pattern: Additional avenues in the search for coronary-prone behavior. In A. W. Siegman & T. M. Dembroski (Eds.), *In search of coronary-prone behavior: Beyond Type A* (pp. 91–116). Hillsdale, NJ: Erlbaum.

Smith, T. W., Pope, M. K., Rhodewalt, F., & Poulton, J. L. (1989). Optimism, neuroticism, coping, and symptom reports: An alternative interpretation of the life orientation test. *Journal of Personality and Social Psychology, 56*, 640–648.

Sommers-Flanagan, J., & Greenberg, R. P. (1989). Psychosocial variables and hypertension: A new look at an old controversy. *Journal of Nervous and Mental Disease, 177*, 15–24.

Stein, M. J., Wallston, K. A., Nicassio, P. M., & Castner, N. M. (1988). Correlates of a clinical classification schema for the arthritis helplessness subscale. *Arthritis and Rheumatism, 31*, 876–881.

Stephens, M. A. P., Kinney, J. M., Norris, V. K., & Ritchie, S. W. (1987). Social networks as assets and liabilities in recovery from stroke by geriatric patients. *Psychology and Aging, 2*, 125–129.

Stern, M. J., Pascale, L., & Ackerman, A. (1977). Life adjustment postmyocardial infarction: Determining predictive variables. *Archives of Internal Medicine, 137*, 1680–1685.

Storer, J. H., Frate, D. M., Johnson, S. A., & Greenberg, A. M. (1987). When the cure seems worse than the disease: Helping families adapt to hypertension treatment. *Family Relations, 36*, 311–315.

Suls, J., & Sanders, G. S. (1988). Type A behavior as a general risk factor for physical disorder. *Journal of Behavioral Medicine, 11*, 201–226.

Surwit, R. S., & Feinglos, M. N. (1988). Stress and autonomic nervous system in Type II diabetes: A hypothesis. *Diabetes Care, 11*, 83–85.

Taylor, C. B., Houston-Miller, N., Ahn, D. K., Haskell, W., & DeBusk, R. F. (1986). The effects of exercise training programs on psychosocial improvement in uncomplicated postmyocardial infarction patients. *Journal of Psychosomatic Research, 30*, 581–587.

Taylor, S. E. (1983). Adjustment to threatening events: A theory of cognitive adaptation. *American Psychologist, 38*, 1161–1173.

Taylor, S. E., & Brown, J. D. (1988). Illusion and well-being: A social psychological perspective on mental health. *Psychological Bulletin, 103*, 193–210.

Taylor, S. E., Falke, R. L., Shoptaw, S. J., & Lichtman, R. R. (1986). Social support, support groups, and the cancer patient. *Journal of Consulting and Clinical Psychology, 54*, 608–615.

Taylor, S. E., Lichtman, R. R., & Wood, J. V. (1984). Attributions, beliefs about control, and adjustment to breast cancer. *Journal of Personality and Social Psychology, 46*, 489–502.

Taylor, S. E., Lichtman, R. R., Wood, J. V., Bluming, A. Z., Dosik, G. M., & Leibowitz, R. L. (1985). Illness-related and treatment-related factors in psychological adjustment to breast cancer. *Cancer, 55*, 2506–2513.

Telch, C. F., & Telch, M. J. (1985). Psychological approaches for enhancing coping among cancer patients: A review. *Clinical Psychology Review, 5*, 325–344.

Telch, C. F., & Telch, M. J. (1986). Group coping skills instruction and supportive group therapy for cancer patients: A comparison of strategies. *Journal of Consulting and Clinical Psychology, 54*, 802–808.

Temoshok, L. (1987). Personality, coping style, emotion and cancer: Towards an integrative model. *Cancer Surveys, 6*, 545–567.

Tempelaar, R., de Haes, J. C. J. M., de Ruiter, J. H., Bakker, D., van den Heuvel, W. J. A., & van Nieuwenhiujzen, M. G. (in press). The social experiences of cancer patients under treatment: A comparative study. *Social Science and Medicine*.

Thoits, P. A. (1987). Gender and marital status differences in control and distress: Common stress versus unique stress explanations. *Journal of Health and Social Behavior, 28*, 7–22.

Thomas, C. B., & Duszynski, K. R. (1974). Closeness to parents and the family constellation in a prospective study of five disease states: Suicide, mental illness, malignant tumor, hypertension, and coronary heart disease. *Johns Hopkins Medical Journal, 134*, 251–270.

Thompson, D. R., & Cordle, C. J. (1988). Support of wives of myocardial infarction patients. *Journal of Advanced Nursing, 13*, 223–228.

Thompson, D. R., Webster, R. A., Cordle, C. J., & Sutton, T. W. (1987). Specific sources and patterns of anxiety in male patients with first myocardial infarction. *British Journal of Medical Psychology, 60*, 343–348.

Thompson, S. C., Sobolew-Shubin, A., Graham, M. A., & Janigian, A. S. (1989). Psychosocial adjustment following a stroke. *Social Science and Medicine, 28*, 239–247.

Thoresen, C. E., & Mahoney, M. J. (1974). *Behavioral self-control.* New York: Holt.

Turk, D. C., & Meichenbaum, D. (1989). Adherence to self-care regimens: The patient's perspective. In R. H. Rozensky, J. J. Sweet, & S. M. Tovian (Eds.), *Handbook of clinical psychology in medical settings.* New York: Plenum Press.

United States Bureau of the Census. (1989). *U.S. Bureau of the Census Statistical Abstract of the United States 1989* (109th ed.). Washington, DC: Government Printing Office.

van Dam, F. S. A. M., Somers, R., & van Beek-Couzijn, A. L. (1981). Quality of life: Some theoretical issues. *Journal of Clinical Pharmacology, 21*, 166S–168S.

Wallston, B. S., Alagna, S. W., DeVellis, B. McE., & DeVellis, R. F. (1983). Social support and physical health. *Health Psychology, 2*, 367–391.

Waltz, M. (1986). Marital context and post-infarction quality of life: Is it social support or something more? *Social Science and Medicine, 22*, 791–805.

Waltz, M., Badura, B., Pfaff, H., & Schott, T. (1988). Long-term anxiety and depression following myocardial infarct. *Sozial-und Praventivmedizin, 33*, 37–40.

Ware, J. E. (1984). Conceptualizing disease impact and treatment outcomes. *Cancer, 53*, 2316–2323.

Weinberger, D. A. (1990). The construct validity of the repressive coping style. In J. L. Singer (Ed.), *Repression and disassociation.* Chicago: University of Chicago Press.

Weisman, A. D. (1976). Early diagnosis of vulnerability in cancer patients. *American Journal of the Medical Sciences, 271*, 187–196.

Weisman, A., & Worden, J. W. (1976–1977). The existential plight in cancer: Significance of the first 100 days. *International Journal of Psychiatry in Medicine, 7*, 1–15.

Weisman, A., Worden, J. W., & Sobel, H. J. (1980). *Psychosocial screening and intervention with cancer patients: Research report.* Boston: MA: General Hospital.

Welch-McCaffrey, S. (1985). Cancer, anxiety, and quality of life. *Cancer Nursing, 8*, 151–158.

Wellisch, D. K., Jamison, K. R., & Pasnau, R. O. (1978). Psychosocial aspects of mastectomy: II. The man's perspective. *American Journal of Psychiatry, 135*, 543–546.

Whitlock, F. A. (1982). The neurology of affective disorder and suicide. *Australian and New Zealand Journal of Psychiatry, 16*, 1–12.

Wiebe, D. J., & McCallum, D. M. (1986). Health practices and hardiness as mediators in the stress–illness relationship. *Health Psychology, 5*, 425–438.

Wiklund, I., Oden, A., Sanne, H., Ulvenstam, G., Wilhelmsson, C., & Wilhemsen, L. (1988). Prognostic importance of somatic and psychosocial variables after a first myocardial infarction. *American Journal of Epidemiology, 128*, 786–795.

Wilson, W., Ary, D. V., Biglan, A., Glasgow, R. E., Toobert, D. J., & Campbell, D. R. (1986). Psychosocial predictors of self-care behaviors (compliance) and glycemic control in non-insulin-dependent diabetes mellitus. *Diabetes Care, 9,* 614–622.

Wittrock, D. A., Blanchard, E. B., & McCoy, G. C. (1988). Three studies on the relation of process to outcome in the treatment of essential hypertension with relaxation and thermal biofeedback. *Behavioural Research and Therapy, 26,* 53–66.

Woods, P. J., Morgan, B. T., Day, B. W., Jefferson, T., & Harris, C. (1984). Findings on a relationship between Type A behavior and headaches. *Journal of Behavioral Medicine, 7,* 277–286.

Wool, M. S., & Goldberg, R. J. (1986). Assessment of denial in cancer patients: Implications for intervention. *Journal of Psychosocial Oncology, 4,* 1–14.

Worden, J. W. (1984). Psychosocial screening of cancer patients. *Journal of Psychosocial Oncology, 1,* 1–10.

Worden, J. W., & Weisman, A. D. (1984). Preventive psychosocial intervention with newly diagnosed cancer patients. *General Hospital Psychiatry, 6,* 243–249.

Wortman, C. B. (1984). Social support and the cancer patient. *Cancer, 53,* 2339–2360.

Wortman, C. B., & Dunkel-Schetter, C. (1979). Interpersonal relationships and cancer: A theoretical analysis. *Journal of Social Issues, 35,* 120–155.

Wortman, C. B., & Dunkel-Schetter, C. (1987). Conceptual and methodological issues in the study of social support. In A. Baum & J. E. Singer (Eds.), *Handbook of psychology and health* (Vol. 5, pp. 63–108). Hillsdale, NJ: Erlbaum.

Wortman, C. B., & Silver, R. C. (1987). The myths of coping with loss. *Journal of Consulting and Clinical Psychology, 57,* 349–357.

Wortman, C. B., & Silver, R. C. (1989). Coping with irrevocable loss. In G. R. VandenBos & B. K. Bryant (Eds.), *Cataclysms, crises, and catastrophes: Psychology in action* (Master Lecture Series 6) (pp. 189–235). Washington, DC: American Psychological Association.

Zachariah, P. K. (1987). Quality of life with antihypertensive medication. *Journal of Hypertension, 5,* (Suppl.), S105–S110.

Zarski, J. J., West, J. D., DePompei, R., & Hall, D. E. (1988). Chronic illness: Stressors, the adjustment process, and family-focused interventions. *Journal of Mental Health Counseling, 10,* 145–158.

Zich, J., & Temoshok, L. (1987). Perceptions of social support in men with AIDS and ARC: Relationships with distress and hardiness. *Journal of Applied Social Psychology, 17,* 193–215.

Zonderman, A. B., Costa, P. T., & McCrae, R. R. (1989). Depression as a risk for cancer morbidity and mortality in a nationally representative sample. *Journal of the American Medical Association, 262*(9), 1191–1195.

THE CHILD WITH DIABETES: A DEVELOPMENTAL STRESS AND COPING PERSPECTIVE

D onald L. Wertlieb is a clinical–developmental psychologist whose major research interest has been the understanding of the complex processes by which children and families cope with stress. His general research agenda is the articulation of a developmentally informed taxonomy of stress and coping processes, which could serve to guide investigations of child and family development as well as guide our efforts in clinical and social intervention. One specific focus of his recent work has been how children and families cope with the stresses of marital separation and divorce. A second focus, and the topic of his 1989 American Psychological Association Master Lecture, is how children and families cope with chronic illness, with specific emphasis on adaptation to insulin-dependent diabetes mellitus. Reports of his research have appeared in the *American Journal of Orthopsychiatry, Health Psychology, Journal of Applied Developmental Psychology, Journal of Clinical Child Psychology, Journal of Pediatric Psychology,* and *Journal of Personality and Social Psychology,* among others.

Wertlieb is associate professor and chairman at the Eliot-Pearson Department of Child Study, Tufts University, and has been a lecturer at the Department of Social Medicine and Health Policy, Harvard Medical School. At Tufts, he teaches undergraduate and graduate courses in developmental psychopathology, pediatric psychology, and assessment and consultation. His undergraduate education and first master's degree are from Tufts. He is a graduate of the Clinical and Community Psychology Program at Boston University. Prior to joining the Tufts faculty, he served on the faculty of the Judge Baker Guidance Center. He has been active in organized psychology at the national, regional, and state levels, including APA Division of Child, Youth, and Family Services; Section on Clinical Child Psychology; Society of Pediatric Psychology; New England Psychological Association; and Massachusetts Psychological Association. He maintains an independent practice providing consultation and mental health services to individuals, families, schools, and human service agencies.

THE CHILD WITH DIABETES: A DEVELOPMENTAL STRESS AND COPING PERSPECTIVE

First described almost two thousand years ago by Aretaeus the Cappadocian, diabetes mellitus is among the most common of chronic diseases and affects nearly 10 million Americans.[1] Taking into account the various serious complications associated with it, insulin-dependent diabetes mellitus (IDDM) is our nation's third leading cause of death and is responsible for an estimated 300,000 deaths each year (Surwit, Feinglos, & Scovern, 1983). Diabetes affects 1 in every 800 children below the age of 18 years, making IDDM one of the most common childhood endocrine problems. The illness onset can occur throughout the life

---

[1]Most recent work distinguishes between Type I and Type II diabetes. The focus of this chapter, Type I diabetes, is also labeled as *insulin dependent diabetes mellitus* (IDDM), because it involves complete pancreatic failure and requires insulin replacement by injection. IDDM is also the form of diabetes present in childhood, and used to be referred to as "juvenile-onset" diabetes. However, adults can also develop IDDM, and children may develop other types of diabetes. Type II diabetes, or *noninsulin dependent diabetes* (NIDDM) is far more common and characterizes nearly 85% of the population with diabetes. These individuals retain some endogenous insulin and are generally able to maintain homeostatic glycemic control through diet, weight management, and sometimes oral medication to stimulate glucose metabolism. We now have available certain immunologic and genetic markers that distinguish diabetes types, and the discussion that follows will generally focus on Type I (Bradley, 1988; Johnson, 1989).

---

span, although newly diagnosed cases peak between 5 and 6 and 11 and 13 years of age, with equal prevalence for boys and girls (Drash, 1981; Traisman, 1980).

IDDM presents a wide range of stressors and challenges for children and their families. In this chapter, we will examine how children live with diabetes. We begin with an overview of some of the medical and psychological aspects of IDDM. We then offer an analysis using the stress and coping paradigm to convey our current understanding of the illness and of the opportunities for advancing that understanding. We conclude with a consideration of some of the issues in research and intervention.

An IDDM Pathophysiology Primer

Diabetes mellitus is "a collection of several disorders with different underlying causes and with multiple hormonal abnormalities" (Bradley, 1988, pp. 383–384). The hallmark of these disorders is "an absolute or relative insufficiency of insulin secretion for the efficient metabolism of glucose" (Fisher, Delamater, Bertelson, & Kirkley, 1982, p. 993). "The beta cells of the pancreas produce insufficient insulin or the insulin produced may not be used effectively. Relative insufficiency of insulin may be due to hypersecretion or hyperactivity of insulin antagonists such as glucagon from the alpha cells of the pancreas, pituitary, adreno-medullary or thyroid hormones" (Bradley, 1988, p. 384). Among the causal factors implicated in diabetes are heredity, viral infections, auto-immunity, and psychological stress (Turk & Speers, 1983).

Insulin deficiency diminishes the body's ability to store and use glucose, the sugar that is transported in the blood and is the main source of energy for cells under most conditions. In the absence of an adequate insulin effect, blood glucose (or blood sugar) accumulates and spills over into the urine. Osmotic diuresis leads to frequent urination, thirst, and dehydration. The body's cells, hungry, even "starving" for the unavailable glucose, mobilize the body's energy reserves—glycogen, fat, and protein—for sustenance. The child experiences fatigue and weight loss.

Efficient use of these back-up metabolites is derailed. Normal glucose metabolism produces substances central to fat utilization. In the

We appreciate the helpful comments of Barbara Anderson, Janet Milley, Andrew Safyer, Paul Costa, and several anonymous reviewers on earlier versions of this chapter. Partial support for preparation of this work was provided by U.S. Public Health Service grant # NIAMDDK-NIHRO1AM27845. Thanks are expressed to Rose Chioccariello and Laura Cahaly for preparation of the manuscript.

Correspondences concerning this chapter should be addressed to Donald Wertlieb, Eliot-Pearson Department of Child Study, Tufts University, Medford, Massachusetts 02155.

diabetic disease process, this fat metabolism is thus incomplete and the intermediate metabolites, called ketone bodies, accumulate in the blood. As the kidneys clear the blood of excessive glucose and ketone bodies, urine volume rises. The child needs to urinate frequently and experiences thirst as his or her body dehydrates. Excretion of large quantities of the acidic ketones causes coexcretion of the body's buffer base substances (sodium, phosphate, and bicarbonate). Acidosis of the blood ensues; coma, even death, can result.

The child treated for diabetes with insulin can also experience loss of consciousness and coma associated with low blood sugar (hypoglycemia). In managing diabetes, the child must maintain a balance of the amount and timing of his or her insulin intake, carbohydrate consumption, and exercise. Excessively low blood glucose levels lead to insulin shock with disorientation, convulsion, and coma.

So far, our focus has been on the moment-to-moment or day-to-day processes and risks of IDDM. Medical treatment of diabetes strives to prevent both hyperglycemia and hypoglycemia and to maintain blood glucose levels within a relatively "normal" range, with minimum fluctuations. This task involves a regimen of insulin injections, usually once or twice a day, with complex dosage adjustments when needed; regular monitoring of blood glucose levels with reagent strips and a drop of blood from a finger stick; a strict dietary plan with specific types and amounts of food (typically scheduled as three small meals and three snacks); and a program of regular aerobic exercise. The regimen aims not just for day-to-day survival, but for a "near normal" reasonable quality of life and continued mental and physical growth despite the chronic illness. Insulin replacement therapy provides only a crude approximation of normal pancreatic function. The achievement and maintenance of metabolic control (also termed *diabetic control* or *glycemic control*) is also thought to delay or even prevent the very serious long-term manifestations or "complications" of IDDM, most of which appear one or two decades after onset (Davidson, 1981; Johnson, in press-a).

The child with IDDM is at risk for a range of complications in adulthood, many of which may represent the "wear and tear" effect of the illness on the body. Microvascular complications include retinopathy (eye disease), nephropathy (kidney disease), and neuropathy (nerve disease). Hypertension (high blood pressure) is more common among persons with diabetes, and myocardial infarction (heart attack) is twice as prevalent compared with a nondiabetic population. Gangrene and associated limb amputation is five times greater among people with diabetes. Renal failure and blindness exist at a rate 17 to 25 times higher in a diabetic population. Pregnancies are high risk for women with diabetes, with the neonate vulnerable to congenital defects at three times the rate of neonates of nondiabetic births, as well as the likely transmission of the disease given the genetic component of the etiology. Perinatal loss is 5 to 7 times higher for diabetic women relative to nondiabetic women (Bradley, 1988; Davidson, 1981; Johnson, in press-a; Turk & Speers, 1983).

On the horizon are a number of biomedical advances that have potentially powerful implications for how children with IDDM and their families might be living as the century turns and how we as researchers and clinicians will be furthering our understanding of the challenges faced by these families. Examples of these advances suggest some of the most exciting frontiers. One is the introduction of the "insulin pump." A second is the availability of a risk screening technology.

The insulin infusion pump is a small, "beeper" size device, worn externally by the person and attached with a small plastic catheter so that it can supply the body with a continuous supply of insulin. The pump can closely mimic natural pancreatic function, at least relative to the twice-daily injections of the typical regimen of most children with IDDM. The patient can adjust the rate of insulin delivery before meals or in response to changes in glycemic state. Despite the hope and enthusiasm surrounding the introduction of this new technology, there are also the complications and disadvantages that are well summarized by Johnson (in press). For example, the continuous flow of fast-acting insulin puts the individual at greater risk for hypoglycemia, while asleep or if adjustments for meal carbohydrate content are inadequate. Blockage of the catheter, needle displacement, or battery malfunction can quickly lead to hyperglycemia or ketoacidosis. Frequent needle and catheter replacement is required (every 48 hours) and poses a risk (albeit small) of infection. Contact and water sports are precluded. In donning an insulin pump, an "invisible" disability becomes a "visible" disability, drastically altering the perceptions and reactions of the patient and those with whom he or she interacts. "Children typically do not have sufficient cognitive sophistication to carry out the glucose testing and decision making . . . consequently the parent or some other adult would have to closely monitor the child . . . (who) may have negative psychological sequelae in the form of increased dependency. . . . Adolescents may have the cognitive capability to use the pump but are often not sufficiently motivated to carry out the frequent, daily glucose tests demanded by this procedure" (p. 11). Diabetologists and psychosocial researchers are just beginning to evaluate the implications of this new technology, and their evaluations may become useful for the future management of the pump.

A second biomedical advance with important ramifications for future research on psychosocial aspects of IDDM is the new availability of a blood test that reliably detects islet cell antibody (ICA), indicating that an individual is at risk for developing diabetes. Initial data indicate that about 40% of individuals who test islet cell antibody positive (ICA +) develop diabetes within five years, and most of those identified are children (Johnson, in press-b). Thus, a new concern of both diabetologists and psychologists is how children and families cope with learning of their at-risk status. A new opportunity exists for the investigation of preonset biopsychosocial elements of IDDM. The first of these studies is now being carried out within a stress and coping framework (Johnson, in press-b). Along with other innovative work that studies the development of infants at risk for diabetes by virtue of maternal IDDM (e.g., Barglow, Berndt, Burns, & Hatcher, 1986), this broadening window on the developmental course of the child with IDDM and his or her family holds great challenge and promise for enhancing our understanding of how people cope. Having now summarized the pathophysiology of IDDM and having glimpsed some of the newest developments that may have an impact on diagnosis and management of the illness, we will shift our focus to the literature on psychosocial factors.

Psychosocial Factors and IDDM

The role of psychosocial factors in IDDM has long been of interest. In the seventeenth century, Thomas Willis proposed "prolonged sorrow" as a cause of diabetes. However, it was the 1922 discovery of insulin that made the understanding of psychosocial factors more necessary and compelling. Before then, a diagnosis of diabetes amounted to a kind of death sentence. With the advent of insulin treatment, children with diabetes retained a reasonable life expectancy, although certainly a life replete with considerable constraints and challenges.

The earliest work prompted by this new population of individuals living with diabetes involved a quest for the "diabetic personality." A range of psychological and psychosocial variables were investigated in the effort to discover some discriminating characteristic of individuals with diabetes. Such investigations often involved confounded conceptualizations of etiology, disease course, and developmental course. For example, depression was examined as a "causal factor" and concurrently noted as a reaction to the diagnosis and response to the illness, in both normal and pathological dimensions. Early psychosomatic theorists and researchers posed formulations that emphasized the diabetic personality "as one fraught with anxiety, depression, paranoia, dependency conflicts, and sexual problems" (Dunbar, 1954; Menninger, 1935). Researchers began to address the problem by contrasting groups of diabetic patients with a range of comparison groups of "normal," "healthy," or otherwise ill groups on numerous dimensions including self-esteem, ego development, psychopathology, behavior symptoms, anxiety, depression, and social adjustment.

An additional strategy developed by these early researchers was to compare groups of individuals with diabetes in "good control" with groups of individuals with diabetes in "poor control" (e.g., Koski, 1969; Simonds, 1976, 1977). Patients in poor control are more prone to episodes of ketoacidosis and hypoglycemia. Extreme forms of poor control have been labeled *brittle diabetes*. Again, researchers examined an extensive array of psychological variables in an effort to discriminate the groups. An especially important advance associated with this strategy was the broadening of the researcher's focus to include family-level variables, an advance that was stimulated by Minuchin's clinical research defining "psychosomatic" families prone to enmeshment, overprotectiveness, rigidity, lack of conflict resolution, and poor diabetic control (Minuchin et al., 1975).

Recently, this vast literature has been critically reviewed. These reviews surveyed the early work on psychosocial factors in the onset and course of diabetes, as well as implications for psychosocial and family development (Anderson, 1984; Anderson & Auslander, 1980; Anderson & Kornblum, 1984; Dunn & Turtle, 1981; Jacobson & Hauser, 1983; Johnson, 1980). The reviews pointed to pervasive inadequacies and fatal flaws in almost all of the pre-1980 studies. As Johnson (1980) noted, the literature is "inconclusive" (p. 111) and yields "few consistent findings" (p. 110). Dunn and Turtle (1981) concluded by dispelling the myth of the diabetic personality and noted that "in the 40 years of the literature under review, there has been no consistency in the frequency with which any particular methodology was able to define a 'diabetic personality' or personality characteristic. In fact, the frequency of positive results is about that which one would expect by chance in each of the three major comparison methods: random or matched controls, test norms, or clinical assessment" (p. 644). Thus, the 1980s began on a pessimistic note, with lamentation about a literature replete with "uninterpretable findings despite extensive efforts" (Johnson, 1980, p. 113) and even a nihilism prompted by this frustration: "Research into the personality causes, correlates and consequences of diabetes mellitus has been fundamentally on unproductive and unanswerable questions" (Dunn & Turtle, 1981, p. 645).

The efforts of these reviewers were not in vain. Their admonitions and guidance, along with a series of conceptual, technological, and methodological advances, are reflected in the current literature. The conceptual advances most relevant to the present discussions are what we will soon return to in acknowledging the stress and coping paradigm as one of several process-oriented, nonlinear models that provide leverage for research on psychosocial factors in IDDM. The methodological and technological achievements and ongoing work are varied, but certainly include the following strengths: (a) improved assessment of glycemic control, (b) advances in psychosocial and behavioral assessment, and (c) use of more appropriate research designs.

Improved assessment of glycemic control. Early research relied on a range of indices of glycemic control with limited or questionable accuracy, reliability, and validity. These early indices, including infrequent fasting or random glucose determinations, were unsatisfactory in that they "may reflect periodic or unsustained episodes of deterioration in control caused by stress, infection or changes in dietary and exercise routines" (Barglow et al., 1986, p. 788). Variations and concentrations of blood glucose were key elements of hypotheses about disease processes and psychosocial influences. Whether measuring stress and coping, adherence to treatment regimen, or the impact of a medical or psychosocial intervention, the impact on glycemic control is a crucial concern. With the advent of the glycohemoglobin assay in the late 1970s (Blanc, Barnett, Gleason, Dunn, & Soeldner, 1981; Gonen, Rachman, Rubenstein, Tanega, & Horowitz, 1977), a reliable index of metabolic control was available, reflecting an average level of blood glucose over the prior 8 to 12 weeks. Most recent studies use this glycosylated hemoglobin index. Although there is some variation across laboratories, norms are available, and comparability and consensus can now be achieved.

Some concerns have been expressed about an overreliance on this single index of glycemic control, and efforts are under way to construct a battery of indices to measure control using both physiological and behavioral markers (Brand, Johnson, & Johnson, 1986; Daneman, Wolfson, Becker, & Drash, 1981; Johnson, in press).

Another advance in the measurement of glycemic control has been the introduction of corrections for endogenous insulin associated with residual pancreatic function. This is of particular concern in assessing control in recently diagnosed individuals, because the body may continue producing some insulin for several months to as long as two years into the early stages of the illness, a so-called honeymoon period. Serum C-peptide indices reflect levels of endogenous insulin and are beginning to be included in psychosocial research (Bradley, 1988; Delamater, in press; Welborn, Garcia-Webb, Bonser, McCann & Constable, 1983).

An additional advance involves regimen adherence. In recent years, the blood glucose monitoring tasks in the daily regimen of the child with diabetes have become increasingly mechanized, even computerized. Traditionally, patients (or their caretakers) were instructed to monitor and record glucose levels in urine or blood several times a day by wetting reagent strips with the body fluid and matching the strips to a color chart. These procedures remain open for noncompliance and a variety of errors. Portable meters are now available for home blood-glucose monitoring that allow machine reading and memory storage of quantitative data on the time of testing and glucose level. Not only does this equipment open avenues for the study of adherence, but it also potentially generates daily glucose oscillation data that can complement the "average" index in the glycosylated hemoglobin measures so central to current assessment of control (Johnson, in press).

Advances in psychosocial and behavioral assessment. One source of optimism about the yield of contemporary research on psychosocial factors in IDDM lies in recent advances in our operationalization of various constructs that are used in our view of adaptation to illness. Some of these advances are reflected in general concepts and measures such as those captured in our increasingly refined classification of child-hood psychopathology and competence (e.g., Rutter, Tuma, & Lann, 1988). Others are captured in diabetes-specific concepts and measures, which are receiving much attention from researchers with some promising results. Most noteworthy in this latter category is the program by Johnson and her colleagues in which they are developing a multidimensional 24-hour recall measure of diabetes regimen adherence (Johnson, in press). Many of the studies mentioned later illustrate the need for or the use of increasingly valid and reliable assessment instruments.

Use of more appropriate research designs. Contemporary researchers are turning to more sophisticated research designs that are more consonant with the complexity of the field's pressing questions. Multimethod and longitudinal designs, including analyses at the level of the individual, the family, and the health care system are being deployed (Hauser et al., in press; Kovacs, Kass, Schnell, Goldston, & Marsh, 1989).

These advances in the measurement of glycemic control, adherence, and psychological variables as well as the use of more sophisticated methodology and design harmonize with the demands and potentials of the stress and coping paradigm. Having considered some of the crucial medical and psychosocial aspects of IDDM, we will now consider IDDM in terms of the stress and coping paradigm in order to begin to document current understandings and needs.

Stress and Coping Models of IDDM

A number of the current studies of IDDM make explicit use of a stress and coping conceptual framework.[2] Some of the IDDM-specific constructs of this framework are noted in Figure 1 and are discussed here to illustrate the heuristic value of the stress and coping paradigm and to document some of the recent advances in our understanding of child and family adaptation to IDDM. Ultimately, as the model suggests, it is the complex causal relationships among stress, coping, and adaptational

---

[2]Space limitations preclude a general discussion of the stress and coping model. For a more general background, please consult the following reports: Garmezy, 1987; Gersten, Langer, Eisenberg, and Simcha-Fagan, 1977 (pervasiveness or chronicity of stress); Hauser, Vieyra, Jacobson, and Wertlieb, 1985; Hauser et al., 1988; Jandorf, Deblinger, Neale, and Stone, 1986 (the contribution of stress, measured in terms of *hassles*, to physical and mental health); Johnson, 1986 (life events as stressors in childhood and adolescence); Kanner, Coyne, Schaefer, and Lazarus, 1981; Lazarus and Folkman, 1984 (general); Mason, 1975 (a historical view of stress research); McCubbin, 1979 (conceptualizations of the family's coping process); Menaghan, 1983; Moos, 1989; Rolland, 1987 (stress and coping from a life span orientation); Rutter, 1985 (dealing with stress and achieving developmental progress); Thoits, 1986 (social support as coping); and Wertlieb, Weigel, and Feldstein, 1987 (integrating individual and family perspectives).

processes as they unfold over the course of development that must be understood. Currently, we have made some important initial steps toward that goal.

Stress and Diabetes

Traditionally, three dimensions of the relationship between stress and diabetes have interested clinicians and researchers: (a) stress as a cause or trigger of IDDM, (b) stress as a factor in disease course or outcome, and (c) IDDM as a stressor (Bradley, 1988). Findings in each of these areas remain inconsistent, often for the same reasons mentioned in the comprehensive reviews from the early 1980s cited earlier. However, the integration of recent conceptual and methodological advances sustains the interest and productivity in studies with these foci.

The early observations of an association between stressful life events, especially events involving loss, and the onset of IDDM continue to receive empirical attention, despite discounting and harsh methodological critique by several reviewers. Leaverton, White, McCormick,

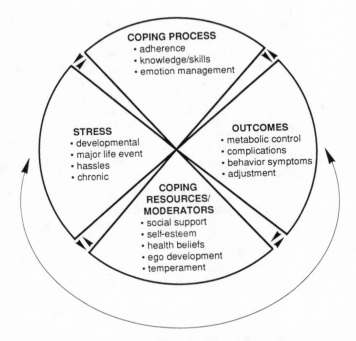

Figure 1. Stress and coping in insulin-dependent diabetes mellitus.

Smith, and Sheikholislam (1980) documented a significantly higher prevalence of parental loss because of death, separation, or divorce in a group of 37 youngsters who subsequently were diagnosed with IDDM when compared with a sociodemographically matched control group. Doubts about such findings often focus on shortcomings of retrospective measures and variability in lag periods between the psychological stress event and the onset or diagnosis of the illness. However, recent identification of individual differences, even idiosyncracies, in psychological stress responses and identification of multiple points of vulnerability in the immunological processes implicated in IDDM may be reviving interest in etiological roles of stress (Barglow et al., 1986; Bradley, 1988). Some of this evidence will be presented later.

Somewhat less controversial, although still inconsistent, are findings that relate stress to disease course or outcome. Conceptualizations vary in positing direct relationships between stress and some index of illness. A range of mediated relationships is hypothesized, most often implicating treatment regimen adherence as a moderator of the impact of stress on disease course (e.g., Hanson, Henggeler, & Burghen, 1987a, 1987b). As is generally the case in child mental health research, there is a reliable, statistically significant association between the accumulation of recent negative major life events and negative health outcomes. In the case of IDDM, negative life event stress is associated with behavior symptoms as well as with poor metabolic control (Barglow et al., 1986).

One of the advances in the conceptualization and measurement of stress mentioned earlier is the consideration of *hassles*—the relatively minor, day-to-day stressors—in contrast or in addition to the more traditional *major life events* stress. Studies that take into consideration hassles are still inconsistent, although enlightening. Hanson and Pichert (1986) documented a relationship between hassles, or minor event stress, and blood glucose levels averaged over a three-day period for 39 youngsters (M age $=$ 13.8 years) at a summer diabetes camp. With the effects of diet and exercise partialed out, the correlation was .38 ($p = .01$), a magnitude consistent with findings in the larger stress–illness literature (Johnson, 1986).

Delamater, Kurtz, Bubb, White, and Santiago (1987) used a similar measure of hassles, a different index of metabolic control, glycosylated hemoglobin, tied to a longer time frame (2–3 months), and a similar age group (M age $=$ 15.4 years) with the same illness duration and found no significant relationship between stress and metabolic control in their group of 27 youngsters with IDDM. However, they did identify some intriguing differences between youngsters in good control and those in poor control in terms of the kinds of hassles identified as stressful. Patients in good metabolic control reported much of their stress to be related to academics and little of it to be related to parents. Patients in poor metabolic control reported diabetes-specific hassles as most stressful. The groups reported similar proportions of peer-related hassles.

The delineation of illness-specific stressors or hassles has been profitably initiated by Kosub and Kosub (1982) in their development of a scale of stresses associated with diabetes. Their inventory included major life events (e.g., "finding out you have diabetes") as well as daily hassles (e.g., "shots"). Allen, Affleck, Tennen, McGrade, and Ratzan (1984) generated some very important data in their cognitive–developmental analysis of the concerns and worries expressed by children 8 to 17 years of age. As they noted, "cognitive development brings the ability to conceptualize future possibilities, implications of the disease, and potential responses of others. This heightened awareness may enable children to prepare for the future and to acquire self-management skills, but it also has a more painful side, increasing the range of anxieties children experience" (p. 216). Incorporation of these more IDDM-specific and developmentally oriented stress assessments should be a goal of future research (e.g., Kanner, Feldman, Weinberger, & Ford, 1987).

One additional approach that shows promise for unraveling the connections between stress and disease course and outcomes uses a more experimental design in which stress responses are induced in a laboratory setting to test hypothesized relationships (Delamater et al., 1988; Gilbert, Johnson, Silverstein, & Malone, 1989). Delamater et al. (1988) compared groups of adolescents (M age $= 14.5$ years) with good ($n = 10$), fair ($n = 10$), and poor ($n = 11$) glycosylated hemoglobin indices. Gilbert et al. (1989) compared groups of adolescents (M age $= 14$ years) with diabetes in good control ($n = 15$), with groups of adolescents with diabetes in poor control ($n = 15$), and with groups of adolescents without diabetes ($n = 15$). Both studies used an extensive battery of physiological, behavioral, and self-report indices of anxiety and arousal administered during stressful manipulations. Gilbert et al. (1989) included a venipuncture and two public speaking tasks. Delamater et al. (1988) used a cognitive quiz and family interaction tasks. The stressors induced several of the expected stress responses, but the pattern of responses was similar across all groups. The groups with diabetes in poor control did exhibit a higher heart rate throughout both studies including higher baseline measures at the studies' inception, suggesting to the authors a link with significant autonomic and cardiac risk in this population. Delamater et al. (1988) summarized their negative findings as failing "to support the hypotheses that short-term, experimentally induced psychological stress acutely worsens metabolic control or that physiological responses to such stress are greater in poorly controlled adolescent patients" (p. 70); nonetheless, they concluded their discussion by hypothesizing "that psychological stress may exert adverse effects on metabolic control if stress is very severe or more chronic in the patient's natural environment, particularly if the patient has limited coping resources and disrupted regimen adherence" (p. 85).

The third dimension of the stress–diabetes relationship emphasizes diabetes as a stressor. Kovacs' ongoing longitudinal study of an onset cohort of children and adolescents with diabetes has generated a very comprehensive and elegant conceptualization and some initial empirical data documenting IDDM as a significant stressor (Kovacs & Feinberg, 1982; Kovacs et al., 1985). Consistent with the stress and coping paradigm introduced at the beginning of this chapter, Kovacs and her colleagues differentiated between objective correlates (in particular the management requirements and their implications) and subjective correlates (in particular the psychological issues posed by IDDM for the child and family). Of course, there may be individual differences in the perception or appraisal of the stressfulness of any of these elements (a topic to which we will return when we examine coping processes): "Every single component of diabetic care is a potential source of stress for the child and parent(s)" (Kovacs & Feinberg, 1982, p. 170).

The management requirements outlined by Kovacs and Feinberg (1982) and others illustrate the enormous complexity of the medical regimen required to sustain life and quality of life for the child with diabetes. Consider the daily insulin injections—pain and discomfort along with multiple tasks such as "access to a hypodermic syringe and prebottled insulin, appropriate measurement of insulin dose, preparation of the injection site, actually administering the injection, varying the site of administration, and keeping a written record of insulin dose, changing the dose, if necessary, based on the integration of information" from glucose testing of blood or urine (p. 170). In addition, effects of diet, exercise, or a destabilization associated with even a minor illness have to be part of the integration. The diet itself is highly structured in terms of timing and types and amounts of foods. The child and caretaker must be skilled at recognizing and responding to insulin reactions or hypoglycemia. The daily scheduling and coordination of each of these tasks is a key challenge requiring sophistication, organization, and regimentation.

Among the nondaily stresses identified in the Kovacs study are the various yearly medical visits, including the blood and urine lab work. From time to time, an inpatient hospitalization might be required if an infection is not healing properly or if metabolic control is disrupted too severely. The prospect of the numerous long-term complications noted earlier—eye disease, vascular disease, kidney disease, limb amputation—and the associated psychosocial and medical implications constitute additional stress potentials.

Determination and negotiation of age-appropriate division of labor or sharing of responsibility for management of the illness represents another chronic stressor. Conventional practice suggests that by ages 10 or 11, most children will be cognitively and emotionally "ready" to measure and administer their own insulin. However, a recent study presented by Fonagy, Moran, Lindsay, Kurtz, and Brown (1987) found that, in children younger than 12 years, "early and independent participation in the implementation of the diabetic regimen was associated with poor (metabolic) control" (p. 1009). These researchers considered their findings to be consistent with observational studies that found inadequacies in diabetes knowledge and skills of children at this age (e.g., Johnson et al., 1982). They concurred with Ingersoll, Orr, Herrold, and Golden (1986) in noting that "parental participation in implementing the regimen may well ensure the provision of resources which are necessary but not sufficient to ensure good glycemic control" (Fonagy et al., 1987, p. 1013).

An additional developmental stressor that is complicated by IDDM can be identified in adolescence, as a youngster "confronts the objective fact that certain career choices will be closed to him or her (e.g., airline pilot) and that other potentially hazardous vocations or avocations are not recommended (sky diving, mountain climbing, etc.)" (Kovacs & Feinberg, 1982, p. 171).

Despite a great deal of clinical and conceptual discussion of IDDM as a stressor, recent empirical data and methodological critiques urge qualification of this view (Delamater, in press). The initial reports from the two existing longitudinal studies provide a basis for tempering our notions of the stressfulness of IDDM. Kovacs et al. (1985) reported a 36% rate of psychiatric disorder in their group ($N = 74$) of 8 to 13-year-old children in their first year after diagnosis. The relatively mild diagnosis of adjustment disorder with depression characterized most of these cases, and a normal level of preexisting psychological problems was assessed in the sample. By nine-months postdiagnosis, 93% of these youngsters had recovered and no longer exhibited the psychopathological pattern. The 64% of the children who were noncases did exhibit some feelings of depression, anxiety, withdrawal and isolation, but these were transient "normative" responses.

A wide range of psychosocial indicators including low self-esteem, behavior problems, and locus of control failed to distinguish children with recent-onset diabetes from a comparison group of children with acute illnesses, with both groups exhibiting normal or nonclinical mean scores on these measures (Jacobson et al., 1986). The children with diabetes did score lower in terms of school-related competence, however. One might interpret this data as nonsupportive of the hypothesis of IDDM as a stressor. Such an interpretation appears premature until longitudinal follow-up data are considered. As the stress and coping paradigm suggests, psychological distress or psychiatric disturbance at the initial postdiagnosis period, although transient, may be predictive of later adaptational difficulties and, more certainly, may be associated with other aspects of later psychosocial development or regimen adherence (Delamater, in press).

To summarize this discussion of stress and diabetes, we have noted data that suggest an etiological relationship, and we have emphasized conceptualizations and data that focus on (a) stress as an influence on illness course and outcome and (b) diabetes itself as a stressor. Among the dimensions of stress identified as salient were the developmental stressors, major life events, and daily hassles. It is useful to distinguish the acute stresses of illness onset, diagnosis, and early management from the chronic stresses of living with diabetes. The stressfulness of any of these elements, as well as any eventual manifestation as a health or illness outcome or as a factor in adaptation, rests heavily on their mediation by the coping processes, coping resources, and coping moderators to which we now turn.

Coping With IDDM

Complementing the stress framework mentioned earlier for IDDM as a stressor, Kovacs and Feinberg (1982) discerned from the literature and from their initial interviews a catalogue of coping responses that children and their families bring to bear on the challenges of IDDM. Again, some of these coping processes focus on the management requirements of diabetes, whereas others emphasize the subjective or psychological correlates. Coping with the management requirements of diabetes constitutes adherence or compliance with the regimen prescribed by the child's health care team. The complexities of adherence and nonadherence, as well as the monumental challenges involved in the study of these processes, are well addressed in Johnson's (in press-a) recent comprehensive review.

Among management-related coping processes, Kovacs and Feinberg (1982) and others described division of labor and sharing of responsibility among family members, including "sibling deployment," which is the involvement of brothers and sisters in certain aspects of the diabetes management routine. Simultaneous to the reorganization within the family in response to the IDDM demands, there are often bids for resources outside the family. This might include enrollment in self-help groups such as the American Diabetes Association or various forms of information seeking that tap the health care team as well as other community resources.

Some more specific examples at the day-to-day level illustrate this coping in behavioral terms. Some families use objective reminders (e.g., posting a schedule and chart for glucose testing results on the bathroom wall). A child may begin to wear a wristwatch with an alarm that is set for snack times. Family activities require additional planning that takes into account the demands of the regimen. (Kovacs and Feinberg, 1982, mentioned a family that shifted to relying on motels with a kitchenette in the room for their vacations.) The parents and the child must become active, effective teachers and inform school teachers and nurses, as well as friends and relatives who might host the child, of his or her special needs. A wide range of family habits and routines get reassessed and changed. In some families where both a parent and child have IDDM, they may synchronize their injection, glucose testing schedules, or both (Kovacs & Feinberg, 1982).

Adherence to the treatment regimen is often a relative matter, and Kovacs and Feinberg (1982, p. 177) designated certain coping processes as "potentially reasonable modified implementation." For instance, "partially attending to tasks," "substituting task components" or otherwise "altering aspects of the daily routine" were noted by many families. Blood tests might be done, but not properly recorded. Sweets might be eliminated, but other crucial diet details overlooked. Weekend or summer routines might be more lax than school-day rituals. Also at play are a range of cognitive strategies including self-deception, lying, imaging, or mental rehearsal to cope with the discomfort of an injection or with anticipation of the management of an insulin reaction.

In understanding how children and families cope with the more subjective and psychological dimensions of IDDM, we must be satisfied with a series of more clinically meaningful descriptions that, only very recently, are being addressed using systematic, empirical methods. Especially in characterizing the initial period of IDDM onset and diagnosis, the coping process has been likened to a grief and mourning process for both parents and child, with "acceptance of diabetes" as the hoped-for outcome (Kovacs & Feinberg, 1982). This may indeed be a crucial immediate task for the child with IDDM and his or her family, but its specific dynamics and alternative implications for subsequent coping, development, and metabolic control remain to be documented.

Kovacs and Feinberg (1982) identified a number of intrapsychic, behavioral, and interpersonal "maneuvers" that appear to operate as dimensions of coping as the crisis of diagnosis is resolved. Among the intrapsychic maneuvers that they described are efforts to manage the continuing or recurring negative affect—anger, depression, anxiety, and fear—associated with the vicissitudes of the illness. *Cognitive distancing*, including detachment or rejection, has also been observed between family members. *Denial* characterizes some of the effort, sometimes with a positive consequence so that "potential upheaval is eliminated, and current functioning enhanced" (p. 191). Risk-taking behavior might increase, sometimes with negative consequences so that the illness and treatment regimen are ignored and life-threatening episodes emerge. *Proportioning* appears to be an important element of appraisal-focused coping, with some children and families "catastrophizing" and seeing only the most dire aspects of the illness, and others "de-catastrophizing or minimizing" the impact of the illness (p. 192). Elements of *omnipotent thinking* may be evident as a child or parent portrays himself or herself as supercompetent in his or her diabetes knowledge or management skill. *Vigilant focusing*, with a selective, narrow emphasis, or even preoccupation, either on the disease or on some tangent, may serve to reduce uncertainty and manage anxiety.

Some coping maneuvers have a spiritual or religious bent, such as the inculcation of hope or a search for meaning. Kovacs and Feinberg (1982) mentioned the case of a mother who described her daughter's illness as a blessing from God and an opportunity to test and portray spiritual and emotional strength and worthiness.

Among the behavior maneuvers characterizing parental coping are "tackling" the illness (Lipowski, 1970) through "behaviors leading to mastery" (Kovacs & Feinberg, 1982, p. 192). Learning about the illness and successfully implementing the treatment regimen can be a source of pleasure and enhanced sense of competence and self-esteem. Kovacs and Feinberg suggested that extremes of this mastery-oriented behavior might manifest as parental overprotectiveness or overnurturance. Some parents reported that "keeping busy" provides relief or distraction. This sometimes involved a belief that healing will come with time. Other coping, perhaps more prone to creating or maintaining problems, involved avoiding or giving up. "Through behavioral passivity, possible confrontations with painful issues are minimized" (Kovacs & Feinberg, 1982, p. 193).

We know considerably less about what coping behaviors children bring to bear on the subjective and emotional issues of IDDM. Currently, we rely on a mixture of clinical lore, case studies, and primitive research. Acceptance of the illness, adherence to the treatment regimen, acknowledgment of challenges, responsibilities, limitations, and more general pursuit of age-appropriate peer and family relationships and success with the developmental tasks such as academic achievement appear to be elements of good coping. Several authors have noted that identification with medical personnel, often expressed in the wish to be a doctor or a nurse, constitutes a "good" coping process (Kovacs & Feinberg, 1982).

Among the interpersonal coping maneuvers identified by Kovacs and Feinberg (1982) are "showing the works" and "instructing others," which are strategies that seem to enhance a child's mastery, acceptance of self, and acceptance by others. Whether demonstrating an insulin self-injection to a curious, fascinated, even admiring friend, or delivering a "lecture" to classmates on some complex medical topic, the child with diabetes capitalizes on his or her uniqueness. A contrasting strategy that is used by many youngsters is active and purposeful concealing of the diabetes from others. The child may refuse to eat school-time snacks, refuse to wear a medic-alert bracelet or necklace, or decline invitations for overnights at a friend's house.

A broader range of behaviors has been noted in children experiencing problems adjusting. Among these elements—or perhaps outcomes—of "maladaptive coping" processes are the following:

. . . anxiety, shame, guilt, denial, passive dependence or manipula-
tiveness, regressive or obsessive compulsive behavior, seclusive-
ness and secretiveness, defiance and rebellion, poor self-esteem,
poor peer relations, and highly noncompliant self-care. . . . These
responses allegedly represent: (a) ways to manage the feeling of
being stigmatized and different from age-mates, or feeling inadequate, overdependent, and physically damaged, (b) the wish to assume control over one's destiny, (c) the inability to balance desire
with the reality demands of the illness or (d) reactions to the parents' attitudes toward the diabetes. (Kovacs & Feinberg, 1982, pp.
195–196)

The first systematic empirical efforts to describe these coping processes are just now appearing in the literature. A preliminary report
from Spirito, Stark, and Tyc (1989) involved their new screening instrument called "Kidcope," which is a checklist that assesses ten common
cognitive and behavioral strategies used by children and adolescents:
distraction, social withdrawal, cognitive restructuring, self-criticism,
blaming others, problem solving, emotional regulation, wishful thinking,
social support, and resignation. These researchers asked a heterogeneous group of boys and girls with chronic illnesses, including IDDM, to
report on the frequency and perceived effectiveness of these various
coping strategies with both medically related and other common problems encountered in their recent experience. As their sample size and
longitudinal assessments evolve, we will have greater understanding of
both general and IDDM specific coping.

Similarly, the recent construction of the Family Coping Coding System (FCCS) by Hauser et al. (1988) holds promise for identifying coping
processes relevant to adaptation to IDDM. The FCCS assesses the appraisal, problem-solving, and emotion-management coping processes
that emerge during family interactions and discussions. As the scale is
developed and applied in our ongoing longitudinal study of children
with diabetes, family coping styles associated with improved compliance, metabolic control, and general adaptation in adolescence and
young adulthood will be better understood.

Some data are already available from another study that support
our theory that these coping processes are indeed relevant to adaptation
to IDDM. Delamater et al. (1987), in the study mentioned earlier, found
that adolescents with poor metabolic control used more wishful thinking,
avoidance, and help seeking, and that they were more likely to endorse
an item reflecting the appraisal that one "must hold back from doing
what you want." Thus, coping process variables do relate to diabetes
adjustment, but the nature and implications of these relationships is just
beginning to be described. Coping transactions are facilitated or ham-

pered by numerous factors, some of which are designated in our model as coping resources and moderators.

Coping Resources and Moderators

Among the coping resources and moderators that have received the most empirical attention in diabetes research to date are social support (both intra- and extrafamilial), self-esteem, ego development, health beliefs, Type A personality characteristics, and other dimensions of temperament. Some resources or moderators are conceived and measured as properties or traits of the individual child or parent. Others are conceptualized and operationalized as characteristics of the environment. In either case, the stress and coping paradigm suggests that it is the transactional process that must ultimately be described and understood. Recent research is providing beginning steps for understanding the roles of these resources and moderators as indicated in the following examples.

Social support. As in the broader health psychology literature, social support in its many and varied forms and functions has been repeatedly implicated in stress and coping processes. Both direct effects and buffering effects have been hypothesized and documented (see Cohen & Willis, 1985; House, Umberson, & Landis, 1988; Thoits, 1986, for recent reviews). Given widespread variation in measurement and data analytic designs, controversy surrounds any effort to summarize or integrate findings; nonetheless, a number of specific implications are suggested for social support in the process of a child or family coping with IDDM.

Some aspects of social support are manifest in the qualities of family relationships, or what has been termed *family environment* (Anderson & Kornblum, 1984; Boyce, 1985; Moos, 1974; Newbrough, Simpkins, & Maurer, 1985; Wortman & Conway, 1985). Preliminary reports from our ongoing longitudinal study noted some differences between families with a child recently diagnosed with IDDM and the comparison group of families with a child with a recent acute illness. The IDDM families, probably reflecting an effort to cope with the IDDM as suggested earlier, were described by the mothers as more highly organized, relative to the acutely ill groups (Hauser, Jacobson, Wertlieb, Brink, & Wentworth, 1985). During the first year of the study, mothers from both groups reported similar levels of behavior symptoms in these children, 9 to 16 years of age, and these levels were generally in the normal, rather than clinical, range (Jacobson et al., 1986; Wertlieb, Hauser, & Jacobson, 1986). However, when relations between family environment factors rated by the children and behavior symptoms rated by the mothers were examined, some interesting differences between the two groups were noted. Family factors were assessed using the Family Environment Scale

(Moos, 1974). Family conflict was associated with more symptoms for both groups, but the correlation was slightly higher in the IDDM group. Low levels of family cohesion were associated with symptoms for the acutely ill children, but not for the IDDM children. Families with IDDM that were described as invested in clear routines, organization, and social and recreational activities had fewer symptoms. This relationship was not significant for the other families. Rather, for the acutely ill families, emphasis on competition, achievement, and control was associated with higher levels of symptoms. In addition, a moral–religious family environment was associated with symptoms in the IDDM group only (Wertlieb, Hauser, & Jacobson, 1986).

Data on ratings of observed family interaction in the first year also revealed distinctions between the two groups in terms of *enabling* and *constraining*. Enabling interactions, usually verbal exchanges that reflected efforts of active understanding and problem solving, were more often evident in family discussions where the child had IDDM. Fathers of children with diabetes also engaged in more constraining behaviors, such as verbal exchanges with a devaluing or judgmental tone. Analyses that focus on the extent to which these differences continue over time or on the nature of the relationship of these variables to adherence, metabolic control, or other outcomes are currently under way (Hauser et al., 1986).

Gustafsson (1987) and his colleagues in Sweden have described salient family interaction variables and demonstrated relationships between what they termed *disturbed interaction* and metabolic control in a prospective design. Glycosylated hemoglobin levels were measured one and five years after the interaction observations of 30 families, with children ages 10 to 14 (M age = 12.4), with diabetes of at least two years duration and no significant endogenous insulin production. Elaborating on the pioneering effort of Minuchin, Rosman, and Baker (1978) mentioned earlier, Gustafsson engaged the families in a series of decision-making tasks (e.g., planning a meal, furnishing an apartment, and a discussion of a recent family conflict). Ratings of family adaptability were coded from scales for assertiveness, discipline, control, and focus. Ratings of family cohesion were coded from scales for emotional expression, attention, support, self-reliance, and decision making. Disturbed interactions were those that were rated either extremely high or extremely low and characterized 25% of these families. Contrasted with disturbed interaction was a *midrange* or *balanced* interaction. In the analysis at the first year postobservation, metabolic control was unrelated to the family interaction category. Five years later, however, disturbance in adaptability (but not cohesion) predicted poorer metabolic control (higher glycosylated hemoglobin) at a statistically significant level. The researchers were able to correctly classify two out of three cases. The relationship held best for the adolescent children rather than for preadolescents or young adults.

Theoretically meaningful contrasts in the nature of social support as a moderator emerged in Varni, Babani, Wallander, Roe, and Frasier's (1989) comparison of children (6 to 12 years of age) and adolescents (12 to 18 years) with IDDM. Peer social support and family social support were significant predictors of fewer behavior symptoms for children; only peer support was significant in the comparable regression model for adolescents.

Developmental differences are also suggested by findings reported by Waller et al. (1986). Their work is also noteworthy in that, rather than assess the general dimensions of family climate and interaction, it uses the authors' Diabetes-Specific Family Behavior Scale (DFBS) to operationalize social support within the family as it directly relates to diabetic care. These researchers studied a group of 42 youngsters at a diabetes summer camp who were 7 to 17 years of age (M age = 12.1) and had a mean diabetes duration of 5 years (range = 1–13 years). The 60 items on their DFBS tapped three dimensions of family support: warmth/caring (e.g., "My parent understands how I feel about diabetes"), guidance/control (e.g., "I take care of my diabetes myself"), and problem solving (e.g., "When we go out to eat, I choose things from the menu in line with my exchange diet). Warmth/caring and guidance/control, but not problem solving, correlated significantly with a glycosylated hemoglobin index. Furthermore, comparison of preteen and teenage children revealed that what might be optimal for children may not be for adolescents. For instance, family guidance/control correlated with metabolic control for the preteens (r = .63, p < .003), but not for the teenagers (r = .07, ns). Some findings reported at the single item level (so they must be interpreted cautiously) suggest crucial developmental factors. For instance the warmth/caring item, "My parent gets angry with me when I make a slip in taking care of my diabetes," was correlated positively with metabolic control in the younger group (r = .75, p < .0001), but inversely related for the older group (r = −.52, p < .03).

An earlier effort by Schafer, Glasgow, McCaul, and Dreher (1983) also constructed a self-report index of *supportive* and *nonsupportive* diabetes family behaviors and found correlations with adherence, but not with metabolic control, in a group (N = 34) of 12- to 19-year-old summer campers. More recently, they conducted a prospective study with 18 adolescents and 54 adults (Schafer, McCall, & Glasgow, 1986). Adherence was measured through self-reports, including 24-hour dietary recalls. Their Diabetes Family Behavior Checklist (DFBC) tapped both supportive behaviors (e.g., "help you decide if changes should be made based on glucose testing results") and nonsupportive behaviors (e.g., nag you about following your diet"). Psychometrically, there were more weaknesses in the scale for the adolescents than for the adults, thus limiting the validity of the findings and reducing the ability to generalize from them. In fact, we do not recommend using the scale for adolescents until it is improved. For adults, significant concurrent and 6-month prospective follow-up correlations were reported between family support (especially nonsupport) and adherence. For adolescents, there was no consistent pattern of relationships between the DFBC and adherence or metabolic control. Further validation of these instruments along with longitudinal designs that consider a range of outcomes—both psychological and physiological—may help delineate the manner in which social support moderates adaptation to diabetes. A likely linkage might be that support affects adherence, which then influences metabolic control. To summarize, environmental factors such as family processes and social support (or more accurately, the perception of family processes and social support, because researchers rely heavily on self-report) relate to IDDM adjustment in complex and important ways. These relationships appear to vary with age, developmental stage, or related variables such as IDDM-onset age or duration of IDDM.

There is another perspective on the body of research on family functioning that deserves further attention. In one of the most important longitudinal follow-up analyses reported to date, Kovacs, Kass, Schnell, Goldston, and Marsh (1989) found that their family and marital functioning measures did not correlate significantly with metabolic control over a six-year study of an onset cohort ($N = 85$) of 8- to 14-year-old children with IDDM. However, about 8% of the sample had "coexisting" family and medical problems (e.g., poor control). In concluding their report, they suggested that "perhaps such a group . . . is so striking in clinical practice that it accounts for the persistence of beliefs concerning the causal relationship between aspects of the family and metabolic control" (p. 414).

Other studies have focused on specific personality variables as coping moderators or resources. Again, findings to date are fragmented and inconsistent, yet they suggest important links in stress and coping processes. Among the personality variables that we might consider for continued investigation are self-esteem, ego development, health beliefs, and Type A personality factors.

Self-esteem. Self-esteem has been indexed as higher, lower, and equivalent in comparisons between groups of children with and without diabetes. Gross, Delcher, Snitzer, Bianchi, and Epstein (1984); Jacobson, Hauser, Powers, and Noam (1984); Jacobson et al. (1986); and Ryan and Morrow (1986) found negligible differences on a range of self-esteem and self-concept indices in four distinct samples of children and adolescents. When self-esteem is found to be higher for a group of children with diabetes, as it was for boys studied by Ryan and Morrow (1986), it is interpreted in terms of a clinical impression that these youngsters "may have made excessive use of denial as a primary coping strategy" (p. 731).

One way researchers are attempting to clarify the findings on self-esteem in children with IDDM is to refine their conceptualizations and measures of self-esteem and to provide a context of relationships with other relevant variables. For instance, Hauser, Jacobson, Noam, and Powers (1983) identified a specific dimension of self-image disturbance in early adolescents with diabetes, a "more polarized," future-oriented perspective. This difference may reflect healthy realism rather than psychopathology when placed in the context of the understandable apprehension and anxiety about the future, given the higher mortality for people with diabetes (Barglow et al., 1986).

Ryan and Morrow (1986) examined the hypothesis that age-at-onset and gender related to self-esteem differences in their group ($N = 125$) of 10- to 19-year-old children with diabetes. Using the Piers–Harris Self Concept scale, they found a "striking interaction," so that girls who developed diabetes before age 5 had poorer self-concepts than "early onset" boys. When diabetes onset was after age 5, boys and girls did not differ from each other or from nondiabetic controls. Analysis of the self-concept subscales revealed that the difference was accounted for in the domains of physical appearance and anxiety. Ryan and Morrow interpreted the findings in terms of how boys and girls might cope differently with IDDM, with girls being "more affected by changes in physical appearance . . . perhaps because girls are more likely to believe that their popularity will be determined primarily by how they look, whereas boys are more likely to believe that it will be determined primarily by what they do" (p. 731). The early onset risk factor might reflect a compromise in early body image, leaving the girls affected less able to cope with IDDM. In addition, there may be an association of longer illness duration with shorter stature, heavier weight, and maturational lag that might be a more proximal influence on self-esteem ratings (Clifford, 1971).

Ego development. Two teams of researchers have focused on ego development as a crucial coping moderator or resource. Ego development is a manifestation of integrative functioning involving impulse control, moral development, and quality of interpersonal relationships. Youngsters with diabetes have lower levels, impaired, or slowed rates of ego development (Hauser, Jacobson, Noam, & Powers, 1983; Hauser et al., in press). Barglow et al. (1983) found ego development to be their best predictor of responsiveness to a brief intensive effort to enhance adherence, as reflected in the magnitude of improved metabolic control. Whereas a life events stress index predicted the groups' initial Hemoglobin A1 (HgA1) indices, it was the ego development score that best predicted the change in control. Measures of psychopathology and self-esteem were not significantly related to either initial or follow-up metabolic control indices.

Health beliefs. Health beliefs have been examined as coping moderators with links to regimen adherence and metabolic control in both general terms (e.g., Health Locus of Control) and illness-specific terms (e.g., Diabetes Health Belief Questionnaire, Brownlee-Duffeck et al., 1987). In a general assessment of beliefs about their own abilities to influence their health, a group of children with diabetes ages 9 to 12 (M age $= 11$) (illness duration 1 to 10 years, M duration $= 4.2$ years) exhibited a more internal locus of control, compared with a nondiabetic sample. Health locus of control was not, however, correlated with a glycosylated hemoglobin index (Gross et al., 1984).

Using a more comprehensive design and illness-specific indices of Health Belief Model variables, some relationships with adherence and metabolic control as well as developmental contrasts have been documented. For what they termed their adolescent group ($n = 54$), ages 13 to 26 (M age $= 18$ years; M age of onset $= 9.6$ years; M duration $= 8.9$ years), Brownlee-Duffeck et al. (1987) reported a multiple regression model controlling for age and diabetes knowledge and predicting glycosylated hemoglobin level using five health belief variables. This model accounted for 27% of glycosylated hemoglobin variation. In particular, the individuals' perceived severity of the diabetes, and their perceived susceptibility to complications were significant predictors. Increased susceptibility was associated with poorer rather than (the predicted) better metabolic control. In predicting self-reported adherence from the health belief variables and controlling for age and knowledge, 52% of the variance was accounted for, with perceived costs of adherence as the significant health belief factor.

In the *adult* group ($n = 89$) of Brownlee-Duffeck et al. (1987), ages 13 to 64 (M age $= 37$ years; M onset $= 25$ years; M duration $= 11.8$ years), the model for glycosylated hemoglobin, controlling for age and knowledge, accounted for 19% of the variance, with perceived costs and benefits emerging as the significant health belief predictors of metabolic control. Adherence in this older sample was predicted with 41% of the variance accounted for, and perceptions of susceptibility to complications, as well as perceptions of costs and benefits of adherence emerged as significant. Numerous methodological issues limit the extent of inferences from these data on how health beliefs moderate adherence and metabolic control. However, the documentation of a series of significant relationships between IDDM moderators and outcomes, along with these yet-to-be replicated age differences, begins to suggest implications for intervention as well as future research. "The differential salience of specific health belief variables between the two samples suggests that older patients may be better able to think and act on the preventive benefits of adherence, whereas the immediate privations of regimen may figure more prominently in younger diabetic's perceptions about their adherence" (p. 143). Diabetes education efforts might be tailored with these distinctions in mind. Researchers will continue to need multidimensional assessments of adherence and control.

Type A behavior. One personality variable whose investigation continues to hold promise is the Type A behavior pattern. Type A individuals exhibit a style that is more competitive, impatient, and hostile than Type B individuals. Further, evidence exists that Type A individuals are more autonomically reactive and exhibit larger changes in catecholamine and cortisol levels when stressed. In an effort to account for individual differences in changes in blood glucose levels in response to stress, Stabler, Morris, Litton, Feinglos, and Surwit (1986) compared blood glucose levels of Type A and Type B children with IDDM, ages 8 to 15, before and after an exciting and stressful encounter with a challenging videogame (Atari Superbreakout). Five of the six Type A children showed an increase in blood glucose during the game. Six of the seven Type B children showed a decrease. Heart rate and blood pressure did not distinguish the groups before, during, or after the game.

The same experiment was then performed with a larger sample of 44 children, ages 8 to 16 (M age = 12.5). Again, the Type A children were more likely to respond to stress with an increase in blood glucose. Further, the Type A children had significantly higher glycosylated hemoglobin values (Stabler et al., 1987). An effort to replicate this latter finding failed to confirm this relationship between glycosylated hemoglobin and Type A behavior in another group of children with IDDM, ages 8 to 19 years (M age = 14.2 years, M onset 9.3 years, M duration 5.9 years) (Stabler et al., 1988).

Temperament. Child development researchers have focused on dimensions of temperament as salient moderators of stress and coping processes (Wertlieb, Weigel, & Feldstein, 1988, 1989; Wertlieb, Weigel, Springer, & Feldstein, 1987). Temperament factors as elements of behavioral or personality style have now been implicated in adaptation to IDDM. In a sample of 51 children with IDDM (M age = 9.8 years, range = 6.1–12.9 years), comparison with healthy siblings did not reveal particular problem areas or a characteristic temperament profile (Rovet & Ehrlich, 1988). However, using nine dimensions of temperament as predictors of glycosylated hemoglobin resulted in a multiple regression model accounting for 42% of the variance. Children with better metabolic control were temperamentally more active, more regular in their routines, less intense in reacting to external stimuli, more distractible, and more prone to negative moods. The findings suggest that individual differences in behavioral organization, energy consumption, and stress modulation are factors in metabolic control. By implication, pending replication with a larger sample in a longitudinal design, these personality dimensions such as the Type A behavior pattern may be appropriate targets for intervention as well as markers for at-risk groups.

The differences or lack of differences between children with and without diabetes on these various personality dimensions is important to document. The questions of whether and how these dimensions or differences relate to metabolic control and other indices of adaptation and outcome are even more significant. Consistent with the stress and coping paradigm, it is this multivariate process view that underlies the most promising of recent empirical efforts. For example, Hanson and colleagues (e.g., Hanson & Henggeller, 1984; Henggeller & Burghen, 1987;

Hanson et al., 1987a, 1987b; Hanson, Henggeler, Harris, Burghen, & Moore, 1989); Hauenstein, Marvin, Snyder, and Clarke (1989); Jacobson et al. (1987); Marteau, Bloch, and Baum (1987); and Varni et al. (1989) are presenting integrative analyses that help describe the process of adaptation to IDDM.

Multivariate perspectives. Cross-sectional studies presented by Hanson's group support a model that relates metabolic control to regimen adherence and chronic life events stress. Rather than directly affecting metabolic control, variables such as age, family relations, and knowledge about IDDM exert their influence through an impact on adherence. For instance, in their sample of 93 adolescents (M age = 14.4 years) with IDDM (M age at onset = 8.9 years), both adherence and stress were significant predictors of metabolic control. Family relations (marital adjustment, cohesion, adaptability, and diabetes-specific social support), diabetes knowledge, and age were significant predictors in a multiple regression model accounting for 18.5% of the variance in a measure of adherence using both self-report and observation. Some of the relationships reported were of marginal significance and the data were all derived from intact families (Hanson, Henggeler, & Burghen, 1987a). The child's social competence is also implicated as a component of the multivariate model. Under conditions of high stress, adolescents with low social competence had relatively poor metabolic control. Stress and metabolic control were not correlated for the highly competent youngsters (Hanson, Henggeler, & Burghen 1987b).

When other family structure variables are introduced into this framework, additional complexities emerge. Hanson, Henggeler, Rodrique, Burghen, and Murphy (1988) compared 30 adolescents with IDDM from intact families with a matched group of 30 adolescents with IDDM from father-absent families (M age = 14.4 years, M IDDM duration = 5.4 years, M age at diagnosis = 9.1 years). (*Father absence* included the following: divorce, 86.7%; death, 10%; and desertion, 3.3% with no adult male currently living in the home.) The groups did not differ in metabolic control, although adherence as indexed by self-report and observation items was greater for the father-absent group. The groups did not differ in terms of social competence. There was some indication of greater perceived diabetes-specific social support in the intact families and some indication of an interaction between effects of gender and family type. In interpreting these findings Hanson et al. suggested that father-absent adolescents adapt to the single-parent situation by effectively taking on greater responsibility for their own health care. Hypotheses such as these require further investigation, especially in light of major conceptual and methodological issues inherent in attributing adjustment and adaptation effects to differences in family processes and structures (e.g., Wertlieb, in press).

For instance, Marteau et al. (1987) reported that metabolic control for children in intact or single-parent families was better than that for children living with stepparents or adoptive parents. Their study of 78 families with children with IDDM 5 to 16 years of age (*M* age = 11.6 years, *M* IDDM duration = 5.2 years) included those family structure variables as well as measures of family processes. Rather than using only the more typical measures of adherence, Marteau et al. (1987) also asked parents to respond to "clinical vignettes" of a child displaying hyperglycemic behavior (a thirsty child frequently emptying his bladder). Families were then classified as *test first* (i.e., ascertain blood glucose level as a prelude to intervention) versus *action first* (i.e., immediate intervention such as giving insulin, encouraging exercise, or phoning the doctor). Among their findings was that the test first group had better diabetic control as rated by the pediatrician. In terms of the range of family factors assessed, only the tendency of nonbiological fathers to be less likely to test first was statistically significant. Family cohesiveness, expressiveness, and harmony, as well as higher child self-esteem were associated with better control. As the researchers noted, the dynamics and causal relationships among family functioning, regimen adherence, metabolic control, and child psychological status remain unknown, but models must include multiple direct and indirect pathways, and investigations will need both longitudinal and intervention components.

Outcomes

Returning to Figure 1, the outcomes of the stress and coping processes described earlier represent both traditional and innovative concepts, some general and some specific to IDDM. Most of the studies rely on traditional single, even isolated, dimensions of outcome. At the general level, some index of psychiatric status is often used to address the question of the extent to which different stress and coping processes might be associated with adjustment or psychological problems (e.g., Kovacs et al., 1985; Wertlieb et al., 1987). At the IDDM-specific level, an index of metabolic control, usually glycosylated hemoglobin, is used to document an association or a prediction by successful or unsuccessful coping (e.g., Delamater et al., 1987; Gustafsson, 1987). Some researchers have used the Diabetes Adjustment Scale (Sullivan, 1979) to assess the more psychological or attitudinal dimensions of outcome (Jacobson et al., 1987). In addition, at the illness-specific level, we have noted studies that investigate psychosocial factors associated with regimen adherence, which is considered to be a necessary condition for successful adaptation to IDDM (e.g., Hanson et al., 1987a, 1987b; Brownlee-Duffeck et al., 1987). As noted earlier, there is an emerging consensus that outcomes in IDDM research will need to be increasingly conceptualized and measured in multidimensional terms with better attention given to distinctions between metabolic control and adherence measures. Both physiological and behavioral markers will be needed, and both short-term (e.g., blood glucose level), intermediate (glycosylated hemoglobin index), and long-term (e.g., physical complications) outcomes must be assessed (e.g., Brand et al., 1986; Johnson, in press).

Neurocognitive impairment, often of a very subtle nature, appears to be an important factor in IDDM adaptation and outcome and is just recently being included in psychosocial research. Noting the increased incidence of EEG abnormalities in children with diabetes, Ryan, Longstreet, and Morrow (1985) investigated relationships among school absences, academic achievement, and neuropsychological functioning. Children with diabetes (onset after 5 years of age) missed more school and scored lower on achievement tests and visuomotor tasks compared with nondiabetic peers. The two groups of 40 teenagers (12 to 18 years old) did not differ in overall intelligence, self-concept, range of learning, memory, problem solving, and visuospatial tasks.

Rovet, Ehrlich, and Hoppe (1987) investigated these neurocognitive factors in 51 younger children (6 to 14 years old) with early IDDM onset (less than 4 years old) and later onset (more than 4 years old). The early onset group, especially girls, showed greater impairment, especially in visuospatial tasks and math. Children with diabetes did not differ from sibling controls on spatial tasks or academic achievement although they scored lower on verbal tasks. A number of explanations may account for some of the emerging findings in neuropsychological development, ranging from the deleterious effects of hypoglycemia, to interactions between disease onset and brain maturation, to more psychosocial explanations relative to parental responses to the child's illness. Neurocognitive factors may need to be considered at various points in the stress and coping framework and outcome assessment just noted.

Implications for Assessment and Intervention

The stress and coping paradigm and the related diabetes research suggest a range of assessment and intervention strategies and opportunities. For instance, each category of coping process, moderator, or resource addressed in the previous discussion as a correlate or predictor of illness outcome or adaptation might present an appropriate focus for intervention. Indeed, many of the contemporary and traditional interventions in diabetes care can be so conceived. For instance, a range of interventions termed *diabetes education* take a generally didactic approach to equipping the child and his or her family with diabetes knowledge and skills involved in carrying out the multifaceted treatment regimen. To date, few efforts to evaluate these educational interventions have incorporated psychosocial variables (Jacobson, 1986).

Another range of traditional interventions involves referral of a child experiencing difficulties in maintaining glycemic control or exhibiting other behavioral or psychological symptoms into the mental health service delivery system. Psychotherapeutic interventions with the child, the family, or both might then focus on enhancing the child's self-esteem or on altering family patterns of communication or conflict, thus targeting intervention on some of the crucial coping moderators identified by the research mentioned earlier.

A third range of contemporary interventions targets individuals or groups experiencing difficulties in maintaining glycemic control and, through applied behavior analysis and modification, including social-learning and cognitive–behavioral techniques, addresses skill deficits and increases adherence behaviors. There are scant empirical data on the effectiveness of the numerous kinds of intervention on which we currently rely.[3] For our present purpose, it is useful to describe a few intervention studies that illustrate the implications of the stress and coping paradigm in a relatively explicit way and that may provide guidance for the much needed systematic intervention evaluation research called for by virtually all reviewers of the field (e.g., Jacobson, 1986).

Barglow et al. (1983) evaluated an intensive multicomponent intervention, in contrast to standard care. Two groups of 21 adolescents were studied over a four-month period, and among the variables assessed were life events stress, self-esteem, ego development, and psychopathology. The intensive intervention group received daily telephone contact with the nurse–educator or physician in which glucose readings were monitored, insulin adjustments were considered, and adherence was reinforced. Every two weeks, these youngsters visited the clinic for review and interpretation of self-monitoring records, behavioral reinforcement, group discussion, mental health, or nutritional consultation. Prizes were awarded for the achievement of a normal glycohemoglobin value at the end of the four-month period. Standard care consisted of three routine visits to the clinic, as well as completion of the study questionnaires. Both groups showed improvement in metabolic control (lower glycosylated hemoglobin scores), with intensive multicomponent intervention yielding greater improvement. In terms of the improvements for both groups, the amount of change was related to the amount of life events stress reported at the beginning of the study ($r = .29, p < .05$) as well as to the level of ego development ($r = .37, p < .01$). Psychopathology and self-esteem were related neither to baseline nor to change in glycosylated hemoglobin.

---

[3]The interested reader is referred to the following sources for more comprehensive cataloging of the intervention methods and limited evaluation data: Bradley, 1988; Delamater, 1986; Glasgow, McCaul, & Schafer, 1986; Rose & Firestone, 1983; Schafer, Glasgow, & McCaul, 1982; Stark, Dahlquist, & Collins, 1987.

Another recent intervention study attempted to adapt understandings generated by contemporary smoking prevention research. This research suggests that educational intervention that focuses on facts seems to have little effect on adolescent health behavior (e.g., diabetes regimen adherence, cigarette smoking, etc.), and social skills such as the capacity to cope with peer pressure might be involved in improved health behavior. Kaplan, Chadwick, and Schimmel (1985) randomly assigned 21 teenagers with IDDM to three weeks of either daily training in social skills or daily lessons in the medical factors of diabetes care. Four months after completion of the project, the social coping skills group showed a slight decline in glycosylated hemoglobin levels, and the education group showed a slight increase, resulting in a statistically significant intervention effect. A measure of social support satisfaction and a measure of social skills (Means–Ends Problem Solving Test) correlated positively with glycosylated hemoglobin, that is, those teenagers "most satisfied with their social support and those with greatest social skill were actually in the poorest control" (p. 154). As the researchers noted, "although intriguing, our results should be interpreted with great caution" (p. 155).

Family-centered intervention has also recently been subjected to systematic evaluation. Satin, LaGreca, Zigo, and Skyler (1989) randomly assigned 32 adolescents to a 6-week multifamily group intervention, a multifamily group plus a parent simulation of diabetes, or a control group. The group meetings included parents and their children with diabetes in discussions of diabetes management and activities and in the exchange of guidance and support. The simulation component involved the child with diabetes teaching the parents various diabetes management tasks, including the use of syringes and calculation of dosage. The improvement in metabolic control was greatest for the multifamily group intervention plus simulation.

Methodological limitations preclude many substantive or obligatory generalizations from these studies. However, the studies alert researchers to opportunities and requirements for the design of the next generation of intervention evaluations. At the most general level, the stress and coping approach identifies several crucial domains of variables to be measured and the necessity for multivariate, multidimensional assessments. Composition of appropriate control and comparison groups is an abiding concern in such research. Options for identification of other relevant groupings are also suggested by the stress and coping paradigm. For instance, it may be that tailoring and matching a diabetes education program to a particular level of ego development would enhance intervention effectiveness. Differentiation of interventions will also be crucial, as evidenced in the contrast noted in the Barglow et al. (1983) study between standard care and intensive multicomponent care. Researchers will need to identify which specific components constitute the active and effective ingredient. Variation in information form and content, skill building technologies, and social support enhancements, among others, all pose considerable challenges for the intervention researcher.

As emphasized by LaGreca (1988), interventions, especially when a child has IDDM, may need to be family oriented and focused, acknowledging this contextual emphasis of our stress and coping approach. In terms of the developmental emphasis of our approach, certain developmental periods may be targeted for particular interventions. For instance, in the context of the data on age differences in the adherence associated with shifting diabetes care responsibilities from family or parent to teenager, LaGreca (1988) suggested "it may be particularly important to target this developmental period [adolescence] for *renewed* education efforts" (p. 145, emphasis added).

Although the thrust of these remarks on intervention research calls for larger-scale, complex designs with larger samples, it is also important to encourage and to capitalize on the significant hypothesis-generating resource inherent in clinical reports and research. Especially noteworthy is an innovative contribution by Moran and Fonagy (1987). In a time–series analysis of a 3½ year, five-times-weekly psychoanalysis of an adolescent girl with IDDM, they were able to predict short-term changes in weekly urine glucose contents with themes abstracted from the psychotherapeutic material. Particular conflicts and symptoms (e.g., feeling unloved or angry with father) were associated with glucose levels in lagged correlations.

To summarize the implications for assessment and intervention research, the stress and coping paradigm focuses the clinician and investigator on stress management and coping enhancement as the crucial intervention targets. A wide range of such targets spans domains such as adherence behavior, diabetes knowledge, personality traits or styles amenable to change, and family processes such as social support or conflict. Whether assessing or treating an individual child or family, or implementing a comprehensive psychosocial treatment program for children with IDDM, the interacting domains described earlier and the elements of the stress and coping paradigm in Figure 1 provide guidance for our efforts.

Concluding Remarks

It is useful to reiterate the manner in which a stress and coping paradigm helps to organize current understandings of psychosocial factors in IDDM and to guide relevant research and practice. The utility and heuristic value of the paradigm lie in its comprehensiveness in capturing some degree of the complexity of the adaptation process. Whether at the general level or at the IDDM-specific level (see Figure 1), there are extant empirical data documenting each of the four domains in relationship to at least one, if not several, of the others that constitute the paradigm. Thus, we have many of the pieces—both conceptually and empirically—and a set of directions for completing this very complex puzzle. Among the pieces that we have is, for example, a relationship between stressful experiences and behavior symptoms—both for children with and without IDDM. We have a beginning taxonomy of some of the specific stressors implicated in "getting" diabetes and in living with diabetes. The aspect of coping with diabetes that involves adherence to the medical regimen appears to be related to the achievement and maintenance of metabolic control and good health. What we have termed *coping moderators* and *resources*—social support and ego development, for instance—appear to play a role in the extent to which coping efforts are effective and in the degree to which the stresses associated with the illness manifest as problems in health outcomes. Furthermore, the stress and coping paradigm requires that a biopsychosocial developmental context be maintained for the description, analysis, and influence of these processes.

The stress and coping paradigm can help us to organize the substantial conceptualization and empirical data that have formed the basis for our current appreciation of psychosocial factors in IDDM. The paradigm's continued application as a stimulus for research and as a framework for practice innovation and evaluation is increasingly warranted in the context of past fruitfulness and future promise.

References

Allen, D. A., Affleck, G., Tennen, H., McGrade, B., & Ratzan, S. (1984). Concerns of children with a chronic illness: A cognitive developmental study of juvenile diabetes. *Child: Care, Health and Development, 10*, 211–218.

Anderson, B. J. (1984). The impact of diabetes on the developmental tasks of childhood and adolescence: A research perspective. In M. Nattras & J. Santiago (Eds.), *Recent advances in diabetes* (Vol. 1, pp. 165–171). London: Churchill Livingstone.

Anderson, B. J., & Auslander, W. F. (1980). Research on diabetes management and the family: A critique. *Diabetes Care, 3*(6), 696–702.

Anderson, B. J., & Kornblum, H. (1984). The family environment of children with a diabetic parent: Issues for research. *Family Systems Medicine, 2*(1), 17–27.

Barglow, P., Berndt, D. J., Burns, W. J., & Hatcher, R. (1986). Neuroendocrine and psychological factors in childhood diabetes mellitus. *Journal of the American Academy of Child Psychiatry, 25*(6), 785–793.

Barglow, P., Edidin, D. V., Budlong-Springer, A. S., Berndt, D., Phillips, R., & Dubow, E. (1983). Diabetic control in children and adolescents: Psychosocial factors and therapeutic efficacy. *Journal of Youth and Adolescence, 12*(2), 77–94.

Blanc, M. H., Barnett, D. M., Gleason, R. E., Dunn, P. J., & Soeldner, J. S. (1981). Hemoglobin A1C compared with three conventional measures of diabetes control. *Diabetes Care, 4*, 349–353.

Boyce, W. T. (1985). Social support, family relations, and children. In S. Cohen & L. Syme (Eds.), *Social Support and Health* (pp. 151–174). New York: Academic Press.

Bradley, C. (1988). Stress and diabetes. In S. Fisher & J. Reason (Eds.), *Handbook of life stress, cognition and health* (pp. 383–401). New York: John Wiley.

Brand, A. H., Johnson, J. H., & Johnson, S. B. (1986). Life stress and diabetic control in children and adolescents with insulin-dependent diabetes. *Journal of Pediatric Psychology, 11*(4), 481–495.

Brownlee-Duffeck, M., Peterson, L., Simonds, J. F., Goldstein, D., Kilo, C., & Hoette, S. (1987). The role of health beliefs in the regimen adherence and metabolic control of adolescents and adults with diabetes mellitus. *Journal of Consulting and Clinical Psychology, 55*(2), 139–144.

Clifford, E. (1971). Body satisfaction in adolescence. *Perceptual and motor skills, 33*, 119–125.

Cohen, S., & Wills, T. A. (1985). Stress, social support, and the buffering hypothesis. *Psychological Bulletin, 98*(2), 310–357.

Daneman, D., Wolfson, D. H., Becker, D. J., & Drash, A. L. (1981). Factors affecting glycosylated hemoglobin values in children with IDDM. *The Journal of Pediatrics, 99*(6), 847–853.

Davidson, M. B. (Ed.). (1981). *Diabetes mellitus: Diagnosis and treatment.* New York: Wiley.

Delamater, A. M. (1986). Psychosocial aspects of diabetes mellitus in children. In B. Lahey & A. Kazdin (Eds.), *Advances in clinical child psychology. Vol. 9.* (pp. 333–375). New York: Plenum.

Delamater, A. M. (in press). Adaptation of children to newly diagnosed diabetes. In C. S. Holmes (Ed.), *Neuropsychological and behavioral aspects of insulin- and non-insulin-dependent diabetes mellitus.* Springer-Verlag.

Delamater, A. M., Bubb, J., Kurtz, S. M., Kuntze, J., Smith, J. A., White, N. H., & Santiago, J. V. (1988). Physiologic responses to acute psychological stress in adolescents with Type I diabetes mellitus. *Journal of Pediatric Psychology, 13*(1), 69–86.

Delamater, A. M., Kurtz, S. M., Bubb, J., White, N. H., & Santiago, J. V. (1987). Stress and coping in relation to metabolic control of adolescents with Type I diabetes. *Developmental and Behavioral Pediatrics, 8*(3), 136–140.

Drash, A. L. (1981). The child with diabetes mellitus. In H. Rifkin & P. Raskin (Eds.), *Diabetes mellitus* (Vol. 5). Bowie, MD: Prentice Hall.

Dunbar, F. (1954). *Emotions and bodily change.* Columbia: New York.

Dunn, S. M., & Turtle, J. R. (1981). The myth of the diabetic personality. *Diabetes Care, 4*(6), 640–646.

Fisher, E. B., Jr., Delamater, A. M., Bertelson, A. D., & Kirkley, B. G. (1982). Psychological factors in diabetes and its treatment. *Journal of Consulting and Clinical Psychology, 30*(6), 993–1003.

Fonagy, P., Moran, G. S., Lindsay, M. K. M., Kurtz, A. B., & Brown, R. (1987). Psychological adjustment and diabetic control. *Archives of Disease in Childhood, 62*, 1009–1013.

Garmezy, N. (1987). Stress, competence, and development: Continuities in the study of schizophrenic adults, children vulnerable to psychopathology, and the search for stress-resistant children. *Journal of the American Orthopsychiatric Association, 57*, 159–174.

Gersten, J. C., Langer, T. S., Eisenberg, J. G., & Simcha-Fagan, O. (1977). An evaluation of the etiologic role of stressful life-change events in psychological distress. *Journal of Health and Social Behavior, 18,* 228–244.

Gilbert, B. O., Johnson, S. B., Silverstein, J., & Malone, J. (1989). Psychological and physiological responses to acute laboratory stressors in IDDM adolescents and non-diabetic controls. *Journal of Pediatric and Psychology, 14,* 571–591.

Glasgow, R. E., McCaul, K. D., & Schafer, L. C. (1986). Barriers to regimen adherence among persons with insulin dependent diabetes. *Journal of Behavioral Medicine, 9*(1), 65–77.

Gonen, B., Rachman, H., Rubenstein, A. H., Tanega, S. P., & Horowitz, D. L. (1977). Hemoglobin A1C: An indicator of the metabolic control of diabetic patients. *Lancet, 2,* 734–737.

Gross, A. M., Delcher, H. K., Snitzer, J., Bianchi, B., & Epstein, S. (1984). Personality variables and metabolic control in children with diabetes. *The Journal of Genetic Psychology, 146*(1), 19–26.

Gustafsson, P. A. (1987). *Family interaction and family therapy in childhood psychosomatic disease.* Linkoping, Sweden: Linkoping University.

Hanson, C. L., & Henggeler, S. W. (1984). Metabolic control in adolescents with diabetes: An examination of systemic variables. *Family Systems Medicine, 2*(1), 5–16.

Hanson, C. L., Henggeler, S. W., & Burghen, G. A. (1987a). Social competence and parental support as mediators of the link between stress and metabolic control in adolescents with IDDM. *Journal of Consulting and Clinical Psychology, 55*(4), 529–533.

Hanson, C. L., Henggeler, S. W., & Burghen, G. A. (1987b). Race and sex-differences in metabolic control of adolescents with IDDM—a function of psychosocial variables. *Diabetes Care, 10*(3), 313–318.

Hanson, C. L., Henggeler, S. W., Rodrigue, J. R., Burghen, G. A., & Murphy, W. D. (1988). Father-absent adolescents with IDDM: A population at risk? *Journal of Applied Developmental Psychology, 9,* 243–252.

Hanson, C., Henggeler, S., Harris, M., Burghen, G., & Moore, M. (1989). Family system variables and the health status of adolescents with IDDM. *Health Psychology, 8,* 239–253.

Hanson, S. L., & Pichert, J. W. (1986). Perceived stress and diabetes control in adolescents. *Health Psychology, 5*(5), 439–452.

Hauenstein, E., Marvin, R., Snyder, A., & Clarke, W. (1989). Stress in parents of children with diabetes mellitus. *Diabetes Care, 12,* 18–23.

Hauser, S. T., Jacobson, A. M., Noam, G., & Powers, S. (1983). Ego development and self-image complexity in early adolescence. *Archives of General Psychiatry, 40, 325–332.*

Hauser, S. T., Jacobson, A. M., Wertlieb, D., Brink, S., & Wentworth, S. (1985). The contribution of family environment to perceived competence and illness adjustment in diabetic and acutely ill adolescents. *Family Relations, 34,* 99–108.

Hauser, S. T., Vieyra, M., Jacobson, A., & Wertlieb, D. (1985). Vulnerability and resilience in adolescence: Views from the family. *Journal of Early Adolescence, 5,* 81–100.

Hauser, S., Jacobson, A. M., Milley, J., Wertlieb, D., Herskowitz, R., Wolfsdorf, J., & Lavori, P. (in press). Ego trajectories and adjustment to diabetes: Longitudinal studies of diabetic and acutely ill patients. In L. Feagens, W. Ray, & E. Susman (Eds.), *Emotion and cognition in child and adolescent health and development.* Hillsdale, NJ: Erlbaum.

Hauser, S. T., Jacobson, A. M., Wertlieb, D., Weiss-Perry, B., Follansbee, D., Wolfsdorf, J. I., Herskowitz, R. D., Houlihan, J., & Rajapark, D. C. (1986). Children with recently diagnosed diabetes: Interactions within their families. *Health Psychology, 5*(3), 273–296.

Hauser, S. T., Paul, E. L., Jacobson, A. M., Weiss-Perry, B., Vieyra, M., Rufo, P., Spetter, L. D., DiPlacido, J., Wertlieb, D., Wolfsdorf, J., & Herskowitz, R. D. (1988). How families cope with diabetes in adolescence. *Pediatrician, 15*, 80–94.

Henggeler, S. W., & Burghen, G. A. (1987). Social competence and parental support as mediators of the link between stress and metabolic control in adolescents with IDDM. *Journal of Consulting and Clinical Psychology, 55*, 529–533.

House, J. S., Umberson, D., & Landis, K. R. (1988). Structures and processes of social support. *Annual Review of Sociology, 14*, 293–318.

Ingersoll, G. M., Orr, D. P., Herrold, A. J., & Golden, M. P. (1986). Cognitive maturity and self-management among adolescents with insulin-dependent diabetes mellitus. *Behavioral Pediatrics, 108*, 620–623.

Jacobson, A. (1986). Current status of psychological research in diabetes. *Diabetes Care, 9*(5), 546–548.

Jacobson, A. M., & Hauser, S. T. (1983). Behavioral and psychological aspects of diabetes. In M. Ellenberg & H. Rifkin (Eds.), *Diabetes mellitus: Theory and practice*, (3rd ed, pp. 1037–1052). New York: Medical Exam Publishers.

Jacobson, A., Hauser, S. T., Powers, S., & Noam, G. (1984). The influences of chronic illness and ego development on self-esteem in diabetic and psychiatric adolescent patients. *Journal of Youth Adolescence 13*, 489–507.

Jacobson, A. M., Hauser, S. T., Wertlieb, D., Wolfsdorf, J. I., Orleans, J., & Vieyra, M. (1986). Psychological adjustment of children with recently diagnosed diabetes mellitus. *Diabetes Care, 9*(4), 323–329.

Jacobson, A. M., Hauser, S. T., Wolfsdorf, J. I., Houlihan, J., Milley, J. E., Herskowitz, R. D., Wertlieb, D., & Watt, E. (1987). Psychologic predictors of compliance in children with recent onset of diabetes mellitus. *The Journal of Pediatrics, 110*(5), 805–811.

Jandorf, L., Deblinger, E., Neale, J. M., & Stone, A. A. (1986). Daily versus major life events as predictors of symptom frequency: A replication study. *Journal of General Psychology, 113*(3), 205–218.

Johnson, J. H. (1986). *Life events as stressors in childhood and adolescence.* Newbury Park, CA: Sage Publications.

Johnson, S. B. (1980). Psychosocial factors in juvenile diabetes: A review. *Journal of Behavioral Medicine, 3*(1), 95–116.

Johnson, S. B. (in press-a). Adherence behaviors and health status in childhood diabetes. In C. Holmes (Ed.), *Neuropsychological and behavioral aspects of insulin and non-insulin dependent diabetes.* New York: Springer-Verlag.

Johnson, S. B. (in press-b). *The psychological impact of risk screening for chronic and life-threatening childhood illnesses.* Gainesville, FL.

Johnson, S. B., Pollack, R., Silverstein, J., Rosenblum, A., Spillar, R., McCallum, M., & Harkany, J. (1982). Cognitive and behavioral knowledge about IDDM in children. *Pediatrics, 69*, 708–713.

Kanner, A. D., Coyne, J. C., Schaefer, C., & Lazarus, R. S. (1981). Comparison of two modes of stress management: Daily hassles vs. major life events. *Journal of Behavioral Medicine, 4*, 1–39.

Kanner, A. D., Feldman, S., Weinberger, D., & Ford, M. (1987). Uplifts, hassles and adaptational outcomes in early adolescents. *Journal of Early Adolescence, 7*, 371–394.

Kaplan, R. M., Chadwick, M. W., & Schimmel, L. E. (1985). Social learning intervention to promote metabolic control in Type I diabetes mellitus: Pilot experiment results. *Diabetes Care, 8*(2), 152–155.

Koski, M. (1969). The coping process in childhood diabetes. *Acta Paediatrica Scandinavica Supplement, 198*, 1–82.

Kosub, S. M., & Kosub, C. (1982). Assessing perceptions of stress in diabetic children. *Children's Health Care, 11*(1), 4–8.

Kovacs, M., & Feinberg, T. (1982). Coping with juvenile onset diabetes mellitus. In A. Baum & J. Singer (Eds.), *Handbook of psychology and health* (Vol. 2, pp. 165–212). Hillsdale, NJ: Erlbaum.

Kovacs, M., Feinberg, T., Paulaskas, S., Finkelstein, R., Pollock, M., & Crouse-Novack, M. (1985). Initial coping responses and psychosocial characteristics of children with IDDM. *Journal of Pediatrics, 106*, 827–834.

Kovacs, M., Kass, R., Schnell, T., Goldston, D., & Marsh, J. (1989). Family functioning and metabolic control of school aged children with IDDM. *Diabetes Care, 12*, 409–414.

LaGreca, A. M. (1988). Children with diabetes and their families: Coping and disease management. In T. Field, P. McCabe, & N. Schneiderman (Eds.), *Stress and coping across development* (pp. 139–159). Hillside, New Jersey: Erlbaum.

Lazarus, R. S., & Folkman, S. (1984). *Stress, appraisal and coping.* New York: Springer.

Leaverton, D. R., White, C. A., McCormick, C. R., Smith, P., & Sheikholislam, B. (1980). *Journal of the American Academy of Child Psychiatry, 19*, 678–689.

Marteau, T. M., Bloch, S., & Baum, D. (1987). Family life and diabetic control. *Child Psychology and Psychiatry, 28*(6), 823–833.

Mason, J. W. (1975). A historical view of the stress field. *Journal of Human Stress, 1*, 6–12, 22–36.

Menaghan, E. G., (1983). Individual coping efforts and family studies: Conceptual and methodological issues. *Marriage and Family Review, 6*, 113–135.

Menninger, W. C. (1935). Psychological factors in the etiology of diabetes. *Journal of Nervous and Mental Diseases, 81*, 1–13.

McCubbin, H. I. (1979). Integrating coping behavior in family stress theory. *Journal of Marriage and the Family, 41*, 237–244.

Minuchin, S., Rosman, B. L., & Baker, L. (1978). *Psychosomatic families.* Cambridge, MA: Harvard University Press.

Minuchin, S., Baker, L., Rosman, B., Liebman, R., Milman, L., & Todd, T. (1975). A conceptual model of psychosomatic illness in children. *Archives of General Psychiatry, 32*, 1031–1038.

Moos, R. (1974). *Family environment scale.* Palo Alto, CA: Consulting Psychologists Press.

Moos, R. (1989). Life stressors and coping resources influence health and well-being. *Psychological Assessment, 4*, 133-158.

Moran, G. S., & Fonagy, P. (1987). Psychoanalysis and diabetic control: A single-case study. *British Journal of Medical Psychology, 60*, 357–372.

Newbrough, J. R., Simpkins, C. G., & Maurer, H. (1985). A family development approach to studying factors in the management and control of childhood diabetes. *Diabetes Care, 8*(1), 83.

Rolland, J. (1987). Chronic illness and the life cycle: A conceptual framework. *Family Process, 26*, 203–221.

Rose, M. I., & Firestone, P. (1983). Behavioral interventions in juvenile diabetes mellitus. In F. Firestone, P. J. McGrath, & W. Feldman (Eds.), *Advances in behavioral medicine for children and adolescents* (pp. 59–73). Hillsdale, NJ: Lawrence Erlbaum.

Rovet, J., & Ehrlich, R. (1988). Effect of temperament on metabolic control in children with diabetes mellitus. *Diabetes Care, 11*, 77–82.

Rovet, J., Ehrlich, R., & Hoppe, M. (1987). Behavior problems in children with diabetes as a function of sex and age of onset of disease. *Child Psychology Psychiatry, 28*(3), 477–491.

Rutter, M. (1985). Resilience in the face of adversity: Protective factors and resistance to psychiatric disorder. *British Journal of Psychiatry, 147*, 598–611.

Rutter, M., Tuma, A., & Lann, I. (1988). *Assessment and diagnosis in child psychopathology*. New York: Guilford.

Ryan, C. M. & Morrow, L. A. (1986). Self-esteem in diabetic adolescents: Relationship between age at onset and gender. *Journal of Consulting and Clinical Psychology, 54*(5), 730–731.

Ryan, C., Longstreet, C., & Morrow, L. (1985). The effects of diabetes mellitus on the school attendance and school achievement of adolescents. *Child: Care, Health and Development, 11*, 229–240.

Satin, W., LaGreca, A., Zigo, M., & Skyler, J. (1989). Diabetes in adolescence: Effects of multifamily group intervention and parent simulation of diabetes. *Journal of Pediatric Psychology, 14*, 259–275.

Schafer, L. C., Glasgow, R. E., McCaul, K. D., & Dreher, M. (1983). Adherence to IDDM regimens: relationship to psychosocial variables and metabolic control. *Diabetes Care, 6*(5), 493–498.

Schafer, L. C., McCall, K. D., & Glasgow, R. E. (1986). Supportive and nonsupportive family behaviors: Relationships to adherence and metabolic control in persons with Type I diabetes. *Diabetes Care, 9*,(2), 179–185.

Schafer, L. C., Glasgow, R. E., & McCaul, K. D. (1982). Increasing the adherence of diabetic adolescents. *Journal of Behavioral Medicine, 5*(3), 353–362.

Simonds, J. (1976). Psychiatric status of diabetic youth in good and poor control. *International Journal of Psychiatry, 7*, 133–151.

Simonds, J. (1977). Psychiatric status of diabetic youth matched with a control group. *Journal of the American Diabetes Association, 26*, 921–925.

Spirito, A., Stark, L., & Tyc, V. (1989). Common coping strategies employed by children with chronic illness. *Newsletter of the Society of Pediatric Psychology, 13*(1), 3–8.

Stabler, B., Lane, J. D., Ross, S. L., Morris, M. A., Litton, J., & Surwit, R. S. (1988). Type A behavior pattern and chronic glycemic control in individuals with IDDM. *Diabetes Care, 11*(4), 361–362.

Stabler, B., Morris, M. A., Litton, J., Feinglos, M. N., & Surwit, R. S. (1986). Differential glycemic response to stress in type A and type B individuals with IDDM. *Diabetes Care, 9*(5), 550–552.

Stabler, B., Surwit, R. S., Lane, J. D., Morris, M. A., Litton, J., & Feinglos, M. N. (1987). Type A behavior pattern and blood glucose control in diabetic children. *Psychosomatic Medicine, 49*(3), 313–316.

Stark, L. J., Dahlquist, L. M., & Collins, F. L. (1987). Improving children's compliance with diabetes management. *Clinical Psychology Review, 7*, 223–242.

Sullivan, B. J. (1979). Adjustment in diabetic adolescent girls: Development of the diabetic adjustment scale. *Psychosomatic Medicine, 41*, 119–126.

Surwit, R. S., Feinglos, M. N., & Scovern, A. W. (1983). Diabetes and behavior: A paradigm for health psychology. *American Psychologist, 38(3), 255–262.*

Thoits, P. (1986). Social support as coping assistance. *Journal of Consulting and Clinical Psychology, 54*, 416–423.

Traisman, H. S. (1980). *Management of juvenile diabetes* (3rd ed.). St. Louis: Mosby.

Turk, D. C., & Speers, M. A. (1983). Diabetes mellitus: A cognitive–functional analysis of stress. In T. Burnish & L. Bradley (Eds.), *Coping with chronic disease* (pp. 191–217). New York: Academic Press.

Varni, J., Babani, L., Wallander, J., Roe, T., & Frasier, S. (1989). Social support and self-esteem effects on psychological adjustments in children and adolescents with IDDM. *Child and Family Behavior Therapy, 11*, 1–17.

Waller, D. A., Chipman, J. J., Hardy, B. W., Hightower, M. S., North, A. J., Williams, S. B., & Babick, A. J. (1986). Measuring diabetes-specific family support and its relation to metabolic control: A preliminary report. *Journal of the American Academy of Child Psychiatry, 25*(3), 415–418.

Wellborn, T. A., Garcia-Webb, P., Bonser, A., McCann, V., & Constable, I. (1983). Clinical criteria that reflect C-peptide status in idiopathic diabetes. *Diabetes Care, 6*, 315–316.

Wertlieb, D., Hauser, S. T., & Jacobson, A. (1986). Adaptation to diabetes: Behavior symptoms and family context. *Journal of Pediatric Psychology, 11*, 463–479.

Wertlieb, D., Weigel, C., Springer, T., & Feldstein, M. (1987). Temperament as a moderator of children's stressful experiences. *American Journal of Orthopsychiatry, 57*, 234–245.

Wertlieb, D., Weigel, C., & Feldstein, M. (1989). Stressful experiences, temperament and social support: Impact on children's behavior symptoms. *Journal of Applied Developmental Psychology, 10*, 487–503.

Wertlieb, D., Weigel, C., & Feldstein, M. (1988). Impact of stress and temperament on children's medical utilization. *Journal of Pediatric Psychology, 13*, 409–421.

Wertlieb, D., Weigel, C., & Feldstein, M. (1987). Measuring children's coping. *American Journal of Orthopsychiatry, 57*, 548–560.

Wertlieb, D. (in press). Children and divorce: Stress and coping in developmental perspective. In J. Eckenrode & S. Gore, (Eds.), *Stress and coping: Crossing the boundaries*. (Vol. 2). New York: Plenum.

Wortman, C. B., & Conway, T. L. (1985). The role of social support in adaptation and recovery from physical illness. In S. Cohen & S. L. Syme (Eds.), *Social support and health* (pp. 281–302). New York: Academic.

GREGORY M. HEREK

ILLNESS, STIGMA, AND AIDS

G regory M. Herek is an associate research psychologist at the University of California at Davis. He received his PhD in social/personality psychology from the University of California in 1983 and then completed a two-year postdoctoral fellowship at Yale University. Herek subsequently was a lecturer at Yale for one year and then an assistant professor in the Social/Personality Psychology Program at the Graduate Center of the City University of New York for three years.

Herek is a leading expert on antigay prejudice and AIDS-related stigma. He has published numerous scholarly articles on these topics and has spoken frequently on university campuses and on national television and radio. He also has addressed these issues in his teaching. In 1984, he offered a seminar at Yale University on antigay prejudice, and in 1987, he collaborated in a seminar on the psychosocial aspects of AIDS at the C.U.N.Y. Graduate Center. Both courses were among the first of their kind to be offered at major universities in the United States.

In his current research, Herek is assessing the effects of stigma and prejudice on public reactions to the AIDS epidemic and on the effectiveness of AIDS-education efforts. He has received funding from the National Institute of Mental Health for two projects: a) a national survey of attitudes associated with the AIDS epidemic and b) an extensive social psychological analysis of existing AIDS-educational videotapes.

Photo by K. Hancock

Herek's other professional involvements also have focused on lesbian and gay issues and, more recently, AIDS issues. In 1986, he testified on behalf of the American Psychological Association (APA) for the House Criminal Justice Subcommittee's hearings on antigay violence. He also has assisted the APA in preparing amicus briefs in court cases challenging the constitutionality of state sodomy laws (*Bowers v. Hardwick*, U.S. Supreme Court) and military policies excluding lesbians and gay men (*Watkins v. U.S. Army*, Ninth Circuit Court of Appeals).

Herek was chairperson of APA's Committee on Lesbian and Gay Concerns in 1987. During that year he also was national president of the Association of Lesbian and Gay Psychologists. He served on the Task Force on Avoiding Heterosexist Bias in Research, which was convened by the Board of Social and Ethical Responsibility in Psychology (BSERP), and the APA Task Force on AIDS, which was convened by the Board of Directors. He is a coeditor of the Division 44 annual, *Contemporary Perspectives on Lesbian and Gay Psychology*, and a consulting editor for the *Journal of Homosexuality* and the *Journal of Gay and Lesbian Psychotherapy*. He recently edited (with Kevin Berrill) a special issue of the *Journal of Interpersonal Violence* on violence against lesbians and gay men.

GREGORY M. HEREK

ILLNESS, STIGMA, AND AIDS

Imagine a disease that arouses great fear throughout the United States, especially in New York and other large cities where it is rampant. Imagine that the disease has no cure and is fatal to most people who manifest its symptoms. Physicians prescribe a variety of treatments but with little success.

Imagine that people who get sick are widely assumed to have engaged in immoral behaviors—probably related to sexual behavior or consumption of drugs. Imagine that the illness strikes disproportionately among Blacks, ethnic minorities, immigrants, and the poor. Many members of these groups even believe the epidemic to be the product of a conspiracy against them by the powerful of society. If someone famous gets sick or dies from the illness, considerable speculation arises about that person's secret life.

Imagine that the lack of effective treatments leads society to focus on prevention efforts. Attempts are made to change "immoral" behaviors that are thought to predispose people to the disease. A movement arises to shut down public establishments where such behaviors occur, because they are viewed as breeding grounds for the disease. Imagine that many people explain the disease as a punishment from God for sin, while others claim it is Nature's retribution for maladaptive behavior. Some commentators regard the epidemic as fortunate: It has provided a dramatic opportunity for battling unnatural and unhealthy behaviors.

Imagine that, despite assurances by public health authorities and physicians, the general public assumes the illness to be highly contagious. Consequently, the sick are viewed as dangerous. Calls arise for their quarantine. Hospitals are reluctant to accept them because of the public outcry by neighborhood residents. Some medical professionals refuse to treat the stricken. Physicians refrain from reporting cases out of a desire to protect their patients from public stigma.

Imagine that some tolerance emerges from the horrors of the epidemic, as the public observes a stigmatized group taking care of its own who are sick. Other benefits also emerge, including notable advances in medicine, science, and public health.

The events described here all occurred in the United States during the 1832 cholera epidemic (Rosenberg, 1987). The similarities between cholera in the 1830s and AIDS (acquired immune deficiency syndrome) in the 1990s are striking. In both epidemics, the social meanings of a disease included stigmatization of those who manifested its symptoms. Historically, other illnesses have displayed similar patterns. In this chapter, I shall discuss some of the cultural, social, and psychological processes through which an illness becomes stigmatized, and the consequences of these processes for individuals with the disease.

Stigma and Illness: Historical and Cultural Background

History and Usage

Originally, the term *stigma* referred to a visible marking on the body that was usually made by a branding iron or a pointed instrument.[1] The mark signified social ostracism, disgrace, shame, or condemnation. Its bearers typically were considered criminals or villians. Stigma could also refer to nonphysical characteristics. For example, a 1907 textbook of psychiatry described a form of psychopathology known as a Stigmata of Degeneration, and the *Oxford English Dictionary* (*OED*) notes a reference in 1859 to the "stigmata of old maidenhood." The *OED* also records that the word was used in 1597, apparently humorously, to describe the mark bestowed upon a person by an academic degree. In

Preparation of this chapter was supported in part by research grants to the author from the National Institute of Mental Health (#MH43253 and #MH43823). Correspondence should be directed to Gregory M. Herek, Department of Psychology, University of California, Davis, CA 95616.
[1]My comments on the history and usage of the word *stigma* are based on the 1971 edition of the *Oxford English Dictionary* (*OED*), p. 954.

none of these cases was the word's meaning limited to a physical mark or blemish.

Stigma has also carried positive connotations. For Christians, stigmatic markings could signify special grace. Catherine of Siena and other Catholic saints reportedly manifested wounds on their own bodies corresponding to those of the crucified Jesus. Some of these wounds regularly appeared or bled in conjunction with important feast days. For example, the thirteenth-century saint, Francis of Assisi, was said to have received the stigmata while praying during the Feast of the Exaltation of the Cross.

Modern social scientists have used stigma to denote a socially undesirable characteristic and have been interested primarily in its effects on social interactions. A recent review, for example, identified stigmatized individuals as members of social groups "about which others hold negative attitudes, stereotypes, and beliefs, or which, on average, receive disproportionately poor interpersonal and/or economic outcomes relative to members of the society at large due to discrimination against members of the social category" (Crocker & Major, 1989, p. 609).

In what is perhaps the best known and most enduring theoretical analysis of stigma, Goffman (1963) defined it as "an attribute that is deeply discrediting within a particular social interaction" (p. 3). He described stigma as a special discrepancy between social expectations and reality. Stigma arises during a social interaction when an individual's *actual social identity*—the attributes she or he possesses—falls short of normative expectations about what that individual should be—her or his *virtual social identity*. This discrepancy is in an unfavorable direction. The individual is perceived, whether accurately or not, as unable to fulfill the role requirements of ordinary social interaction with "normals," and is consequently "reduced in our minds from a whole and usual person to a tainted, discounted one" (p. 3). According to Goffman, stigma spoils an identity by preventing the stigmatized person from meeting expectations for particular kinds of social interaction. Goffman stressed that stigma is not inherent in an attribute itself, but rather arises in social interactions where the attribute is relevant to the participants' expectations about what the other person should be. Being Black is a source of stigma at a social gathering of White supremacists, but not in an African American church congregation. Having AIDS is a source of stigma in many settings, but not in an AIDS support group.

Because a discrepancy between virtual and actual social identities can appear in many ways, various dimensions have been proposed on which different stigmas can be ordered. One of them is a stigma's *concealability*, the extent to which the stigmatized condition is hidden or obvious (Jones et al., 1984). More concealable conditions permit their holder to avoid stigma with greater ease. The physical manifestations of cerebral palsy and advanced Kaposi's sarcoma are readily evident in social interactions, and consequently these conditions are low on concealability. In contrast, being gay or asymptomatically infected with HIV (human immunodeficiency virus) is usually concealable. A second important dimension on which to locate any stigma is its level of *disruptiveness* (Jones et al., 1984) or *obtrusiveness* (Goffman, 1963), that is, the extent to which it interferes with the normal flow of social interaction. Characteristics that are disruptive elicit high levels of stigma. A third, closely related dimension is that of *aesthetic qualities*; the more that others perceive the condition as repellent, ugly, or upsetting, the more stigma is attached to it. A fourth dimension is the circumstance of the condition's *origin*. This includes the bearer's perceived responsibility for its cause or maintenance. Observers may attach less stigma to a condition whose cause is perceived to be beyond control. A fifth dimension is the *course* of the stigma over time. Less acceptance is extended to those whose condition is unalterable or degenerative. Finally, perceived *peril* from the stigmatized condition is important. Others manifest more negative attitudes toward a stigmatized person to the extent that they believe they can be physically, socially, or morally tainted by interaction with him or her (Goffman, 1963; Jones et al., 1984).

At least five areas of analysis are necessary for understanding any specific instance of stigma. First, we must understand the characteristic or condition that provides the basis for stigmatization. In the case of physical disease, this means understanding its etiology, symptoms, and course. Second, we must examine the processes through which the culture attaches stigma to the condition, that is, the cultural construction of an ideology of stigma. Third, we must analyze the formation, expression, and maintenance of attitudes toward the stigmatized by those socially defined as "normal." Fourth, we must analyze the subjective experience of having the stigma: how one interprets and understands it, negotiates socially around it, and constructs an identity that incorporates it. Fifth, at the interpersonal level, we must analyze the interaction processes through which stigmatized individuals are identified, and through which the nonstigmatized and stigmatized negotiate their respective roles in a social interaction. These five areas of analysis can be useful in considering further the nineteenth-century American epidemic of cholera.

A Case Study: Cholera in the United States

Prior to 1800, cholera was endemic in some parts of India and regularly was spread throughout the country by Hindu pilgrims and religious travelers. By the early nineteenth century, traders and military troops from Britain and other nations intercepted the traditional routes of transmission and spread cholera throughout the world. The epidemic reached the United States in 1832, and again in 1849 and 1866. The disease probably was carried by Irish emigrants traveling to Canada. Cholera is

> caused by a bacillus that could live as an independent organism in water for lengthy periods of time. Once swallowed, if the cholera bacillus survives the stomach juices, it is capable of swift multiplication in the human alimentary tract, and produces violent and dramatic symptoms—diarrhea, vomiting, fever, and death, often within a few hours of the first signs of illness. The speed with which cholera killed was profoundly alarming, since perfectly healthy people could never feel safe from sudden death when the infection was anywhere near. In addition, the symptoms were peculiarly horrible: radical dehydration meant that a victim shrank into a wizened caricature of his former self within a few hours, while ruptured capillaries discolored the skin, turning it black and blue. The effect was to make mortality uniquely visible: patterns of bodily decay were exacerbated and accelerated, as in a time-lapse motion picture, to remind all who saw it of death's ugly horror and utter inevitability. . . . (McNeill, 1976, pp. 230–231)

Rosenberg's (1987) history of three nineteenth-century cholera epidemics in the United States clearly illustrates the evolution of the social construction of disease. Cultural understanding of cholera shifted from viewing it as a moral punishment for sinners in the 1832 epidemic to understanding it as the result of poor sanitation and public health practices by 1866.

When the 1832 epidemic struck, neither physicians nor the general public understood the bacterial transmission of the disease. Physicians believed that cholera was caused by the introduction of poisons into the atmosphere, for example, from decaying matter. Certain conditions were thought to predispose people to succumb to these poisons. Excessive sexual activity, for example, was viewed as a predisposing factor for cholera because it "left its devotees weakened and 'artificially stimulated,' their systems defenseless against cholera" (Rosenberg, 1987, p. 41). Consequently, prostitutes and their customers were considered to be at high risk.

The poor, Blacks, and immigrants all comprised additional "risk groups" for cholera. Many members of the upper middle classes explained the poor's susceptability to cholera as a consequence of idleness and intemperance. In reality, the poor were stricken chiefly because they lived in crowded and unsanitary conditions without clean water. Rosenberg (1987) reported that so few deaths occurred in Paris outside of the lower classes that the poor regarded the epidemic as "a poison plot fomented by the aristocracy and executed by the doctors" (p. 56). In the case of Black Americans, who suffered disproportionately from both poverty and cholera, victim blaming was accompanied by racism. "Whether he was free or slave, [White] Americans believed, the Negro's innate character invited cholera. He was, with few exceptions, filthy and careless in his personal habits, lazy and ignorant by temperament. A natural fatalist, moreover, he took no steps to protect himself from disease. . . ." (pp. 59–60). Newly arrived European immigrants, the majority of whom were Catholic, also were feared. Many were kept out of the country and thereby condemned to wander "starved and half-naked along the Canadian border" (p. 62). Nevertheless, although they often were viewed as ignorant, superstitious, and distasteful, immigrants were also pitied by many Americans. The work of priests and nuns to care for sick Catholic immigrants even may have moderated anti-Catholic prejudice, if only temporarily.

Because no effective treatment was available for cholera, public attention centered on prevention efforts, which often took a highly moralistic tone. A Connecticut physician, for example, demanded that boards of health have "the power to *change the habits of the sensual, the vicious, the intemperate*" (Rosenberg, 1987, p. 96). Temperance reformers argued with some success that if consumption of alcohol predisposed one to cholera, then the saloons were legally dispensing poison and should be closed. This moralism interfered with scientific observation. Physicians who could detect no clear differences in susceptibility between drinkers and nondrinkers did not broadcast their observation "for the sake of temperance and good order" (p. 97).

To their credit, many Americans perceived the epidemic as revealing a disturbing extent of poverty, which they blamed on society rather than God or the poor. For most, however, cholera seemed to demonstrate the power of God and the futility of earthly values. It functioned to "'promote the cause of righteousness, by sweeping away the obdurate and the incorrigible,' and 'to drain off the filth and scum which contaminate and defile human society.' The great majority of those who fell before the destroyer were the enemies of God" (Rosenberg, 1987, p. 43). Many who did not view cholera as a direct punishment from God viewed it as the consequence of failure to observe Nature's laws. "Cholera was caused by intemperance and filth and vice—liberals emphasized—conditions which had never been imposed by God. Just as the misuse of a machine must inevitably damage it, so any abuse of our bodies would bring its inescapable punishment" (p. 45).

Although physicians proclaimed (incorrectly) that cholera was not contagious, many members of the public disregarded them and responded to the epidemic by attacking and avoiding sick persons. "In Chester, Pennsylvania, several persons suspected of carrying the pestilence were reportedly murdered, along with the man who had sheltered them. Armed Rhode Islanders turned back New Yorkers fleeing across Long Island Sound. At Ypsilanti, the local militia fired upon the mail stage from cholera-infested Detroit. Everywhere there were stringent quarantines" (Rosenberg, 1987, p. 37).

Hospitals for cholera patients also provoked protest. Workers in a shipyard adjoining a cholera hospital "left work so unanimously and precipitately at its establishment that their employers were unable to fulfill their contracts" (Rosenberg, 1987, p. 87). "Neighbors resorted to everything from humble petitions to arson in their efforts to have them removed. Not that respectable folk opposed cholera hospitals. Everyone agreed they were necessary—but on someone else's street" (p. 94).

In the subsequent 1849 and 1866 cholera epidemics, public attitudes changed as scientific understanding of the disease increased. Once the cholera bacillus was known to spread primarily through the vomitus and excrement of infected individuals, massive public health campaigns were mounted to destroy contaminated bedding and clothing, to improve sewage disposal and purify public water supplies, and to clean up cities. Outmoded moralistic conceptualizations of the disease yielded to a new respect for public health and medicine as Americans realized that purely material practices could prevent the spread of cholera. As Rosenberg pointed out, this shift in the paradigm for cholera did not reflect the culture's decrease in piety; rather, it was based on advances in scientific understanding that made the moralistic approach to cholera increasingly irrelevant.

Stigma and the Social Construction of Illness

In his discussion of cholera, Rosenberg (1987) observed, "A disease is no absolute physical entity but a complex intellectual construct, an amalgam of biological state and social definition" (p. 5n). In other words, illnesses are socially constructed. Symptoms are noticed, correlated, and categorized as related or unrelated to the illness. The disease is labeled. Theories of cause, transmission, prevention, and cure are formulated, promulgated, criticized, and revised. This process involves a series of social interactions among epidemiologists, physicians, patients and their loved ones, journalists, insurance companies, government officials, and others.

In addition to identifying symptoms and naming the disease, the social construction of illness typically includes four components. The *origin* of the disease is identified. Frequently, as knowledge about it accrues, increasingly complex systems of causes are articulated. In this process, *responsibility* for the disease often is assigned. Simultaneously, the *"victim"* or "patient" is constructed as guilty or innocent, dangerous or benign, heroic or pitiful. Finally, *responsibility for cure* is assigned. These four components of the construction of illness can be identified both for individual manifestations of illness and for illness as a societal phenomenon. Immediate sources of infection as well as ultimate or evolutionary origins are identified. Responsibility is assigned to individuals for their own illness and to groups for bringing the disease into the community or society. Cultural images develop of individual patients as well as communities of victims. Responsibility for an individual's cure as well as responsibility for eradicating the illness from society are assigned.

During this definitional process, the culture imbues the disease with meaning by integrating it into a larger ontology. At least two dimensions of conflict pervade this constructive process. The first is a conflict between moralistic and secular worldviews. In his historical account of American reactions to venereal disease, Brandt (1987) labeled these competing views *moralism* and *secular rationalism*. In my own empirical research (described below), I have labeled them *moralism* and *pragmatism*. Moralists seek to define illness as a manifestation of spiritual or supernatural forces in the material world. Disease is viewed as divine punishment or as a test from God. The appropriate response, therefore, is increased piety, adherence to religious teachings and, in some cases, expiatory rituals. The secular or pragmatic construction, in contrast, views disease as the result of purely physical processes which threaten the public welfare and can be eliminated through direct intervention. The appropriate response is to do whatever is necessary to interfere with the disease process, for example, through the use of drugs or vaccines, behavior change, or elimination of hazardous environmental conditions.

Moralists constructed cholera as a punishment inflicted on sinners and prescribed virtuous behavior (e.g., temperance, abstention from excessive sexual activity) as the proper prevention. Pragmatists identified the sources of cholera in the unsanitary living conditions of its victims. Once the cause of the disease was understood, the pragmatists instituted procedures that laid the groundwork for many modern public health practices, for example, removal of garbage from streets and maintenance of sanitary water supplies (Rosenberg, 1987). The pragmatic construction of illness should not be equated automatically with science and medicine, however, since medical approaches to disease have often been infused with moralism. This is especially true in the early constructions of disease before scientific knowledge has advanced. Similarly, moralists may well understand and accept the scientific explanations of disease while considering them to be incomplete. For example, a leading physician offered the following comments on venereal disease in 1950.

> Mere treatment of venereal disease is certainly not the answer. And were it the answer, and were venereal diseases wiped out, it is now clear that the accomplishment would have heavy costs in the social, moral, and material life of man. A world of accepted, universalized,

> safeguarded promiscuity is something to look at searchingly before
> it is accepted. (Brandt, 1987, p. 172)

The conflict between moralism and secular rationalism in public discourse on venereal disease was described by Brandt (1987). Advocates of a secular rationalist approach typically accepted sexual behavior outside of marriage as inevitable. They sought to reduce the incidence of venereal disease through distribution of prophylactics and, when effective antibiotics became available, through nonjudgmental treatment of infected individuals. In contrast, moralists have advocated abstinence and have appealed to moral values and fear of disease to encourage it. Moralists have considered venereal disease to be symptomatic of a deeper social disorder.

The ongoing conflict between moralism and secular rationalism has been apparent in contemporary debates about preventing the spread of AIDS through distributing condoms, instituting needle exchange programs, and developing safer sex education materials for gay and bisexual men. Proponents of these policies take a nonjudgmental stance toward risk behaviors, accept that they occur, and focus on the primary goal of preventing HIV transmission. Opponents reject the interventions as promoting or condoning what they feel is immoral behavior. Their solution is summarized by the "Just say no" slogan of the Reagan administration. For those who subscribe to this moralistic view, "the way to control sexually transmitted disease is not through medical means but rather through moral rectitude. A disease such as AIDS is controlled by controlling individual conduct" (Brandt, 1987, p. 202). The primary goal of the secular rationalists is to prevent disease. The primary goal of the moralists is to prevent behavior that they consider sinful or wrong.

A second conflict pervading the social construction of illness concerns the appropriate response to persons identified as ill. Should they be cared for with compassion by the community, or should they be excluded and viewed as dangerous? This conflict is not necessarily related to that between moralism and pragmatism. Compassionate care for the sick can be justified on either moral or pragmatic grounds, as can ostracism and retribution. Social constructions concerning responsibility for an illness are especially salient in this conflict. As Brandt (1987) framed the question: Is disease "merely the result of an individual's willful exposure, or should external, environmental, and social factors that might contribute to a tendency to exposure be considered?" (p. 169). Writing about herpes, whose mention disappeared from the mass media when the implications of the AIDS epidemic were recognized, Brandt noted that when a disease results from voluntary behavior, victims are often viewed as having gotten what they deserve. He pointed to our culture's underlying assumption that behavior is entirely voluntary and that, once informed about risks, individuals should modify their behavior. "The assumption that an individual's behavior is free from external forces—that life-style is strictly voluntary—is explicit" (p. 202).

Many Americans, including psychologists, take this highly individualistic view of human beings as rational and agentic. We have two reactions when people don't change their riskful behavior: puzzlement and hostility. We are puzzled that everyone who "learns the facts" does not immediately alter her or his behavior. We assume that prevention (of AIDS, lung cancer, heart disease) is both a possibility and a priority for all individuals. We assume that prevention takes precedence over all other physical, psychological, social, and cultural needs. We attribute responsibility entirely to the individual, ignoring the situation and culture in which that individual lives. We ignore historical relationships between communities of the ill and the larger society, disregarding the possibility that communities "at risk" may not trust or believe medical experts and government officials, or that they may have different priorities for which problems must be solved. After our puzzlement abates, we relegate those who cannot (or will not) change to their fate, and we sometimes tolerate punitive actions against them. I shall return to these two dimensions of public debate about prevention later in my discussion of individual attitudes toward people with AIDS.

AIDS and Stigma

Keeping in mind these common themes in the cultural construction of illness and stigma, we now can turn to a more systematic discussion of AIDS-related stigma.[2] As used here, *AIDS-related stigma* refers to all unfavorable attitudes, beliefs, behaviors, and policies directed at persons perceived to be infected with HIV, whether or not they actually are infected and regardless of whether or not they manifest symptoms of AIDS. I purposely avoid using terms that inappropriately individualize and pathologize this social phenomenon, such as "AIDS phobia" or "AIDS hysteria." Instead, I propose that individuals' hostility toward people with AIDS can best be understood through psychological and sociological perspectives on stigma, prejudice, and attitudes. Individual manifestations of AIDS-related stigma represent the intersection of psychological processes with the cultural construction of the illness.

AIDS-related stigma is manifested in a variety of ways. HIV-infected people continue to be rejected by friends and relatives, fired or forced to resign from their jobs, and subjected to violent assault. Calls are still

---

[2]To better understand the social psychological phenomena discussed in the remainder of the paper, readers who lack personal experience with AIDS and AIDS-related stigma may wish to read the accounts provided by Monette (1988), Peabody (1986), and Whitmore (1988).

issued for their quarantine. As the number of people requiring medical care increases, making ever larger demands on already limited health care and government funds (Bloom & Carliner, 1988; Hay, Osmond, & Jacobson, 1988; Scitovsky, Cline, & Lee, 1986; Scitovsky & Rice, 1987; Seage et al., 1986), we can only expect that the problem will be further exacerbated. AIDS-related stigma can best be discussed by considering each of the five areas of analysis described earlier: the biomedical manifestations of AIDS, the cultural construction of AIDS, attitudes of the nonstigmatized, experiences of the stigmatized, and social interactions between the two groups.

The Biomedical Perspective[3]

AIDS is diagnosed when infection with HIV has caused a person's immune system to break down to such a degree that he or she manifests conditions caused by various viruses, fungal infections, and parasites—organisms that people with healthy immune systems are able to repel successfully. Most common among these are a protozoan infection of the lung, called *Pneumocystis carinii pneumonia* (PCP) and *Kaposi's sarcoma* (KS), a previously rare form of cancer that appears as purplish lesions on and in the body.[4] Frequently, HIV also infects the brain. Consequently, many persons with advanced cases of AIDS display marked neurological impairment.

The amount of time between infection with HIV and diagnosis of PCP or KS can be as long as 10 years. In the interim, symptoms such as chronic lymphadenopathy, night sweats, and oral thrush are used to diagnose *AIDS-Related Complex (ARC)*. Many physicians now question the medical usefulness of ARC as a diagnosis, however, and instead have begun to think in terms of *HIV disease*, which ranges along a continuum from initial infection to AIDS. This shift in terminology, which emphasizes that HIV infection itself signals a disease state regardless of whether symptoms have appeared, reflects both pessimism and optimism. In the absence of effective therapies, most people infected with HIV will progress to AIDS; however, early identification and intervention may be effective in slowing or preventing the breakdown of the immune system.

The history of AIDS in the United States is usually traced to 1981, when several cases of PCP and KS were reported in previously healthy

---

[3]Unless otherwise noted, the information in this section is taken from the Institute of Medicine (1988).

[4]Some researchers and physicians have suggested that Kaposi's sarcoma is not a cancer, that it is caused by a sexually transmitted agent other than HIV, and that it is not necessarily an indication of AIDS (Perlman, 1990).

gay men (see, e.g., Fettner & Check, 1985; Shilts, 1987). HIV infection has probably been with the human race for considerably longer. In some parts of Africa, HIV appears to have been endemic for decades, although the lack of medical care in those areas, along with worldwide indifference, prevented AIDS from being noticed there. When the U.S. Public Health Service, through its Centers for Disease Control (CDC), began to name the puzzling phenomenon around 1982, they initially called it GRID: Gay-related immune deficiency (Shilts, 1987). The name eventually adopted, however, was acquired immune deficiency syndrome: *acquired* because the people who had it were previously healthy—it was not congenital; *immune deficiency* because the condition was characterized by immunological weakness; and *syndrome* because the immune deficiency left people vulnerable to a cluster of infections and KS.

HIV is transmitted when infected blood or semen is introduced directly into a healthy person's bloodstream. Transmission can occur during unprotected anal or vaginal (and possibly oral) sexual intercourse, as well as when drugs are injected intravenously with apparatus that already contains another person's AIDS-infected blood (many IV drug users share their needles and syringes). Infections also have resulted from transfusions with contaminated blood or blood products, although new screening procedures have drastically reduced transmission through this route. Additionally, a fetus or neonate can be infected by its mother.

By the end of 1989, the Centers for Disease Control had recorded 117,781 diagnosed cases of AIDS in the United States. Among the 115,786 adults reflected in that statistic, most (61%) were men who were infected through unprotected homosexual behavior. In most of these cases, transmission probably occurred through anal intercourse. The second-most common route of HIV transmission in adult U.S. AIDS cases has been through sharing intravenous needles for illegal drugs (21%). Another 7% of adult cases fit both categories. This pattern differs from that observed in Africa, where most adult transmission appears to have occurred through heterosexual intercourse. The vast majority of the 1,995 cases of pediatric AIDS reported in the United States at the end of 1989 apparently resulted from infection by the mother (81%); 11% were linked to blood transfusions; and another 5% contracted AIDS from blood products for coagulation disorders.

In the United States, Blacks and Hispanics are disproportionately represented in all transmission categories except hemophiliacs. Although African Americans constitute only 12% of the U.S. population, they represent 16% of adult AIDS cases among gay or bisexual men, 50% of the adult cases among IV drug users, 26% of the adult cases among drug-using gay or bisexual males, 62% of the adult cases traced to heterosexual contact, and 53% of pediatric AIDS cases. Similarly, Latin/Hispanic Americans constitute 6% of the U.S. population, yet they account for 11% of the adult AIDS cases among gay or bisexual men, 29%

of the adult cases among IV drug users, 14% of the adult cases among drug-using gay or bisexual males, 17% of the adult cases traced to heterosexual contact, and 25% of pediatric AIDS cases (Centers for Disease Control, 1990; see also Hopkins, 1987; Peterson & Marin, 1988; Rogers & Williams, 1987). In addition to people already diagnosed, the CDC now estimates that approximately one million Americans are infected with HIV (e.g., "Estimates of HIV Prevalence," 1990; see also Garrison, 1990).

Individuals diagnosed with AIDS in the United States have a median life expectancy of about 18 months. This estimate is potentially misleading, however, because it combines individuals who have access to high-quality medical care with those who have no resources for treatment. Currently, therapy with zidovudine (AZT), aerosolized pentamidine, and other drugs can considerably prolong life expectancy after diagnosis. As new treatments become available in the near future, AIDS eventually may become less a fatal illness and more a chronic, treatable condition (for regular updates on new treatments, the reader is referred to *AIDS Treatment News* and other resources listed in Appendix A). Nevertheless, an individual's chances for survival will depend to a large extent on her or his access to good medical care. More than 70,000 Americans had died from AIDS by the end of 1989 (Centers for Disease Control, 1990).

The Cultural Construction of AIDS

As an illness, AIDS is a likely candidate for high levels of stigmatization. Although asymptomatic HIV infection is concealable and unlikely to be disruptive, the symptoms of AIDS-related illnesses are often visible; are perceived by others as repellent, ugly, or upsetting; and can interfere with an individual's social interactions, for example, by reducing mobility, stamina, and endurance. Further, both AIDS and HIV infection are widely viewed as incurable and progressive (*negative course*) and as posing a risk to others through transmission (*high peril*). Additionally, engaging in homosexual intercourse and injecting illegal drugs are widely perceived as intentional, riskful behaviors. HIV contracted through these routes is assigned a blameful origin (I shall consider so-called blameless victims presently).

The intensity of AIDS-related stigma, however, cannot be accounted for solely on the basis of the characteristics of HIV disease. Additionally, we must recognize that the American epidemic of AIDS has occurred primarily among marginalized groups, especially gay men, and that the epidemic has been defined socially as a disease of these groups. Consequently, the stigma attached to AIDS as an illness is layered upon preexisting stigma and, to some extent, is equated with it. AIDS has become a symbol. Reactions to AIDS are reactions to gay men, drug users, racial minorities, or outsiders in general.

The frequent use of the phrase "the general public" as a counterpart to "risk groups" conveys this distinction between the dominant in-group and the stigmatized out-group. Gay men, IV drug users, and their sexual partners are not part of "the general public." Similarly, persons who did not contract AIDS through homosexual behavior or drug use often have been categorized as "innocent victims" (Albert, 1986). A *Newsweek* caption early in the epidemic, for example, described a teenage hemophiliac and an infant with AIDS as "the most blameless victims" ("Social Fallout From an Epidemic," 1985). Of course, the opposite of a blameless victim is a "blamable" victim. Guilt is assigned if HIV infection occurred during stigmatized behavior.

In the past, the treatment and prevention of epidemic diseases have often been hampered by stigma attached to both the illness and to social groups manifesting the illness. Social ostracism and hostility toward bubonic plague in the fourteenth century, for example, encouraged diseased persons to hide their illness from members of their own community or to flee to other towns, spreading infection in the process (e.g., Defoe, 1960). Plague-inspired anti-Semitic riots drove healthy and infected Jews alike to eastern Europe, often spreading illness (McNeill, 1976). In a similar fashion, AIDS-related stigma, layered upon preexisting prejudice against gay men and others, has hindered effective societal response to the epidemic in several ways. Negative reactions have shaped the behavior of policymakers, legislators, caregivers, and infected individuals and have limited the effectiveness of prevention efforts. The Centers for Disease Control withheld funding for educational programs that included explicit instructions for engaging in male homosexual behavior without transmitting HIV (Panem, 1987). The U.S. Senate twice endorsed an amendment by Senator Jesse Helms of North Carolina that prohibited federal funds for AIDS education materials that "promote or encourage, directly or indirectly, homosexual activities" ("Limit Voted on AIDS Funds," 1987, p. B12). By constricting the scope of risk-reduction education, such actions contribute to the epidemic's spread.

The use of AIDS as an ideological and political issue was exemplified by the comments of columnist Patrick Buchanan (1987): "There is one, only one, cause of the AIDS crisis—the willful refusal of homosexuals to cease indulging in the immoral, unnatural, unsanitary, unhealthy, and suicidal practice of anal intercourse, which is the primary means by which the AIDS virus is being spread through the 'gay' community, and, thence, into the needles of IV drug abusers" and to others. Buchanan further suggested that the "Democratic Party should be dragged into the court of public opinion as an unindicted co-conspirator in America's AIDS epidemic" for "seeking to amend state and federal civil rights laws to make sodomy a protected civil right, to put homosexual behavior, the sexual practice by which AIDS is spread, on the same moral plane with being female or being black" (p. 23). AIDS and gay rights were thus equated with and linked to the opposition party.

The federal government's slow response to AIDS can be understood in part as a result of the politics of stigma. Antigay sentiment appears to have played an important role in the Reagan administration's failure to confront the epidemic. Shilts (1987) documented in painful detail the federal government's refusal to respond to AIDS during the Reagan administration—the cutbacks in funding to the CDC, followed by refusals to allocate resources to AIDS research, followed by refusals to request congressional funding for AIDS research, followed by refusals to spend the funds that Congress had allocated over the Reagan administration's objections (see also Panem, 1987).

Then-President Reagan did not even make explicit public statements about AIDS until 1987—more than five years and tens of thousands of lives into the epidemic. The Administration's reasoning was evident in remarks made at the 1985 International Conference on AIDS by then-Secretary of the Department of Health and Human Services, Margaret Heckler: "We must conquer AIDS before it affects the heterosexual population and the general population. . . . We have a very strong public interest in stopping AIDS before it spreads outside the risk groups, before it becomes an overwhelming problem" (quoted in Shilts, 1987, p. 554). Although AIDS already afflicted more than 9,000 people at the time, and more than 4,000 people had died—most of them gay or bisexual men—Heckler and the Reagan administration did not see it as an "overwhelming problem," because it had not affected the "general population" (which did not include gay men).

A similar pattern can be seen in responses by the news media to the epidemic. Initially, AIDS received very little press coverage. When it did, the new disease was often referred to as a "gay plague" (Kinsella, 1989). The *New York Times* published only six stories about AIDS during 1981 and 1982, a period when 634 Americans had been diagnosed with AIDS, 260 of whom had died—most of them in New York. None of the six stories made the front page. In contrast, the *Times* printed 54 stories in 1982 (four of them on the front page) about the discovery of poisoned Tylenol capsules in Chicago in October of that year. Only seven people died from poisoned Tylenol (Shilts, 1987). In 1983, however, infected individuals were discovered outside of the "risk groups" of homosexual/ bisexual men and IV drug users. AIDS was reported in female partners of IV drug users, blood transfusion recipients, and babies born to women with AIDS. Around this time, scientists also realized that infected people could "carry" and transmit the virus without themselves manifesting any physical symptoms of AIDS. In other words, AIDS had "innocent" victims. Suddenly, the previously minimal AIDS coverage in the *New York Times* (measured by number of stories devoted to AIDS each week) took a major jump (Baker, 1986; Panem, 1987). As Shilts (1987) argued, the epidemic was virtually ignored by the nongay media as long as it was merely a "story of dead and dying homosexuals" (p. 191).

Reactions of the Nonstigmatized

The cultural construction of AIDS as a stigmatized condition of stig-matized groups is clearly expressed in the behaviors and attitudes of many nonstigmatized individuals. Healthy people make hurtful and in-sensitive remarks; tell or laugh at AIDS jokes; reject or isolate people with AIDS; vote for quarantine laws or for politicians who support them; and perpetrate or tolerate discrimination, harassment, and even violence (see Herek & Glunt, 1988). Survey research consistently shows that a significant minority of the American public endorses quarantine of HIV-infected persons, universal mandatory testing, and even such draconian measures as tattooing of infected individuals, even though public health officials consistently have argued against such measures as ineffective and repressive (e.g., Blendon & Donelan, 1988; Schneider, 1987; Singer & Rogers, 1986; Stipp & Kerr, 1989). People with AIDS are more negatively evaluated than are persons with other diseases, even by health care workers (Katz et al., 1987; Kelly, St. Lawrence, Smith, Hood, & Cook, 1987; Triplet & Sugarman, 1987). Avoidance of people with AIDS and overestimation of the risks of casual contact are common among care-givers (Blumenfield, Smith, Milazzo, Seropian, & Wormser, 1987; Kelly, St. Lawrence, Smith, Hood, & Cook, 1987; Knox, Dow, & Cotton, 1989; Mejta, Denton, Krems, & Hiatt, 1988; O'Donnell, O'Donnell, Pleck, Snarey, & Rose, 1987; Rubin, Reitman, Berrier, & Sacks, 1989; Wallack, 1989; Werzt, Sorenson, Liebling, Kessler, & Heeren, 1987; Wiley, Heath, & Acklin, 1988). Two complementary social psychological approaches to understanding such attitudes and behavior are discussed here. The first approach is drawn from social cognition research and decision-making theory. The second derives from research on attitudes and prejudice.

AIDS, Anxiety, and Social Cognition

The first approach suggests that many seemingly irrational reactions to AIDS reflect simple errors of judgment, inappropriate use of cognitive heuristics, and stress-related defective decision making. This approach begins with several observations about the AIDS epidemic: AIDS is a new illness that is uniformly fatal; it is caused by an unseen infectious agent that can remain latent in the body for an unknown period of time; the epidemic is perceived as both out of control and potentially catastrophic. Because they are likely to arouse anxiety (Slovic, 1987), such perceptions can affect public reactions to AIDS in several ways. They lead to estima-tions of ever higher levels of risk associated with AIDS and to a strong desire to have that risk reduced; this, in turn, can lead to a willingness to impose strict regulation to achieve such a reduction (Slovic, Fischoff,

& Lichtenstein, 1981). Personal decisions made under the influence of such anxiety are likely to be defective: They fail to consider available information adequately, to seek needed new information, and to evaluate the likely consequences of any proposed action in terms of the full array of one's short-term and long-term goals (Herek, Janis, & Huth, 1987; Janis & Mann, 1977).

One pattern of defective decision making that probably occurs in connection with AIDS is *hypervigilance* (Janis & Mann, 1977). Consider the following example. A person learns that one of her coworkers has been diagnosed with AIDS. She knows that AIDS is a life-threatening disease. She has been bombarded with public education messages that AIDS is incurable but preventable. She believes these messages but is unclear about exactly *how* to prevent HIV infection. Lacking a clear understanding of how HIV is transmitted, she recalls other viral illnesses with which she has experience, such as influenza. She also recalls that experts never say that casual transmission (e.g., through saliva) cannot occur; they simply say that such transmission hasn't been observed. She calculates that her own risk of infection from her coworker is high. She feels that she must do something to protect herself but perceives serious drawbacks to every alternative that she can call to mind (e.g., she could quit her job but would suffer financially; she could continue to interact with her coworker but might get infected this way). Discovering that some other employees are demanding that the coworker with AIDS be forced to take a disability leave and fearful that she will become infected unless she does *something*, she joins the protest. When challenged with expert opinion and company policy concerning nondiscrimination on the basis of HIV status, she states her newly adopted guiding rules: "Better safe than sorry" and "You can't be too careful."

This example includes the key antecedents of hypervigilance. The decision maker experienced intense stress due to several simultaneous perceptions: (a) that severe losses are imminent if she does nothing; (b) that losses are also imminent if she takes action; (c) that a satisfactory solution is possible; but (d) that she must do something now—sufficient time is not available to search carefully for a solution. Time pressures also led the woman in our example to use the *availability* heuristic inappropriately: Lacking information about AIDS, she relied on comparisons to an easily recalled situation (influenza) with which she had experience (Tversky & Kahneman, 1974). Janis (1989) summarized the hypervigilant pattern as "Try anything that looks promising to get the hell out of this agonizing dilemma as fast as you can. Never mind any other consequences" (p. 80). Hypervigilance may underlie a "do something" syndrome observed in some public opinion surveys about AIDS, that is, a willingness to endorse any AIDS-related policy that promises action regardless of its likely costs, consequences, or effectiveness (Schneider, 1987).

AIDS, Attitudes, and Prejudice

Along with anxiety, AIDS evokes prejudice. Social psychological research on attitudes, therefore, also is relevant to understanding AIDS-related stigma. In the sections below, I discuss the cognitive dimensions along which AIDS-related attitudes appear to be organized, the motivations underlying those attitudes, and the relationship of AIDS-related attitudes to antigay prejudice.

The dimensions of attitudes concerning AIDS. In my own research with Eric Glunt at the Graduate Center of the City University of New York (Herek & Glunt, 1988, in press), I have found that public reactions to AIDS appear to be organized principally along two psychological dimensions. These dimensions, which have emerged repeatedly in factor analyses of responses from different samples, correspond to the two levels of conflict that Brandt (1987) observed in the history of public response to sexually transmitted diseases in the United States. One factor focuses on issues of blame and responsibility, as well as the conflict between compassion and coercion in perceptions of people with AIDS. We labeled this factor the *coercion/compassion* dimension of AIDS-related attitudes. The other factor includes items that pit the opposing philosophies of moralism and secular rationalism against each other. We labeled this factor *pragmatism/moralism.* These two dimensions of AIDS-related attitudes were not highly correlated in preliminary research, suggesting that an individual's position on one dimension does not predict her or his position on the other.

Although the same two dimensions emerged in separate analyses of responses from White and Black respondents, we observed racial differences in the variables that predict individuals' positions on the dimensions. Among Whites, individual attitudes toward gay men were among the best predictors of responses to the attitude items. Whites who expressed general prejudice against gay men were also more likely to view people with AIDS as responsible for their illness and to endorse measures such as a quarantine for dealing with AIDS (elements of the coercion/compassion dimension). These people were also more likely to reject governmental policies such as distributing condoms and clean needles (elements of the pragmatism/moralism dimension). Blacks' reactions to AIDS, in contrast, appeared to reflect deep distrust of scientists and the government, as well as a perception of the epidemic in terms of its effect on the African American community. Whites' attitudes appeared to be premised on an "outsiders'" view of the AIDS epidemic, whereas Blacks' attitudes reflected the perspective of "insiders." This did not seem to result from some affinity between Black respondents and gay people: Indeed, we suspect that many of the African Americans in our sample equated "gay men" with "gay *White* men." Rather, Blacks focused on the disproportionate representation of African Americans among people with AIDS. Although many Black males with AIDS contracted HIV through unprotected homosexual behavior, our data do not permit us to assess whether the African American respondents in our sample were aware of this fact. Because of the relatively small representation of African Americans in our research to date, all of our conclusions about their attitudes must be stated provisionally here. Data collection with a larger national Black sample currently is in progress.

From these findings, we concluded that public attitudes concerning AIDS reflect conflicts that have been present in policy debates concerning other illnesses, especially sexually transmitted diseases. We also concluded that the attitudes of Whites and Blacks may have different antecedents. Understanding AIDS-related stigma among White Americans requires understanding the social psychological bases for heterosexuals' attitudes toward gay people. Understanding AIDS-related stigma among African Americans, in contrast, requires an analysis of individuals' perceptions of how AIDS fits in the historical context of African Americans' treatment by White society.

Two conceptualizations of attitudes. At least two social psychological conceptualizations of attitudes are relevant to understanding AIDS-related stigma. The first is exemplified in the work of Fishbein and Ajzen (1975; Ajzen & Fishbein, 1980). Their theory of reasoned action conceives of behavior as shaped largely by the intention to behave, which results from attitudes toward the specific behavior which, in turn, are shaped by beliefs about the utility of the behavior for meeting personal goals and by perceived social norms governing the behavior. Within this framework, attitudes are assumed to be primarily instrumental, that is, strategies for organizing thought and behavior based on the inherent benefits or detriments associated with the attitude object. Broader ideologies or general attitudes are assumed to have minimal immediate relevance to understanding specific behaviors.

A contrasting perspective can be derived from research on symbolic politics, which generally has focused on racial attitudes (e.g., Kinder, 1986; Kinder & Sears, 1981, 1985; see also Sniderman & Tetlock, 1986a, 1986b). Symbolic racism is conceptualized to be a general ideology that is abstracted from specific situations and specific calculations of an individual's own self-interest. Its origins lie in the "preadult acquisition of traditional values (particularly individualism and self-reliance), and of racial fears and stereotypes" (Kinder, 1986, p. 154). It is not simply racism, but rather the conjunction of racism with traditional values. An example would be Whites' anti-Black attitudes based on the belief that Blacks receive unfair preferential treatment in affirmative action hiring programs.

Applied to AIDS, each perspective emphasizes different variables as antecedent to attitudes. The reasoned action perspective highlights the importance of concerns about personal health and safety, such as the fear of becoming infected with HIV. The symbolic politics perspective highlights the importance of AIDS as a symbolic issue that juxtaposes fears and stereotypes of out-groups (gay men, IV drug users, racial minorities) and traditional American values (e.g., sexual morality, beliefs that people get what they deserve). Using these two perspectives in a series of empirical studies, Pryor, Reeder, and Vinacco (1989) examined two kinds of reactions to AIDS: willingness to have one's own child in a classroom with a child with AIDS, and willingness to be enrolled in a course with a professor with AIDS. They observed that their respondents' AIDS-related attitudes included both symbolic (operationalized as attitudes toward homosexuality) and instrumental components.

Such a finding inevitably raises the question of how the relative importance of symbolic and instrumental issues differs among individuals. In this regard, I have found the *functional approach* to attitudes to be very useful. The functional approach is based on the premise that people hold and express particular attitudes because they derive psychological benefit from doing so, and that the type of benefit varies among individuals. Attitudes are understood according to the psychological needs they meet—the functions they serve. These functions are different for different people. Two people can hold the same attitude for very different reasons (see Herek, 1986, 1987; Katz, 1960, 1968; Katz & Stotland, 1959; Sarnoff & Katz, 1954; Smith, 1947; Smith, Bruner, & White, 1956).

In my own research, I have found that attitude functions can be classified into two broad types. Instrumental attitudes, those that benefit people primarily by helping them to organize the various objects of the world according to their own self interests, serve *evaluative functions*. These functions derive from the actual characteristics of the attitude object, that is, whether it provides rewards or punishments. Alternatively, the functions of symbolic attitudes derive principally from consequences of their *expression*—that is, speaking them aloud, writing them down, communicating them to another person, or even simply articulating them to oneself. In the case of *expressive functions*, the attitude object is a means to an end. By expressing a particular attitude, the person receives psychological benefit: increased self-esteem from affirming values central to self-concept (the *value-expressive* function), increased social support from expressing opinions consonant with those of important others (the *social-expressive* function), or a reduction in anxiety (the *defensive* function).

Applied to AIDS, the evaluative functions are most clearly related to concerns about personal risk of exposure to HIV. The expressive functions are associated with the metaphorical (Sontag, 1988) or symbolic aspects of AIDS. These functions are not always distinct. Consider parents' attitudes about sending their children to school where an HIV-infected student is enrolled. At first glance, such attitudes clearly involve evaluative functions. They reflect the parents' assessment of the risks faced by their children in the classroom with an infected child.

Such attitudes probably also serve expressive functions. They provide an opportunity for parents to affirm their feelings of love for their children as well as an occasion to assert to the community, "I am a good parent." If other parents are banding together to respond to the infected student (whether to protest the child's presence or to welcome her or him), the parent can receive support by expressing socially approved sentiments.

Attitude functions are affected by characteristics of the person and the situation. Someone with a strong need for affiliation, for example, is likely to hold attitudes concerning AIDS that increase his or her acceptance by friends, while someone else who is strongly committed to a political ideology is likely to hold attitudes about AIDS that reinforce that commitment. Additionally, situational cues can increase the salience of individual needs and thereby affect attitudes. A situation that makes personal values salient will lend itself to a value expressive function more than will a situation that highlights intrapsychic conflicts (Herek, 1986).

AIDS and attitudes toward gay people. Because of the ways in which AIDS has been socially constructed in our culture, most individuals do not respond to AIDS simply as a lethal and transmissible disease. Rather, they respond to it as a lethal and transmissible disease *of gay men and other minorities*. AIDS thus provides many with a metaphor for prejudice—a convenient hook upon which to hang their preexisting hostility toward out-groups. Approximately one fourth of the respondents to *Los Angeles Times* polls, for example, consistently have agreed that "AIDS is a punishment God has given homosexuals for the way they live"—28% on December 5, 1985, 24% on July 9, 1986, and 27% on July 24, 1987[5] (see also Blendon & Donelan, 1988). Respondents who express negative attitudes toward gay people are more likely than others to be poorly informed about AIDS and are more likely to stigmatize people with AIDS (D'Augelli, 1989; Goodwin & Roscoe, 1988; Herek & Glunt, 1990; Pryor, Reeder, & Vinacco, 1989; Stipp & Kerr, 1989). Further, gay men with AIDS are more likely to be negatively evaluated than are heterosexuals with AIDS (Triplet & Sugarman, 1987).

Antigay hostility has long existed in the United States. Despite their achievement of greater visibility and acceptance in recent years, lesbians and gay men continue to be targets of widespread institutional prejudice. Whereas racial, ethnic, and religious minorities also suffer from such prejudice, gay people are unique in that overt discrimination and intolerance against them are officially condoned by governmental, religious, and social institutions. Discrimination in housing and employ-

---

[5]I thank Bliss Siman, of Baruch College of the City University of New York, for her assistance in obtaining these data through the Roper Center, University of Connecticut at Storrs.

ment on the basis of sexual orientation currently is prohibited by statute only in two states, Wisconsin and Massachusetts. Lesbian and gay male couples generally are denied the community recognition, legal protection, and economic benefits accorded to married heterosexual partners. Indeed, sexual intimacy between same-sex partners remains illegal in one half of the states, and the constitutionality of such laws was upheld by the United States Supreme Court in 1986 in the case of *Bowers v. Hardwick* (Melton, 1989).

This climate of condemnation fosters antigay attitudes and behavior among heterosexuals and discourages gay women and men from disclosing their homosexual orientation to those around them. Yet, great variability can be observed in the attitudes expressed by individuals in American culture. Some heterosexuals are much more hostile toward gay people than seems to be required by social norms. Others defy the norms and accept gay people. These differences can be explained in part through examination of the psychological functions served by attitudes toward lesbians and gay men (see Herek, 1984, 1987).

Given the empirical relationship between AIDS-related stigma and attitudes toward gay people, the psychological functions served by the two types of attitudes might be closely related. For example, people with AIDS may be assigned to a cognitive category already existing for gay people. The affect resulting from negative experiences with gay people then may be transferred to people with AIDS (one of the evaluative functions). Negative stereotypes of gay people (e.g., as preying on young people) may be imputed to people with AIDS as well. Alternatively, a fundamentalist Christian might condemn homosexuality as a way of affirming her or his sense of self as a good Christian and thereby increasing self-esteem (a value-expressive function). AIDS might be interpreted as God's punishment for homosexuality; expressing condemnation for people with AIDS might similarly bolster self-esteem. Yet another possibility is that a person whose hostility toward gay people is based on unresolved intrapsychic conflicts may experience similar anxieties associated with AIDS. Because AIDS links homosexuality with death, it offers a focus for anxieties associated with both (a defensive function).

AIDS, Attitudes, and Education

The social psychological approaches described here point to the need for AIDS education programs to address variables that interfere with receptivity to factual information about AIDS. Although providing accurate information about AIDS and HIV is absolutely necessary, it is not enough for at least five reasons. First, the audience for educational programs may be unable to use the information they receive because of their high levels of anxiety associated with AIDS. One approach to this problem is to address specific types of errors that people are likely to make in thinking about AIDS under conditions of stress. Misuse of the availability heuristic, for example, might be reduced by providing clear information about how AIDS differs from other illnesses easily called to mind, such as influenza. Another important approach is to avoid overstating the risks of HIV infection for audience members. An educator designing an AIDS education program for middle-class, White, heterosexual college students (a group at fairly low risk of encountering a sexual partner infected with HIV), for example, may be tempted to inflate audience members' risk for HIV infection as a way of increasing their sense of urgency and overcoming their illusions of invulnerability. Although based on good intentions, this approach may create anxiety levels so high that audience members adopt a hypervigilant pattern for responding to AIDS. If ineffective, this approach may damage the credibility of the educator with her or his audience.

A second reason why factual information is not enough is that audiences for AIDS education programs may experience conflicts between their own basic values and proposed strategies for preventing HIV transmission. For example, advocating the use of condoms to people whose religious values strictly prohibit nonmarital sex may be ineffectual or counterproductive. Such value conflicts must be recognized by the educator and confronted in the education program (e.g., Rokeach, 1973).

Third, audiences for AIDS education may believe that people with AIDS are only getting what they deserve for engaging in behaviors that are socially condemned. This application of the "just world hypothesis" (Lerner, 1970) probably reflects a priori condemnation of gay men and intravenous drug users. It also may represent a need to believe that the epidemic is controllable and that one can be safe by avoiding certain behaviors and following certain rules. In this sense, the notion of "innocent victims" may reflect concern about the loss of control (people can become infected with HIV even if they don't have sex with men or share needles) as much as it reflects condemnation of "guilty victims."

Fourth, audiences for AIDS education may be skeptical rather than ignorant or uninformed. My own observation from focus group discussions about AIDS is that many Americans know the official story that HIV cannot be transmitted through casual contact, but they do not believe it. African Americans and members of other minority groups that historically have reported less trust in the government than Whites (e.g., Howell & Fagan, 1988) may be especially unwilling to trust White-identified government officials and scientific experts concerning AIDS. Effective AIDS education programs must overcome this barrier, for example, by communicating information through trusted sources (church and community leaders, celebrities).

A fifth reason why information alone is not enough is that although people are concerned about their own vulnerability to HIV infection, AIDS-related attitudes also serve expressive functions. Educators must address the symbolic aspects of AIDS (e.g., rejection of persons with AIDS as a way of increasing in-group solidarity). A person whose AIDS-related prejudice serves a social-expressive function, for example, might be placed in a situation where acceptance and compassion for persons with AIDS are the norm. In such a setting (e.g., one's own classroom), disparaging remarks or jokes about AIDS would receive social disapproval, and expressing prejudice against persons with AIDS would not bring social support or acceptance. Educators can work to change social norms outside the classroom by teaching their students how to speak up against expressions of AIDS-related stigma by friends or family members.

Of all the issues symbolized in AIDS-related stigma, perhaps the most prevalent is that of attitudes toward gay men and, indirectly, attitudes toward lesbians. As described above, the cultural construction of AIDS has focused on the epidemic's early manifestations in the gay male community. The dominant cultural images of AIDS probably will continue to equate the disease with male homosexuality even as the demographic realities of the epidemic shift to heterosexual people of color. Thus, the linkage between reactions to AIDS and attitudes toward gay men should be addressed explicitly in education programs.

The Experience of AIDS-Related Stigma

I have discussed how stigma has been attached to AIDS at the cultural level and how that stigma translates into individual attitudes. But what of the experiences of a person who has AIDS, is infected with HIV, or is presumed by others to be infected? For such people, AIDS-related stigma adds an additional layer to the challenges of coping with a chronic and potentially lethal condition. Sensitivity to the mental health consequences of AIDS-related stigma is important for care givers, researchers, and policymakers. A review of the vast literature on the psychological ramifications of AIDS and HIV infection is beyond the scope of this paper (see Kelly & St. Lawrence, 1988, in this regard). Instead, I shall consider some ways in which being stigmatized by AIDS can affect psychological functioning and mental health. (For discussions of mental health interventions with people with AIDS, see Adler & Beckett, 1989; Barret, 1989; Barrows & Halgin, 1988; Dane, 1989; Morin & Batchelor, 1984; Sheridan & Sheridan, 1988).

Persons with AIDS bear the burden of societal hostility at a time when they are most in need of social support. The stigma attached to the illness also subjects them to suspicion about previously private aspects of their lives. "Indeed, to get AIDS is precisely to be revealed, in the majority of cases so far, as a member of a certain 'risk group,' a community of pariahs" (Sontag, 1989, pp. 24–25).[6] Thus, disclosure of HIV infection is likely to lead others to wonder: Is he homosexual? Did she use drugs? Widespread awareness among American gay men of this discrediting process was reflected in an early AIDS joke: "What's the hardest thing about being diagnosed? Convincing your parents that you're Haitian" (Dundes, 1987). People at risk may compromise their own health when they attempt to avoid these multiple levels of stigma. Fears of harassment, job discrimination, and loss of insurance coverage may deter them from being tested for HIV infection; seeking early treatment for symptoms; or securing help from friends, relatives, or AIDS support organizations.

Stigma and Psychological Functioning

The anxiety, anger, and depression commonly experienced by people with HIV disease (Kelly & St. Lawrence, 1988) are likely to be exacerbated by AIDS-related stigma. Anxiety results not only from fears about the physical effects of HIV disease, but also from fears about others' responses; infected and sick individuals appropriately anticipate rejection, discrimination, hostility, and even physical violence from others who learn of their condition (Herek & Glunt, 1988). Anger at the loss of one's health and mobility can be intensified by perceptions that the federal government, the Catholic Church, and other institutions have failed to respond adequately to the AIDS epidemic because of their hostility toward gay men and other minorities (Herek & Glunt, 1988). Depression can be intensified by self-blame and internalization of societal stigmas concerning AIDS, homosexuality, drug use, and race. Depression also may result from feelings of "universal helplessness." Such feelings are likely when people with AIDS perceive themselves as being treated unfairly and attribute the cause to forces that are external, stable, and global, that is, widespread and enduring prejudices (Abramson, Seligman, & Teasdale, 1978; Crocker & Major, 1989).

Stigma, Self-Concept, and Self-Esteem

In addition to these affective responses, AIDS-related stigma may affect an individual's overall self-concept and level of self-esteem. In general,

---

[6]Conversely, to be a homosexual or bisexual man, an IV drug user, and, to some extent, Black, or a Latin in the United States today is to be perceived as a member of the "AIDS community," whether or not one is infected with HIV. AIDS constitutes a new master category that subsumes these stigmatized groups. Even lesbians, who are at the lowest risk of anyone for sexual transmission of HIV, are categorized with the AIDS community by virtue of their homosexuality.

a stigma is most extensively incorporated into the self-concept when it generates extreme and consistent negative reactions on the part of others. These reactions are most likely to occur when the stigma is nonconcealable, aesthetically displeasing, and socially disruptive. A stigmatized characteristic also affects the bearer's self-concept to the extent that it is related to some domain of behavior or experience over which the bearer feels he or she should have control (Jones et al., 1984). AIDS frequently manifests these characteristics.

Nevertheless, members of stigmatized groups appear to use a variety of strategies to safeguard their self-esteem (Crocker & Major, 1989). First, members of stigmatized groups are able to maintain higher levels of self-esteem to the extent that they attribute negative social experiences to their stigma (an external attribution), while attributing positive social experiences to their own qualities or abilities (an internal attribution). A man with AIDS who is fired from his job, for example, will be less likely to have his self-esteem diminished if he attributes his employer's action to prejudice rather than to his own competence. He still must face the problem of being unemployed, but he may be better able to confront this problem if he does not blame himself for bringing it on. A second successful strategy for maintaining self-esteem in the face of stigma is to devalue the abilities or qualities that one is likely to lack by virtue of one's stigmatized condition. After they have been (literally) marked by Kaposi's sarcoma and other AIDS-related illnesses, for example, many gay men learn to discount the importance of physical attractiveness in defining self-worth. Instead, they may emphasize their capabilities for compassion, sociability, or humor, which are less likely to be impaired by their illness. A third strategy described by Crocker and Major (1989) for maintaining or enhancing self-esteem is to select others who are stigmatized for social comparison. People with AIDS are less likely to feel despair about their physical condition if they compare themselves with others who are sick rather than with healthy friends or their prediagnosis selves.

Generally, these three coping strategies are most readily used by people whose self-concept is structured around the stigmatized group and who have extensive contact with a community of similarly stigmatized individuals. Many communities of people with AIDS, their families, friends, and volunteers exist around the country. In addition to providing services and social support, these groups help people with AIDS to understand and overcome their stigmatization. They provide contexts in which people can formulate alternative analyses of AIDS to counteract those of the larger society. Many groups sponsor publications in which the ideology of the members is formulated. AIDS organizations present the case of people with AIDS to the noninfected public. They have influenced the terminology attached to AIDS, for example, by discouraging the use of the label "AIDS victim" in favor of "person with AIDS."

Some people with AIDS have found that the movement absorbs all of their time and that a new career has been thrust upon them. They have become "professionals." They spend much of their time organizing social services and demonstrations, fundraising, attending meetings, and speaking to the public. This professionalization consolidates belief in AIDS or HIV-status as a basis for identity (Goffman, 1963). Professionals, by recounting their own stories, offer others with AIDS a doctrine for making sense out of their own stigmatized situations. They provide advice and offer norms for behavior. They often urge others to "come out" with their AIDS diagnosis, and to reject others' negative attitudes. Their prescriptions provide others with guidelines for behavior, the basis for an in-group alignment, and an appropriate attitude toward the self. Membership in an AIDS group even may enable individuals to achieve a level of self-esteem higher than that manifested by the majority non-stigmatized group; they may turn their diagnosis into a virtue or asset (Jones et al., 1984).

Simultaneously, however, some people with AIDS may feel that membership in the AIDS community also makes change and growth difficult by decreasing the number of alternative views of the self that are available from others; the pressure to be "politically correct" can feel limiting (Jones et al., 1984). Because they have internalized societal attitudes, others may experience ambivalence about their identity as a person with AIDS. They may feel hostility toward others with AIDS who are more obviously stigmatized than themselves. For example, a person who was infected through a blood transfusion may feel contempt for a gay man with AIDS who, in turn, may express hostility toward an IV drug user with AIDS. Or a person with AIDS might dislike AIDS activists because of their visibility and stridency. In each case, the ambivalent individual may feel both repulsed by others and shameful at being repulsed (Goffman, 1963).

Psychological Consequences of Acute Victimization

People with AIDS are at risk for several kinds of victimization, ranging from interpersonal rejection and ridicule, to job and housing discrimination, to violence (Dalton, Burris, & Yale AIDS Law Project, 1987; Dundes, 1987; Herek, 1989; Herek & Glunt, 1988). The aftermath of criminal victimization is likely to be similar for persons with AIDS to that for other survivors of crime or assault (Garnets, Herek, & Levy, 1990). It may be complicated, however, by several factors. First, physical injuries received in an assault may compound existing health problems of persons with AIDS. Second, trauma related to the assault may interact with the experience of the AIDS diagnosis itself as a major trauma. Third, the dependency that inevitably follows criminal victimization may compound the loss of personal control already experienced by the person with AIDS. Fourth, in searching for a cause for their victimization, many crime victims blame themselves; a victimized person with AIDS may feel responsible for her or his victimization, which may magnify feelings of guilt or responsibility for being sick in the first place. Fifth, to be a victim in our society is itself a stigmatized status; thus, the victimized person with AIDS must cope with yet another level of stigma (see Bard & Sangrey, 1979; Janoff-Bulman & Frieze, 1983a, 1983b).

Managing Social Interactions

Interactions between people who are infected with HIV (or are presumed to be infected) and nonstigmatized others are shaped by all of the factors previously discussed. Because extensive empirical data about such interactions are not yet available, much of the following section derives from Goffman's (1963) impressive theoretical discussion. A starting point is his distinction between the *discredited* (those whose HIV status is known to other parties in the interaction) and the *discreditable* (those whose HIV status is hidden from one or more parties). A discreditable person who is "passing" must concentrate on managing information about her or his stigma. The primary focus of an interaction involving a discredited person, in contrast, is upon managing discomfort and tension. Each of these situations will be discussed in turn.

Managing Information: The Experience of Passing

In addition to reasons already mentioned, people with AIDS or HIV infection may wish to hide their status from others because of a fear of straining family relationships and friendships, a wish to maintain normalcy in their own lives, or a desire to avoid revealing their homosexuality or use of intravenous drugs (Herek & Glunt, 1988; Kelly & St. Lawrence, 1988). Most people with AIDS regularly find themselves in social settings where passing is more or less necessary. In extreme situations, any disclosure of one's health status would mean immediate expulsion (e.g., some employment or housing situations). Goffman (1963, p. 81) refers to these as "forbidden places." At the other extreme are places like the physician's examining room, the hospital, and the AIDS support group, where no need exists to pass. In such "back places," the stigmatized individual, like an actor backstage, can stop playing the role of the healthy person. Between these extremes are "civil places," where others make a visible attempt to treat the person with AIDS like anyone else, even though they may remain uncomfortable and do not completely accept or understand her or him.

People with AIDS who are passing face continual hazards. They can be discredited either by information that becomes apparent about them during an interaction or by others who already know about their diagnosis. Consequently, they must carefully structure social situations to minimize the risk of exposure. Gay people and others with previous experience at hiding a stigmatized condition are likely to have already developed useful skills in this regard.

Passing is stressful to anyone who must do it. People hiding their diagnosis experience a great discrepancy between their public and private identities. They may feel that they are living a lie (Jones et al., 1984). They may have the distressing experience of being exposed to others' insensitivity or prejudice against people with AIDS. They do not face direct prejudice against themselves; rather, they face unwitting acceptance of themselves by individuals who are prejudiced against people with AIDS (Goffman, 1963). People hiding their AIDS diagnosis also may experience what Goffman called "the Cinderella syndrome" (p. 90). They feel that they are living on a leash because they must stay close to home where medicines can be taken, makeup can be reapplied and, in short, their disguise can be refurbished and they can rest up from having to wear it.

People with AIDS use a variety of techniques in passing. Sometimes they present the signs of their illness as signs of another, less stigmatized attribute. The persistent cough is dismissed as a cold, or the lack of energy is attributed to being "stressed out." This process inevitably requires further and further elaboration to prevent disclosure and can give rise to hurt feelings and misunderstandings on the part of others. A man with KS may alienate his gym buddies in the process of avoiding the exposure of his lesions that would occur if he undressed. The woman who cannot eat solid food without vomiting may offend friends and relatives by refusing their invitations to dinner.

People with AIDS who are passing are likely to divide the world into a large group to whom nothing is told and a small group to whom everything is told. Those who know about their diagnosis are then relied on for help in keeping the secret. Sometimes these intimates put themselves in the role of protecting the individual from any manifestation of prejudice or rejection by others. In the course of filling this role, friends and family may be more alive to the diagnosis and its attendant problems than even the person with AIDS (Goffman, 1963).

People with AIDS also may find themselves having to rely for help in protecting their secret upon others who, although they are not known personally, are able to detect their condition. These might include other people with AIDS and the "wise," such as health care professionals and lay individuals active in the gay or AIDS communities. The wise are "persons who are normal but whose special situation has made them intimately privy to the secret life of the stigmatized individual and sympathetic with it, and who find themselves accorded a measure of acceptance, a measure of courtesy membership in the clan" (Goffman, 1963, p. 28). The wise can provide a model for how far normals could go in treating stigmatized people as if they did not have a stigma.

Obviously, the demands of passing are likely to disrupt relationships. People with AIDS who are passing may find that they consciously create distance in order to avoid disclosing their diagnosis to others. They may avoid social contact with specific others and, when together, keep the conversation at a superficial level. They may develop entirely new friendship networks, consisting of people in the AIDS community and service providers.

Even people with AIDS who are relatively open about their diagnosis may experience problems when they encounter acquaintances or family members who know them from an earlier time in their life. These pre-stigma contacts may have difficulty replacing their preexisting conceptions of the person with an understanding of her or his present situation. They may be unable either to accept the person with AIDS or to respond with formal tact of the sort displayed by strangers (Goffman, 1963).

Managing Interpersonal Tension: Social Interactions After Disclosure

General characteristics of social interactions. Although most people with AIDS have had the experience of passing in at least some situations, many also participate in interactions in which their stigmatized status is known to others. Disclosure of their diagnosis may occur against their wishes, for example, by a breach of confidentiality or by an inadvertent disclosure during an interaction. Alternatively, individuals may voluntarily disclose their status because they reject society's stigma and feel that if they accept and respect themselves, they will feel no need to conceal their condition. Additionally, disclosing one's diagnosis to others increases opportunities for much-needed social support (Adelman, 1989; Wolcott, Namir, Fawzy, Gottlieb, & Mitsuyasu, 1986; Zich & Temoshok, 1987). "Coming out" can be accomplished through direct disclosure or through offering indirect evidence to others (e.g., purposeful slips in the conversation, by displaying the logo of an AIDS organization on a button, badge, or article of clothing).

Once their status has been disclosed, persons with AIDS no longer need to worry about passing, but new problems are created. They may now feel uncertain as to what others "really" are thinking of them. They probably will feel that they are under closer scrutiny than are others in the same situation. Their minor accomplishments may be considered too remarkable, while minor failings may be interpreted as a direct expression of their illness. Others may stare at them if they manifest lesions or hair loss due to chemotherapy. Strangers may feel free to strike up personal conversations about AIDS or offer unwanted and unneeded help.

Others' reactions will be influenced by their feelings toward the person with AIDS, their beliefs and attitudes concerning AIDS in general, and their beliefs about appropriate behaviors to display in the company of persons with AIDS (Dunkel-Schetter & Wortman, 1982). Some will have unequivocally positive feelings toward the person with AIDS, will be well-informed, unprejudiced, and will have had experience interacting with persons with AIDS. Others will be unequivocally negative and will terminate their relationship with the person with AIDS. From a social psychological perspective, the interactions (or noninteractions) resulting from such unambiguous responses are fairly simple to understand.

More complicated, however, are interactions with those who have no experience with AIDS and who know little about it. These people are likely to experience ambivalence resulting from the clash of their negative feelings concerning AIDS and their positive (or possibly ambivalent) feelings toward the person with AIDS. Ambivalence may result in exaggerated positive responses to persons with AIDS when they manifest positive characteristics, or it may result in overly harsh rejections when they display negative characteristics (Katz, 1981). Ambivalent individuals may feel unable to discuss their discomfort out of the belief that they should remain positive and optimistic around the person with AIDS. They may worry about whether they are being overly sympathetic or are making impossible demands in an effort to carry on as though nothing was wrong. They may adopt a cheerful facade in the presence of the person with AIDS, both as a strategy for reducing their own anxiety and in response to their beliefs about how one "should" behave in the presence of a seriously ill person. They may fear that they will break down in the presence of the person with AIDS, or betray their feelings, or say the wrong thing (Dunkel-Schetter & Wortman, 1982). The person with AIDS may wish not to burden her or his family, and therefore may hesitate to express her or his concerns about illness, physical discomfort, and death.

Everyone involved in the interaction may feel so uncomfortable that the healthy individual and person with AIDS alike may arrange to avoid or minimize contact with each other. Alternatively, they may maintain social contact while avoiding open discussion of AIDS. In either case, the person with AIDS feels isolated, and the healthy person does not learn how to interact comfortably with someone with AIDS.

Conflicts can also occur concerning the emergent identity of the person with AIDS. For reasons already mentioned, people with AIDS are likely to derive considerable benefit from incorporating their diagnosis into their identity, and from joining various AIDS support groups and organizations. Well-intentioned healthy people, however, may advise friends with AIDS to downplay their newly formed identities. They may encourage people with AIDS to help "normals" in dealing with their diagnosis, for example, by using levity to put them at ease. Goffman (1963) summarized society's criteria for "good adjustment": A stigmatized individual should "cheerfully and unself-consciously accept himself as essentially the same as normals, while at the same time he voluntarily withholds himself from those situations in which normals would find it difficult to give lip service to their similar acceptance of him" (p. 121). Goffman noted that, from the point of view of the nonstigmatized, this prescription means "that the unfairness and pain of having to carry a stigma will never be presented to them; it means that normals will not have to admit to themselves how limited their tactfulness and tolerance is; and it means that normals can remain relatively uncontaminated by intimate contact with the stigmatized, relatively unthreatened in their identity beliefs" (p. 121).

People with AIDS, strongly in need of social support, may try to fit this prescription for adjustment. They may hide their problems from others, conveying the impression that they are coping well. This covering strategy, however, requires the person with AIDS to present a false front. Others' acceptance is perceived to be based on the self that is presented rather than the true self. Thus, the person with AIDS may continue to feel that she or he is not truly worthy of positive regard.

Interactions with family members. Despite these impediments to interaction, most people with AIDS have frequent contact with others, especially with family members. "Family member" here refers to anyone with whom the person with AIDS is involved in a long-term, committed, and caring relationship. This definition includes lovers or life-partners, regardless of the legal status of their relationship, as well as friends. Family members experience considerable anxiety associated with changes in a patient's health status and physical appearance (Frierson, Lippmann, & Johnson, 1987; Greff & Porembski, 1987). Family members who have had unprotected sexual contact with a person with AIDS must cope with their own anxieties about being infected with HIV. Additionally, all family members, whether or not they have had a sexual relationship with the person with AIDS, are likely to experience stigma themselves (Cline, 1989). This can create additional worries for the person with AIDS. Stigma-related stress is especially likely for same-sex lovers, who often are the primary care givers for gay men with AIDS, but whose status is not legally recognized (Morin & Batchelor, 1984). Stress may be especially pronounced after the person with AIDS has died, leaving the lover and other family members to grieve, often without adequate community supports (Bérubé, 1988; Martin, 1988; Trice, 1988).

"Paradoxical stigma" and AIDS. To round out this discussion of social interactions between people with AIDS and healthy others, I wish to note a type of interaction that differs from the negative manifestations of AIDS-related stigma discussed throughout this chapter. In this kind of interaction, AIDS is treated as a sign of special "holiness," and people with AIDS are treated like "saints" by those close to them or politically

supportive of them. I use religious terminology here to draw a parallel between AIDS and the stigmata manifested by certain saints in Catholic teachings. This phenomenon, which I shall refer to as "paradoxical stigma," was illustrated in a column written by Chuck Grochmal, head-lined "Patronizing My Disease," in the Toronto magazine, *Xtra* (June, 1989).[7] After noting that, before his diagnosis, agreeing with his friends on a movie or restaurant required extensive negotiation, he described a change that occurred:

> It dawned on me that my friends were patronizing me or, more correctly, my disease. Because I had aids, in their zeal they were bending over backwards (no dirty comments, please) to make sure my "remaining time" was pleasant on my terms—not theirs. In the process they were compromising their opinions, a cornerstone of our friendship, and also that special quality only gay men ex-perience, known to us as "sisterhood." My friends, John and Jack, being closest to me, were the guiltiest of the lot. When I would suggest a movie that we might go to see, no matter what they really thought of the idea, they agreed that my selection was brilliant and that's the movie we would go to see. . . .It was the same story when it came to a choice of restaurants for eating out. And on and on *ad nauseam* . . . .I certainly have changed because of aids, but there is no good reason for the changes that Jack and John were inflicting on me. It said to me that they were spineless if they couldn't say "no" to me any more, especially since I enjoy a good fight over insignificant details. Well, once they grasped what I was trying to beat into them. . .things improved. I've got a lot of fight left in me and now we're back to fighting. (p. 26)

Our culture tends to portray illness as an occasion for self-transcen-dence, when the virtuous become more so and the less virtuous get an opportunity to behave well (Sontag, 1978). Goffman (1963, p. 28) ob-served that this "cult of the stigmatized" can cause difficulties for all concerned. Although sainthood may have some appeal, it prevents people with AIDS from being treated as normal. Lovers, friends, and colleagues may try to minimize their own relationship needs unrealis-tically—experiencing guilt when they argue with or criticize the person with AIDS. This in turn may create serious strains for loved ones while the person with AIDS is alive, and serious guilt after she or he has died. This paradoxical form of AIDS-related stigma, like the negative forms to which most of this chapter has been devoted, should be considered undesirable.

---

[7] I am grateful to Barry Adam for this example.

The AIDS Epidemic: Challenges and Opportunities

When considering possible future trends in the AIDS epidemic, we inevitably must feel a strange mix of hopeful optimism and overwhelming worry. We can be optimistic based on the amazing pace of scientific progress in understanding AIDS, its etiology, and its natural history. Improvements in treatments mean that persons with AIDS who have access to good medical care today can live longer and better lives than was the case even a few years ago. Although many scientists and activists believe that research to find a cure could proceed more rapidly, promising new experimental treatments all justify hope that HIV infection will become a chronic, treatable condition someday soon.

We also can be optimistic based on the social history of AIDS. Despite the worst fears of many, and the best efforts of some, AIDS-related stigma generally has not become the basis for public policy. Calls for quarantine are now widely considered unrealistic and extreme. The fight against universal mandatory testing has been successful to date, although testing continues in the military, prisons, and other settings. The Americans With Disabilities Act, which protects the civil liberties of persons with AIDS and other disabled Americans, has been passed by Congress with strong bipartisan support and has been signed by President Bush. Perhaps most important, the American public displays increasingly greater sophistication in its knowledge concerning AIDS. In many places, tolerance and compassion appear to be the social norm, rather than fear and persecution.

Despite these hopeful signs, current trends in the epidemic also justify considerable concern about the future. AIDS is not yet a chronic, treatable disease. People continue to die from it every day. Even with advances in treatment and research, the number of people with AIDS soon will increase dramatically. Most of the hundreds of thousands of Americans who now are infected but asymptomatic can be expected to start displaying symptoms within the next 5 to 10 years. This may mean a tenfold increase in the number of AIDS cases over those that have been reported so far during the entire epidemic in the United States. Although early intervention with AZT, aerosolized pentamidine, and other medications may delay or prevent many infected people from developing symptoms, these treatments currently are available only to a minority. Local hospitals and health care systems, already inadequate for meeting the needs of many Americans, will be more severely stressed by AIDS. Even in San Francisco, which is considered a model of effective community response to the epidemic, the present system is not expected to be adequate for meeting the increased demands placed on it as the number of AIDS cases inexorably rises. And if one looks beyond the borders of the United States to AIDS in developing countries, the future is indeed bleak.

Even if all transmission of HIV were to stop immediately, visions of the coming decade would be frightening. But transmission continues. A remarkable amount of risk reduction has been observed in gay male communities in large cities (e.g., Becker & Joseph, 1988; Martin, 1987; Siegel, Bauman, Christ, & Krown, 1988; Winkelstein et al., 1987). Comparable levels of behavior change are not apparent, however, in smaller cities, towns, and rural areas. Despite increased concern about AIDS prevention among intravenous drug users, transmission of HIV remains largely unchecked among them. Available resources and resolve are currently insufficient for dealing effectively with AIDS in this group, which is largely poor and disproportionately made up of people of color (Turner, Miller, & Moses, 1989).

The United States soon will face a second wave of the epidemic as the thousands of gay men who are now infected begin to manifest symptoms and require medical care. Then a third wave will break as symptoms of HIV disease appear among more and more IV drug users, their homosexual and heterosexual partners, and their infants. As the third wave washes over us, the epidemic will become more ghettoized among poor Americans, especially those of color.

Today, in the minds of most Americans, AIDS is primarily a disease of homosexuality, and it carries with it the particular stigma attending that perception. As the social profile of the epidemic changes, so too will AIDS-related stigma. AIDS will continue to be a disease of the "other," but the specific character of that other will evolve from gay males to the poor and people of color. Unfortunately, the history of prejudice in the United States suggests that this shift in the cultural construction of AIDS will be accompanied by changes in the form and manifestations of AIDS-related stigma, rather than a reduction in its intensity.

How should psychologists respond to AIDS-related stigma? As with so many other areas of human behavior, we should each begin by identifying our own personal relationship to HIV disease. Even though our training as scientists, practitioners, and educators provides us with tools and strategies for approaching phenomena far removed from our own experience, AIDS and AIDS-related stigma are not so removed. They are integral parts of our social reality in contemporary America, whether or not we realize it. I propose, therefore, that we each explicitly recognize our own relationship to the epidemic, recognize how that relationship might limit our perspective, and allow it to enrich our understanding. At the same time, psychologists also should clarify their relationships to the many communities affected by the epidemic. As appropriate, we each must recognize our own ignorance about some or all of these groups and learn about them as a prerequisite for working with them.

Obviously, psychologists who are themselves infected with HIV (or who think they may be infected) have a different perspective on the disease than do their uninfected and unworried colleagues. Those who are not concerned about their own personal HIV status may nevertheless have friends and loved ones who are infected. Or HIV may have touched their professional relationships through colleagues, clients, students, staff, or research participants who are HIV-positive. Some psychologists have not yet been touched directly by AIDS, although that is likely to change. Whatever their personal relationship to the epidemic, psychologists must evaluate how it affects their professional involvement with AIDS. Those most intimately involved may have the greatest difficulty maintaining sufficient distance and objectivity in their work, or they may risk rapid burnout as AIDS touches all parts of their lives. Psychologists more distant from the personal consequences of AIDS may fail to appreciate its intellectual, emotional, and social complexities, which ultimately shape their own attitudes and beliefs and thus affect their research, practice, and teaching.

After clarifying their personal and professional relationship to the epidemic, psychologists can begin to approach AIDS and its attendant stigma in each of the five areas I have described. First, in the biomedical realm, they can educate themselves about the physical realities of AIDS and HIV disease. Although reading about the medical aspects of AIDS (e.g., Institute of Medicine, 1988) is an important starting point, psychologists also should develop a first-hand understanding of the disease. Psychologists who are themselves infected with HIV or whose loved ones are infected cannot avoid such an understanding. Others may benefit from volunteering to work for a local AIDS service organization, perhaps after first reading one or more personal accounts of the disease (e.g., Monette, 1988; Peabody, 1986; Whitmore, 1988). I am suggesting here that psychologists purposely seek experience with AIDS outside of their professional role. Aside from making us more empathic and compassionate human beings, such experience will vastly increase our understanding of AIDS and AIDS-related stigma, and thereby improve our research, therapeutic, and diagnostic skills considerably.

The second area of my discussion was the cultural construction of AIDS and its stigmatizing properties. I have tried throughout this chapter to "deconstruct" AIDS, to identify some of its symbolic and metaphorical uses. Psychologists should continue this process for themselves by confronting images of AIDS in daily conversations, in the popular media, and, most important, in their own work. Help with this task can be found in the alternative constructions provided in the newsletters and newspapers of AIDS organizations and in the publications of the gay, African American, and Hispanic communities. As well as deconstructing, psychologists can play important roles in reconstructing AIDS through speaking out as individuals and through professional and academic organizations. Congressional and local lobbying by psychologists, for example, have influenced legislation concerning appropriations, HIV testing, and discrimination. Additionally, psychologists have confronted AIDS-related stigma by speaking out in court rooms and through mass media.

The third and fourth areas of this chapter were attitudes of the nonstigmatized toward persons with AIDS and the subjective experience of being the target of those attitudes. Here again, one's personal relationship to the epidemic is a starting point in developing a critical understanding of these phenomena. Psychologists infected with HIV already know too well the experience of AIDS-related stigma; nevertheless, they can benefit from using their professional skills to analyze critically the dynamics of that stigma. Some uninfected psychologists can draw upon their experiences as a member of another stigmatized minority (e.g., as a gay person or a person of color) to gain an initial understanding of the consequences of AIDS-related stigma. Others who are not themselves at risk for AIDS nevertheless will experience a degree of stigma when their professional involvement with AIDS becomes publicly known. In all cases, these experiences provide lenses through which existing knowledge and theory can be filtered.

The final focus of this chapter was interactions between persons with AIDS and those without. Once again psychologists can begin with their own experiences. Regardless of our own HIV status, how do we feel differently interacting with a person with AIDS in contrast to a person who is not HIV-infected? From this level of questioning, we can move to a critical understanding of the effects of AIDS-related stigma on general social interactions, on relationships between persons with AIDS and family members, and on family members themselves.

If the AIDS epidemic had never occurred, this chapter might instead have focused on the stigma related to cholera. I might have discussed how the cultural construction of that disease in 1832 affected medical responses to the epidemic and how it inflicted hardships upon the sick. Alternatively, I might have discussed social constructions of some other illness: the plague, influenza, or cancer. In any of these cases, many of my general observations and conclusions about the nature of illness and stigma would have been similar to those presented here.

But, of course, the AIDS epidemic did occur and continues to shape our reality. As a result, illness-related stigma is not simply an abstract phenomenon to be considered with scholarly detachment. Instead, it impinges upon our daily lives and work. Rather than being interesting historical trends that we can dispassionately discuss, the conflicts between moralistic and secular constructions of disease, or between coercive and compassionate responses to it have become literally life and death struggles played out in policy arenas as we watch and, in many cases, participate. A chapter on AIDS and stigma, therefore, cannot be limited to analysis but must also include a call to action.

Today, AIDS-related stigma is itself an epidemic, one that infects individual attitudes, beliefs, behaviors, and, ultimately, public policy and the health of society. In many of its broad patterns, AIDS-related stigma resembles past couplings of illness and stigma. In many of its particulars, it is new and different. Because we psychologists can integrate our own subjective experiences of AIDS with our perspectives as researchers, practitioners, and teachers, we can achieve a unique understanding of the many manifestations of AIDS-related stigma described in this chapter. Consequently, we also have unique opportunities and responsibilities to combat not only AIDS, the physical illness, but also AIDS, the stigmatized illness.

References

Abramson, L. Y., Seligman, M. E. P., & Teasdale, J. (1978). Learned helplessness in humans: Critique and reformulation. *Journal of Abnormal Psychology, 87* 49–74.

Adler, G., & Beckett, A. (1989). Psychotherapy of the patient with an HIV infection: Some ethical and therapeutic dilemmas. *Psychosomatics, 30*(2), 203–208.

Adelman, M. (1989). Social support and AIDS. *AIDS & Public Policy Journal, 4*(1), 31–39.

Ajzen, I., & Fishbein, M. (1980). *Understanding attitudes and predicting social behavior.* Englewood Cliffs, NJ: Prentice-Hall.

Albert, E. (1986). Illness and deviance: The response of the press to AIDS. In D. A. Feldman & T. M. Johnson (Eds.), *The social dimension of AIDS* (pp. 163–178). New York: Praeger.

Baker, A. J. (1986). The portrayal of AIDS in the media: An analysis of articles in *The New York Times.* In D. A. Feldman & T. M. Johnson (Eds.), *The social dimension of AIDS* (pp. 179–194). New York: Praeger.

Bard, M., & Sangrey, D. (1979). *The crime victim's book.* New York: Basic.

Barret, R. L. (1989). Counseling gay men with AIDS: Human dimensions. *Journal of Counseling and Development, 67,* 573–575.

Barrows, P. A., & Halgin, R. P. (1988). Current issues in psychotherapy with gay men: Impact of the AIDS phenomenon. *Professional Psychology: Research and Practice, 19*(4), 395–402.

Becker, M. H., & Joseph, J. G. (1988). AIDS and behavioral change to reduce risk: A review. *American Journal of Public Health, 78*(4), 394–410.

Bérubé, A. (1988). Caught in the storm: AIDS and the meaning of natural disaster. *OUT/LOOK, 1*(3), 8–19.

Blendon, R. J., & Donelan, K. (1988). Discrimination against people with AIDS: The public's perspective. *New England Journal of Medicine, 319*(15), 1022–1026.

Bloom, D. E., & Carliner, G. (1988). The economic impact of AIDS in the United States. *Science, 239,* 604–610.

Blumenfield, M., Smith, P. J., Milazzo, J., Seropian, S., & Wormser, G. P. (1987). Survey of attitudes of nurses working with AIDS patients. *General Hospital Psychiatry, 9,* 58–63.

Brandt, A. M. (1987). *No magic bullet: A social history of venereal disease in the United States since 1880* (expanded ed.). New York: Oxford University Press.

Buchanan, P. J. (1987, December 2). AIDS and moral bankruptcy. *The New York Post,* p. 23.

Centers for Disease Control. (1990, January). *HIV/AIDS surveillance report.* Atlanta, GA: Author.

Cline, R. J. W. (1989). Communication and death and dying: Implications for coping with AIDS. *AIDS & Public Policy Journal, 4*(1), 40–50.

Crocker, J., & Major, B. (1989). Social stigma and self-esteem: The self-protective properties of stigma. *Psychological Review, 96*, 608–630.

Dalton, H. L., Burris, S., & Yale AIDS Law Project. (1987). *AIDS and the law: A guide for the public.* New Haven, CT: Yale University Press.

Dane, B. O. (1989). New beginnings for AIDS patients. *Social Casework, 70,* 305–309.

D'Augelli, A. R. (1989). AIDS fears and homophobia among rural nursing personnel. *AIDS Education and Prevention, 1,* 277–284.

Defoe, D. (1960). *A journal of the plague year.* New York: New American Library.

Dundes, A. (1987). At ease, disease: AIDS jokes as sick humor. *American Behavioral Scientists, 30*(1), 72–81.

Dunkel-Schetter, C., & Wortman, C. B. (1982). The interpersonal dynamics of cancer: Problems in social relationships and their impact on the patient. In H. S. Friedman & R. DiMatteo (Eds.), *International issues in health care* (pp. 69–100). New York: Academic Press.

Estimates of HIV prevalence and projected AIDS cases: Summary of a workshop, October 31–November 1, 1989. (1990). *Morbidity and Mortality Weekly Report, 39*(7), 110–119.

Fettner, A. G., & Check, W. A. (1985). *The truth about AIDS: Evolution of an epidemic* (rev. ed.). New York: Holt, Rinehart & Winston.

Fishbein, M., & Ajzen, I. (1975). *Belief, attitude, intention, and behavior.* Reading, MA: Addison-Wesley.

Frierson, R. L., Lippmann, S. B., & Johnson, J. (1987). AIDS: Psychological stresses on the family. *Psychosomatics, 28,* 65–70.

Garnets, L., Herek, G. M., & Levy, B. (1990). Violence and victimization of lesbians and gay men: Mental health consequences. *Journal of Interpersonal Violence, 5,* 366–383.

Garrison, J. (1990, January 28). AIDS experts stumped by slowdown in epidemic. *San Francisco Examiner,* pp. A1, A18.

Goffman, E. (1963). *Stigma: Notes on the management of spoiled identity.* Englewood Cliffs, NJ: Prentice-Hall.

Goodwin, M. P., & Roscoe, B. (1988). AIDS: Students' knowledge and attitudes at a Midwestern university. *Journal of American College Health, 36*(4), 214–222.

Greif, G. L., & Porembski, E. (1987). Significant others of I.V. drug abusers with AIDS: New challenges for drug treatment programs. *Journal of Substance Abuse Treatment, 4,* 151–155.

Grochmal, C. (1989, June). Patronizing my disease. *Xtra,* p. 26.

Hay, J. W., Osmond, D. H., & Jacobson, M. A. (1988). Projecting the medical costs of AIDS and ARC in the United States. *Journal of Acquired Immune Deficiency Syndromes, 1,* 466–485.

Herek, G. M. (1984). Beyond "homophobia:" A social psychological perspective on attitudes toward lesbians and gay men. *Journal of Homosexuality, 10*(1/2), 1–21.

Herek, G. M. (1986). The instrumentality of attitudes: Toward a neofunctional theory. *Journal of Social Issues, 42*(2), 99–114.

Herek, G. M. (1987). Can functions be measured? A new perspective on the functional approach to attitudes. *Social Psychology Quarterly, 50*(4), 285–303.

Herek, G. M. (1989). Hate crimes against lesbians and gay men: Issues for research and policy. *American Psychologist, 44*, 948–955.

Herek, G. M., & Glunt, E. K. (1988). An epidemic of stigma: Public reactions to AIDS. *American Psychologist, 43*, 886–891.

Herek, G. M., & Glunt, E. K. (1990). AIDS-related attitudes in the United States: A preliminary conceptualization. *Journal of Sex Research,* in press.

Herek, G. M., Janis, I. L., & Huth, P. (1987). Decision-making during international crises: Is quality of process related to outcome? *Journal of Conflict Resolution, 31*(2), 203–226.

Hopkins, D. R. (1987). AIDS in minority populations in the United States. *Public Health Reports, 102*, 677–681.

Howell, S. E., & Fagan, D. (1988). Race and trust in government: Testing the political reality model. *Public Opinion Quarterly, 52*, 343–350.

Institute of Medicine. (1988). *Confronting AIDS: Update, 1988.* Washington, DC: National Academy Press.

Janis, I. L. (1989). *Crucial decisions: Leadership in policymaking and crisis management.* New York: Free Press.

Janis, I. L., & Mann, L. (1977). *Decision making: A psychological analysis of conflict, choice, and commitment.* New York: Free Press.

Janoff-Bulman, R., & Frieze, I. H. (Eds.) (1983a). Reactions to victimization [Entire issue]. *Journal of Social Issues, 39*(2).

Janoff-Bulman, R., & Frieze, I. H. (1983b). A theoretical perspective for understanding reactions to victimization. *Journal of Social Issues, 39*, 1–18.

Jones, E. E., Farina, A., Hastorf, A. H., Markus, H., Miller, D. T., & Scott, R. A. (1984). *Social stigma: The psychology of marked relationships.* New York: W.H. Freeman.

Katz, D. (1960). The functional approach to the study of attitudes. *Public Opinion Quarterly, 24*, 163–204.

Katz, D. (1968). Consistency for what? The functional approach. In R. P. Abelson et al. (Eds.), *Theories of cognitive consistency: A sourcebook* (pp. 179–191). Chicago: Rand-McNally.

Katz, D., & Stotland, E. (1959). A preliminary statement to a theory of attitude structure and change. In S. Koch (Ed.), *Psychology: A study of a science* (Vol. 3, pp. 423–475). New York: McGraw Hill.

Katz, I. (1981). *Stigma: A social psychological analysis.* Hillsdale, NJ: Erlbaum.

Katz, I., Hass, G., Parisi, N., Astone, J., McEvaddy, D., & Lucido, D. J. (1987). Lay people's and health care personnel's perceptions of cancer, AIDS, cardiac, and diabetic patients. *Psychological Reports, 60*, 615–629.

Kelly, J. A., & St. Lawrence, J. S. (1988). *The AIDS health crisis: Psychological and social interventions.* New York: Plenum.

Kelly, J. A., St. Lawrence, J. S., Smith, S., Hood, H., & Cook, D. J. (1987). Stigmatization of AIDS patients by physicians. *American Journal of Public Health, 77*, 789–791.

Kinder, D. R. (1986). The continuing American dilemma: White resistance to racial change 40 years after Myrdal. *Journal of Social Issues, 42*(2), 151–171.

Kinder, D. R., & Sears, D. O. (1981). Prejudice and politics: Symbolic racism versus racial threats to the good life. *Journal of Personality and Social Psychology, 40*, 414–431.

Kinder, D. R., & Sears, D. O. (1985). Political behavior. In G. Lindzey & E. Aronson (Eds.), *Handbook of social psychology* (3rd ed., Vol 2, pp. 659–741). New York: Random House.

Kinsella, J. (1989). *Covering the plague: AIDS and the American media.* New Brunswick, NJ: Rutgers University Press.

Knox, M. D., Dow, M. G., & Cotton, D. A. (1989). Mental health care providers: The need for AIDS education. *AIDS Education and Prevention, 1*, 285–290.

Lerner, M. J. (1970). The desire for justice and reactions to victims. In J. Macauley & L. Berkowitz (Eds.), *Altruism and helping behavior* (pp. 205–229). New York: Academic Press.

Limit Voted on AIDS Funds. (1987, October 15). *The New York Times*, p. B12.

Martin, J. L. (1987). The impact of AIDS on gay male sexual behavior patterns in New York City. *American Journal of Public Health, 77*, 578–581.

Martin, J. L. (1988). Psychological consequences of AIDS-related bereavement among gay men. *Journal of Consulting and Clinical Psychology, 56*(6), 856–862.

McNeill, W. H. (1976). *Plagues and peoples.* Garden City, NY: Anchor.

Mejta, C. L., Denton, E., Krems, M. E., & Hiatt, R. A. (1988). Acquired Immuno-deficiency Syndrome (AIDS): A survey of substance abuse clinic directors' and counselors' perceived knowledge, attitudes and reactions. *Journal of Drug Issues, 18*, 403–419.

Melton, G. B. (1989). Public policy and private prejudice: Psychology and law on gay rights. *American Psychologist, 44*, 933–940.

Monette, P. (1988). *Borrowed time: An AIDS memoir.* New York: Harcourt Brace Jovanovich.

Morin. S. F., & Batchelor, W. F. (1984). Responding to the psychological crisis of AIDS. *Public Health Reports, 99*, 4–9.

O'Donnell, L., O'Donnell, C. R., Pleck, J. H., Snarey, J., & Rose, R. M. (1987). Psychosocial responses of hospital workers to Acquired Immune Deficiency Syndrome (AIDS). *Journal of Applied Social Psychology, 17*(3), 269–285.

Panem, S. (1987). *The AIDS bureaucracy.* Cambridge, MA: Harvard University Press.

Peabody, B. (1986). *The screaming room.* New York: Avon.

Perlman, D. (1990, January 24). AIDS virus may not cause Kaposi's Sarcoma lesions. *San Francisco Chronicle*, pp. A1, A10.

Peterson, J. L., & Marin, G. (1988). Issues in the prevention of AIDS among Black and Hispanic men. *American Psychologist, 43*, 871–877.

Pryor, J. B., Reeder, G. D., & Vinacco, R. (1989). The instrumental and symbolic functions of attitudes toward persons with AIDS. *Journal of Applied Social Psychology, 19*, 377–404.

Rogers, M. F., & Williams, W. W. (1987). AIDS in Blacks and Hispanics: Implications for prevention. *Issues in Science and Technology, 3*(3), 89–94.

Rokeach, M. (1973). *The nature of human values.* New York: Free Press.

Rosenberg, C. E. (1987). *The cholera years: The United States in 1832, 1849, and 1866* (2nd ed.). Chicago: University of Chicago Press.

Rubin, H. C., Reitman, D., Berrier, J., & Sacks, H. S. (1989, June). *Attitudes about Human Immunodeficiency Virus (HIV) among health care workers and medical students.* Paper presented at the Fifth International Conference on AIDS, Montreal.

Sarnoff, I., & Katz, D. (1954). The motivational bases of attitude change. *Journal of Abnormal and Social Psychology, 49,* 115–124.

Schneider, W. (1987, July/August). Homosexuals: Is AIDS changing attitudes? *Public Opinion, 10*(2), 6–7, 59.

Scitovsky, A. A., Cline, M., & Lee, P. R. (1986). Medical care costs of patients with AIDS in San Francisco. *Journal of the American Medical Association, 256,* 3103–3106.

Scitovsky, A. A., & Rice, D. P. (1987). Estimates of the direct and indirect costs of Acquired Immunodeficiency Syndrome in the United States, 1985, 1986, and 1991. *Public Health Reports, 102,* 5–17.

Seage, G. R., III, Landers, S., Barry, A., Groopman, J., Lamb, G. A., & Epstein, A. M. (1986). Medical care costs of AIDS in Massachusetts. *Journal of the American Medical Association, 256,* 3107–3109.

Sheridan, K., & Sheridan, E. P. (1988). Psychological consultation to persons with AIDS. *Professional Psychology: Research and Practice, 19,* 532–535.

Shilts, R. (1987). *And the band played on: Politics, people, and the AIDS epidemic.* New York: St. Martin's.

Siegel, K., Bauman, L. J., Christ, G. H., & Krown, S. (1988). Patterns of change in sexual behavior among gay men in New York City. *Archives of Sexual Behavior, 17,* 481–497.

Singer, E., & Rogers, T. F. (1986). Public opinion and AIDS. *AIDS and Public Policy Journal, 1,* 1–13.

Slovic, P. (1987). Perception of risk, *Science, 236,* 280–285.

Slovic, P., Fischoff, B., & Lichtenstein, S. (1981). Perceived risk: Psychological factors and social implications. *Proceedings of the Royal Society of London, A376,* 17–34.

Smith, M. B. (1947). The personal setting of public opinions: A study of attitudes toward Russia. *Public Opinion Quarterly,* 507–523.

Smith, M. B., Bruner, J. S., & White, R. W. (1956). *Opinions and personality.* New York: Wiley.

Sniderman, P. M., & Tetlock, P. E. (1986a). Symbolic racism: Problems of motive attribution in political analysis. *Journal of Social Issues, 42*(2), 129–150.

Sniderman, P. M., & Tetlock, P. E. (1986b). Reflections on American racism. *Journal of Social Issues, 42*(2), 173–187.

Social Fallout From an Epidemic. (1985, August 12). *Newsweek,* pp. 28–29.

Sontag, S. (1978). *Illness as metaphor.* New York: Farrar, Straus & Giroux.

Sontag, S. (1988). *AIDS and its metaphors.* New York: Farrar, Straus and Giroux.

Stipp, H., & Kerr, D. (1989). Determinants of public opinion about AIDS. *Public Opinion Quarterly, 53,* 98–106.

Trice, A. D. (1988). Posttraumatic stress syndrome-like symptoms among AIDS caregivers. *Psychological Reports, 63,* 656–658.

Triplet, R. G., & Sugarman, D. B. (1987). Reactions to AIDS victims: Ambiguity breeds contempt. *Personality and Social Psychology Bulletin, 13*(2), 265–274.

Turner, C. F., Miller, H. G., & Moses, L. E. (Eds., 1989). *AIDS: Sexual behavior and intravenous drug use.* Washington, DC: National Academy Press.

Tversky, A., & Kahneman, D. (1974). Judgement under uncertainty: Heuristics and biases. *Science, 185*, 1124–1130.

Wallack, J. J. (1989). AIDS anxiety among health care professionals. *Hospital and Community Psychiatry, 40*, 507–510.

Wertz, D. C., Sorenson, J. R., Liebling, L., Kessler, L., & Heeren, T. C. (1987). Knowledge and attitudes of AIDS health-care providers before and after education programs. *Public Health Reports, 102*, 248–254.

Whitmore, G. (1988). *Someone was here: Profiles in the AIDS epidemic.* New York: New American Library.

Wiley, K., Heath, L., & Acklin, M. (1988). Care of AIDS patients: Student attitudes. *Nursing Outlook, 36*, 244–245.

Winkelstein, W., Jr., Samuel, M., Padian, N. S., Wiley, J. A., Lang, W., Anderson, R. E., & Levy, J. A. (1987). The San Francisco Men's Health Study: III. Reduction in human immunodeficiency virus transmission among homosexual/bisexual men, 1982–86. *American Journal of Public Health, 76*, 685–689.

Wolcott, D. L., Namir, S. Fawzy, F. I. Gottlieb, M. S., & Mitsuyasu, R. T. (1986). Illness concerns, attitudes towards homosexuality, and social support in gay men with AIDS. *General Hospital Psychiatry, 8*, 395–403.

Zich, J., & Temoshok, L. (1987). Perceptions of social support in men with AIDS and ARC: Relationships with distress and hardiness. *Journal of Applied Social Psychology, 17*, 193–215.

Appendix A:
Resources for Current Information on AIDS

In addition to general academic and professional journals, psychologists wishing to find the most recent information on AIDS-related issues may wish to consult the following.

Newsletters

AIDS Treatment News (semimonthly). ATN, c/o John S. James, P. O. Box 411256, San Francisco, CA 94141.
AIDS/HIV Record (semimonthly). BioData Publishers, P. O. Box 66020, Washington, DC 20035.
Treatment Issues (10 times yearly). Gay Men's Health Crisis, 129 West 20 Street, New York, NY 10011.
FOCUS: A Guide to AIDS Research and Counseling (monthly). UCSF AIDS Health Project, P. O. Box 0084, San Francisco, CA 94143-0884.
MIRA: Multicultural Inquiry and Research on AIDS Newsletter (quarterly). MIRA Newsletter, 74 New Montgomery Street, San Francisco, CA 94105.

AIDS Journals

AIDS & Public Policy Journal (quarterly). 107 East Church Street, Fredrick, MD 21701.
AIDS Education and Prevention (quarterly). Guilford Publications, 72 Spring Street, New York, NY 10012.

SALVATORE R. MADDI

PROLONGING LIFE BY HEROIC MEASURES: A HUMANISTIC EXISTENTIAL PERSPECTIVE

G rowing up in New York City as the son of Sicilian immigrants, Maddi attended Brooklyn College for his B.A. (1954) and M.A. (1956) in psychology. The next step was a PhD (1960) in clinical psychology at Harvard, where he worked with David C. McClelland, Robert W. White, and Jerome Bruner, while encountering Henry A. Murray and Gordon W. Allport. Taking up his academic career, he went through the ranks, starting as an instructor in 1959 at the University of Chicago, where he stayed until 1986. After a varied and productive period there, he joined the University of California at Irvine, in order to participate in the exciting growth of the campus and its area, Orange County. After serving as director of that campus' Program in Social Ecology, Maddi is currently concentrating again on research, writing, and teaching in health psychology, existential personality theory, psychopathology, and creativity.

Maddi has steadfastly valued a wedding of academic and practical efforts and an interdisciplinary approach to inquiry. His academic inclinations have produced influential theory and research on personality hardiness as a factor maintaining wellness as stressors mount, creativity and exploratory behavior as expressive of the need for novelty, a psychosocial analysis of the Catholic religious vocation, interpretations of existential psychology that have informed relevant research, and a classic treatise on personality that is now in its fifth edition. In these efforts, he has striven to integrate knowledge and approaches from the various fields of psychology and the social sciences as well.

He has expressed his practical inclinations by doing existential psychotherapy with clients as diverse as business managers and ministers. Also, he is founder and president of the Hardiness Institute, Inc., a psychological consulting company providing planning, assessment, and training services expressing the hardiness model to organizations and individuals. In this regard, Maddi hopes to simultaneously humanize the workplace and improve productivity.

Serving on many boards and committees, Maddi has been president of Divisions 1 (General Psychology) and 10 (Psychology and the Arts) of the American Psychological Association and a visiting professor at the Educational Testing Service (1963–1964), Harvard University (1969–1970), and the University of Rome (1987–1988). In addition, he was a Fulbright scholar at the Escola Paulista de Medicina in Sao Paolo, Brazil (1984–1985). Well known in this country among clinicians and academicians, Maddi has also emerged as an international figure through his work on hardiness, existential psychotherapy, and personality theory and research. In Poland, he was recently named among the top 180 psychologists in the world.

PROLONGING LIFE BY HEROIC MEASURES: A HUMANISTIC EXISTENTIAL PERSPECTIVE

In our time, the vexing issues that preoccupy humankind revolve around nuclear war, environmental damage, and, paradoxically, the implications of advances in medical technology (Toulmin, 1988). I want to focus here on the last of these issues. Advances in medical technology are forcing us to consider a range of existential issues concerning the meaning of life and death and our responsibility to each other—issues that we have been more or less able to avoid until now. Because the practical impetus to resolve these issues was largely absent before, we now find ourselves confronted with major questions and problems for which we have no ready answers or solutions. Nonetheless, emergency decisions have to be made every day, and psychologists, as health providers who are especially concerned with psychosocial matters, will be pushed to center stage whether or not they are prepared to perform.

Psychologists need to be protagonists in the human drama unfolding around the prolongation of life through heroic measures. Although specialists from many disciplines need to interact in a general effort to use new medical technology wisely, psychologists are among the few participants who are well positioned to guide usage toward a deepening of human character. In this, there is much for all of us to learn about how we want to lead our lives, not only at the point of worsening health, but long before that as well.

Dimensions of the Problem

The first step in this psychosocial analysis is to consider the dimensions of the problem of prolonging life in terms defined by current practice: What is involved? What has already taken place? Where do we seem to be going?

The Emerging Meaning of Heroic Measures

Heroic measures are extraordinary, so-called aggressive procedures for prolonging life when someone is at risk of imminent death or for reinstating life when death can be regarded as actually having occurred. These procedures are considered heroic in the sense that they are a radical departure from what might be termed *natural* or *conventional* care. Heroic measures are technologically advanced, require special knowledge and skill on the part of the health professional, and tend to be both expensive and limited in availability. Sometimes they have significant side effects on the life that is prolonged, and sometimes they do not.

The major examples of heroic measures have become surprisingly familiar in popular parlance. For breathing difficulties, there are endoctracheal intubation and respirators. For ingestion difficulties, there is hydration and nutrition accomplished, for example, by intravenous feeding. When vital organs threaten to fail, they may be assisted to function or actually replaced with transplants or artificial organs. Thus, there are monitors and coronary artery bypass grafting for hearts and their systems and in-center hemodialysis or continuous ambulatory peritoneal dialysis for kidneys. Heart and kidney transplants are coupled with immunosuppressive therapy to decrease risk of rejection, and artificial organs are improving rapidly. To impede cancerous growth, there are various surgical procedures and chemotherapy. And, immediately after death has occurred, there is cardiopulmonary resuscitation.

Heroic measures like these are quite remarkable. We are light years away from the image of a person propped up in bed, at home, surrounded by relatives, drifting off into a "natural" death. As remarkable as the heroic measures themselves is the speed with which they have been accepted as standard features of everyday life. It is understandable that health professionals who are committed to preserving life would embrace heroic measures. The alacrity with which the rest of us trans-

My heartfelt thanks to David Easton, Paul Feldstein, Deborah Khoshaba, William Lillyman, Frederic Ludwig, William Thompson, and Pathik Wadhwa for their encouragement and assistance in the preparation of this chapter.

form these measures into something almost natural, regardless of attendant psychosocial and ethicolegal problems, is a significant testament to our denial of death (Becker, 1973).

Two recent additions to the list of heroic measures are still so new that we are able to observe the struggle going on between the skepticism concerning their effectiveness and the hope that they will help. One of these is cryonics, the deep freezing of whole bodies or severed heads of just-deceased persons in the hope that they can be unfrozen and cloned at some future time, presumably when a cure has been found for what ailed the deceased. The other form of heroic measure involves the human mind itself. Some health professionals (e.g., Pelletier, 1977; Siegel, 1986, 1989; Simonton, Mathews–Simonton, & Creighton, 1978) have suggested that certain patterns of thought, emotion, and action can prolong life and perhaps even reestablish health in the case of serious physical illness.

Regarding cryonics, most physicians and scientists are currently skeptical of the procedure, agreeing with the following remarks of Rowe (cf. Williams, 1989), editor in chief of *Cryobiology*:

> We take a dim view of people involved in freezing whole bodies or heads. We haven't yet learned how to freeze anything like an entire body successfully. . . . To believe in (cloning it), you would have to believe you could make a cow from hamburger. (p. 27)

To make matters worse, the frozen body might still harbor the original cause of death when unfrozen. It has been estimated, for example, that the temperature necessary to preserve body cells would also preserve the AIDS virus and many others (Williams, 1989). Cryonics is currently of questionable value to us and to the future generations that might not wish to be bound by our decision to use it. However, the admirable history of human ingenuity requires us to remain open to the possible perfection of this heroic measure in the future. Meanwhile, many dying people and their families are currently paying huge sums for access to cryonics. The gathering lawsuits surrounding this procedure may or may not be resolved, even if technological advances solve current problems.

Regarding the human mind itself as a vehicle for heroic effort, there is considerable anecdotal and some systematic research evidence to bolster this view. Most physicians and scientists doubt that the mind has such power, however, and regard those who believe in this concept with considerable skepticism. The public now appears to display a spectrum of views, from uncritical acceptance that the mind can cure illness to bitter condemnation of those who would be so cruel as to ascribe physical illness to mental failure.

Terminal and Curable Diseases

Clearly, an illness is terminal when there is no known cure for it and when it regularly results in death. The most salient example in recent times is acquired immune deficiency syndrome (AIDS). Frequently, however, it is difficult to determine whether a condition is terminal in any practical sense. Even in such a serious disease as cancer, many factors interact in determining whether there is a cure. In addition to the nature of the treatment, these factors include the bodily site affected, the extent and rate of growth of the abnormality, and the general vigor of the patient. So complicated is the interaction among these factors that judgments as to whether and when the patient will die are often quite inaccurate. To add to these formidable complications, there are occasional instances of spontaneous remission, as well as the question of how long a patient must be rendered free of disease symptoms to be regarded as cured.

A major reason for determining curability is that this may influence treatment decisions. Because heroic measures tend to be scarce, costly, and invasive, perhaps they are unjustified treatments in terminal illnesses. On the other hand, any prolongation of life may be regarded as its own justification, especially because it is possible that at any time a cure for a currently incurable disease will be found. This argument in favor of heroic measures even in incurable diseases is strengthened by the unreliability of predictions about length of life remaining—unless those predictions are made when death is very close.

Diseases and the Aging Process

Another ingredient in the psychosocial considerations of prolonging life is the aging process. Where adequate health care is applied throughout the life span, a telltale process emerges: An exponential increase in diseases begins for people in their 40s and continues through their later years. According to Ludwig (1989), "If one assents to the existence of such a process, common to all cells, extracellular structures or organs, the majority of ailments emerging from adulthood onwards would be only mere complications of an ubiquitous disease. Its name is aging" (p. 1).

To judge from what has already been demonstrated in experimental animals, a significant postponement of senescence will probably be possible in human beings (Ludwig, 1989). It may not be too long before slowing the aging process qualifies as a heroic measure.

To some health professionals postponement of the aging process seems to be an unwarranted, unwise tampering with the natural order in which organisms and their environment survive and thrive (e.g., Kalish, 1974; Ludwig, 1989). In this view, every effort should be made to cure the diseases that threaten to produce premature death, but natural death through the aging process should be accepted. There are practical difficulties with this position. Because of the exponential increase in diseases that start at age 40, one expensive, scarce heroic measure will be followed by another as our population becomes increasingly older. As this happens, expected life span will also increase, which is occurring at a dramatic rate even now (e.g., Coni, 1989). If we can already increase longevity by preventive and remedial approaches to conventional diseases, will it seem so radically different and unacceptable to slow the aging process itself?

Treatment Options

Even at the current levels of development of heroic measures, the health professional is confronted with a bewildering array of treatment options. These treatment options bring with them complex psychological, social, economic, legal, and ethical issues for which there is not yet a cultural consensus. Nonetheless, born out of the necessity to make decisions every day, a picture of what is currently acceptable is emerging. Before I analyze the psychosocial considerations in greater depth, I will review some of the main issues and current practices regarding them.

Implications of Trying to Save Everyone

A quick way to encounter the major issues is to explore the implications of trying to save everyone with the deployment of medical technology. All of the ethical principles that declare life to be the ultimate value and that support equality among persons in the right to life stand behind this approach. Imagine what would happen: Neither health professionals, nor patients, nor relatives, nor financial, legal, and religious institutions would have any exercise of choice in individual cases. Heroic measures would be used automatically, as often as needed, regardless of the patient's age, condition, or whether the confronting disease was curable. Even if the treatment severely damaged the patient's quality of life, and if he or she pleaded out of unbearable pain and exhaustion to be allowed to die in peace, every effort would be made to prolong that life. Attempts to slow down the aging process would progress as rapidly as possible. The only inhibition in the use of medical technology would be in the case of heroic measures that research had failed to show decreased the threat of death. These would be foregone for fear of actually contributing to the death of patients during the attempt to keep them alive. On the other hand, the use of after-death heroic measures that attempt to bring the patient back to life, such as cryonics, would be rampant, as long as the slightest possibility of success existed.

At the same time, such an unequivocal stance might lead to some positive results. For example, the development of newer and better heroic measures would be supported. Furthermore, no one would have to agonize over treatment decisions. But would we be able to produce long and fantastic lives in the process?

In the short run, the current trend toward longer life spans would probably be accelerated. However, enormous, if not insurmountable, practical problems would overtake us. There would have to be a precipitous increase in hospitals, health professionals, medical research, and relevant supportive and administrative institutions (Wetle, Cwikel, & Levkoff, 1988). This expansion would cost a great deal of money, as would the medical services dispensed. Patients who were too poor, aged, or weak to work would not be able to pay for the medical services that they would need. In our current national health care system, these costs would be borne by individuals and organizations in the work force, either directly (in the case in which the patient is a relative), or indirectly (through taxes and the cost of medical insurance). Estimates make it clear that the burden on those who work would be enormous (e.g., Callahan, 1986). As it became obvious that health costs were swamping all other life-quality costs, those in the work force would speak out against what would seem to be a rank injustice, even when their own poor, aged, or weak relatives were involved.

Our current social system surely could change to accommodate the pressures of heroic measures for all. Perhaps health professionals, hospitals, medical administrators, and their supporting institutions could earn less for their work. At the very least, this would sap the motivation and imagination needed for the dedicated service that is required and would jeopardize the enterprise. Socialized medicine, by itself, would not appreciably alter this prospect, because the working public would have to be taxed in order for the government to offer free or inexpensive medical services for all. Perhaps more of the poor and the aged could enter or remain in the work force and, therefore, be able to shoulder their own medical expenses. This might be feasible for the aged if their health improved and senescence was delayed as a function of deployment of heroic measures. If the poor and the aged were to enter the work force in increasing multitudes, however, they would either displace current workers or else major sources of new jobs would have to be found continually. Moreover, to extrapolate from the proportion of current income deployed for health reasons (cf. Callahan, 1986, 1987; Thomasma, 1986), this hypothetical situation would involve a society (or world) in which people more or less worked in order to pay their medical bills. Perhaps a comprehensive cure to death that obviated continual use of heroic measures could be found before the point of economic suicide was reached, but that would be a risky bet.

To speculate even further, suppose that a way to avoid these problems were found and that people lived longer in unprecedented numbers. On a worldwide basis, this would be a disastrous drain on natural resources and would lead to dangerous levels of pollution and crowding. Solutions to these problems might be found before it was too late, but our current record is not even acceptable (although world population is at a much lower level than it would be if heroic measures were universally available). As a solution to the problems of natural resource depletion, pollution, and overcrowding, novelists have suggested the colonization of other planets (e.g., Heinlein, 1973). For all we know, this might happen, but even if it did, that it would happen in time would again be a risky bet.

Furthermore, there is no guarantee that the lives prolonged would be worthwhile and sufficiently satisfying to justify the effort. Side effects of heroic measures, economic dangers, the necessity of perpetual work, and ecological insufficiency might combine to make life a nightmare. Even if we discovered how to extend life spans on a major scale without destroying economies and ecologies, the discovery by itself would still not guarantee a high quality life. In this respect, Ludwig (1989) argued against the view that aging is like any other disease that can be cured once understood. He asserted "that the aging process, when viewed in a broader perspective than that of the laboratory, differs from disease profoundly. We can imagine life without disease. But can we imagine life with aging?" (pp. 8–9). In place of a Promethean revolt against natural order, he reminded us of Cicero's words shortly before dying in 44 B.C.: "It is not very likely that the last act of the play of life has received less attention from the playwright than the preceding ones which are so admirably well designed" (p. 10). As I will discuss later, quality of life may be substantially bound up with the contrast between health and illness, youth and maturity, life and death. If this is so, prolonging life on a grand scale may not, ipso facto, enhance life psychosocially.

Implications of Selective Treatment

If there are so many imponderable problems with trying to save everyone, is selective treatment a more feasible alternative? Perhaps only those lives that fulfill certain criteria of value justify heroic measures to prolong them. With this approach, it may be possible to avoid economic and ecological catastrophes. The formidable complications of selective treatment, then, are (a) what the criteria of life's value shall be and (b) who shall make the assessments. To assert that value lies with the younger rather than with the older and with the curable rather than the incurable appears commonplace enough, but the assertion is difficult to defend across the board. Some elderly persons and some sufferers of terminal diseases are extraordinarily valuable by virtue of their social influence in matters such as leadership, brilliance, creativity, or power. Once having recognized this, however, the floodgates are open. Is the wealthy person better than the poor person? What of the person who is loved and loves, as opposed to the isolated person who is preoccupied with the self? Moreover, are not some poor, uninfluential persons more humane than the wealthy? Before we know it, there is a bewildering array of criteria of life's worth, and there is little or no consensus about them. Debates on these criteria are age old and are not likely to be resolved, especially if selective treatment decisions are to be tied to resolutions.

Nor is it any simpler to determine who shall make the assessments, even if we were able to agree on a set of life-worth criteria. Will it be clergy, politicians, captains of industry, professors, health professionals, or committees of persons selected at random? Will it be the remarkable or the humble? Implicit in the choice of people to assess us are the same problems encountered in the criteria for assessment. Debates on who is worthy to assess are also age old and unlikely to be resolved.

Heroic treatment for everyone does not seem feasible, and the issues surrounding selective treatment are not easily resolved. So what are we to do? Before further deliberation, let us review current practice in order to appreciate the direction in which we are being led by the thousands of concrete decisions that are made daily by health professionals, patients, relatives, insurance organizations, legislatures, electorates, and judges.

Learning From Current Practice

Although it had long been suspected that health professionals were making ad hoc decisions to withdraw life-sustaining measures from hopelessly ill patients, it was not until 1976 that two major hospitals publicly announced their polices concerning this issue (Fried, 1976).

In the same year, California was the first state to enact a "Natural Death" Act. This Act was a compromise that recognized differences of opinion as to whether there are medical conditions that justify nontreatment and, if so, what they are. In analyzing the Act, Redleaf, Schmitt, and Thompson (1979) indicated that, although the physician was permitted to withhold or withdraw *life-sustaining procedures* only from a patient with a *terminal condition*, these two key terms were left somewhat ambiguous. A terminal condition was defined as something incurable that produces death regardless of whether heroic measures are used. Life-sustaining procedure was defined as a medical practice that uses mechanical or other *artificial means* to artificially prolong the patient's death. No useful examples of artificial means were given, however, thereby leaving the scope of the nontreatment right unclear. Furthermore, the Act indicated that the physician must conclude that "death is imminent whether or not" treatment is given before that treatment can be stopped. This is not to say, however, that the physician can make the decision to forego treatment alone. The Act gave patients substantial control over the treatment decision by indicating that physicians' decisions should be guided by two kinds of directives from their patients. *Advisory directives* can be executed before diagnosis of terminal illness, but do not compel the physician to withdraw treatment. In contrast, *binding directives* do compel the physician, but can only be executed after the patient has been notified of a terminal condition. To guard against hasty decisions, binding directives cannot be executed for two weeks following such notification. Physicians who comply with a valid patient directive cannot be prosecuted, but they must transfer the patient to another physician if they do not wish to obey the directive; otherwise, they can be censured for unprofessional conduct. In an attempt to avoid conflicts of interest, the Act did not extend decision-making power to the patient's relatives or proxies. The resulting weakness was that some patients notified of a terminal condition only when death was imminent would become incompetent (e.g., by lapsing into a coma) to execute a binding directive sometime during the mandatory 14-day waiting period.

Despite the weakness in this Act, it served as a model for other states, of which there are now 38 legitimizing advisory or advance directives from patient to physician concerning withdrawal of treatment (Wanzer et al., 1989). Of these, 15 states specifically indicate that a patient's health-care proxy or spokesperson can authorize withdrawal of life support (Wanzer et al., 1989).

It is apparent that practices concerning care of dying patients that were considered controversial at the beginning of this decade are becoming almost routine (Wanzer et al., 1989). Do-not-resuscitate orders are commonplace now, and even withdrawal of hydration and nutrition is becoming more common in dying, hopelessly suffering, or permanently unconscious patients. The courts have expanded the legal right of patients and their proxies to refuse medical treatment in more than 80 well-known decisions (Wanzer et al., 1989). The justification usually used is the patient's common-law right to autonomy (to decide regarding self) as well as the constitutional right to privacy (to be protected from invasive treatment).

Indeed, the courts now seem to be moving closer to the view that patients have a right to die even if they are not terminally ill or suffering (Wanzer et al., 1989). The notion is that refusing treatment can be used to end unacceptable quality of life, such as permanent unconsciousness, even if the patient is not perceptibly suffering or close to death. These court decisions have dealt with artificial feeding, and the cause of death has been regarded as the underlying disease rather than the withdrawal of treatment. To some ethicists and legal experts (e.g., Larson & Spring, 1987), hydration and nutrition, even if administered artificially, are forms of care rather than treatment. To withdraw care is to kill patients before their time—an act that is not acceptable according to former U.S. Surgeon General C. Everett Koop (Larson & Spring, 1987).

Although laws and courts act as weathervanes, our understanding of current practices would be incomplete without sampling the opinions and actions of the individuals who are directly involved. A good example is a survey of physicians (Redleaf et al., 1979) concerning the first year of operation of the California Natural Death Act. After only one year, some patients appeared to have enacted advisory or binding directives, some of which were carried out by their physicians. By clarifying their legal obligations, the Act made physicians feel more secure about withdrawing treatment. Some problems emerged, however. Fully 8% of physicians were unfamiliar with the Act, and only 22% were clear about the conditions under which the patient directives were and were not binding. Some physicians even admitted to disregarding directives. There were disagreements as to the meaning of the term *terminal disease*. Some physicians did not communicate fully with the patients about their conditions, even when they were considered terminal.

The unwillingness of health professionals to suspend treatment is also shown in the 1985 case of an elderly woman in a leading Christian nursing home who suffered strokes that left her unable to swallow food and water (Larson & Spring, 1987). Her family secured medical certification that there was no chance of recovery and a physician's directive to remove her feeding tube. When three nurses refused to cooperate on ethical and religious grounds, the nursing home at first fired them and then reversed itself, refusing to go along with the withdrawal of treatment directive. Despite a bitter ensuring controversy involving resignations and adverse media coverage, there are still long waiting lists for admission to this nursing home. Nonetheless, results of an opinion pole show that 68% of the sample believed that "people dying of an incurable, painful disease should be allowed to end their lives before the disease runs its course" (Wanzer et al., 1989).

Many health professionals, legal experts, and ethicists are striving to bring more rationality to policies and order to procedures. The direction that this effort is taking involves individualizing treatment plans. If a disease is curable or if there is a reasonable chance to correct an otherwise terminal condition with heroic measures, such measures are used. Officially, the availability and the cost of treatment are not supposed to enter into the decision, although informally these factors play a role (Wetle et al., 1988). If a disease is incurable, then the health professional incurs a responsibility to inform the patient, the proxy, or both and to counsel them concerning their treatment decisions. Counsel needs to be given concerning the implications of relevant heroic measures for prolonging life, and for aspects of quality of life such as pain, mental competence, dependency, and general functioning. If the patient or the proxy insists that every effort be made to prolong life, the health professional has little choice but to agree. When the patient or the proxy decides in favor of accepting death, treatment efforts can shift from heroic measures to ordinary care.

Of relevance when the treatment decision is for ordinary care rather than heroic measures is whether the terminally ill patient is competent (alert although dying), brain dead (existing with irreversible cessation of brain function), vegetative (with the neocortex largely and irreversibly destroyed), or severely and irreversibly demented (Wanzer et al., 1985). Certainly with competent patients (and with the others when relevant), the emphasis is on pain management, even when that hastens death or risks addiction (Angell, 1982). If a patient is willing to tolerate some level of pain in order to remain alert, the health professional accepts this (Payne & Foley, 1987). What remains unclear at this time is whether hydration and nutrition administered artificially are to be regarded as ordinary care or as heroic measures. On this issue hangs the speedy or prolonged death of the terminally ill patient.

Currently, hospitals are tending toward reliance on internal ethics committees in trying to arrive at diagnostic, prognostic, treatment, and counseling stances in complicated cases. Dominated by physicians, these committees tend to include ethicists (e.g., clergy) and, occasionally, counseling specialists (e.g., social workers, psychologists). When courts become involved in treatment-decision cases, they take into account deliberations of in-hospital ethics committees.

Alternatives to hospital residence for terminally ill patients opting for ordinary care are now available. If they do not require the use of heroic measures, patients can be nursed at home or in hospices, where the ambience, love, and expressed compassion may be greater as death approaches (Bulkin & Lukashak, 1988; Wallston, Burger, Smith, & Baugher, 1988). Although the cost of dying in nonhospital settings will be less than in hospitals, medical insurance plans are not yet uniform in reimbursing nonhospital treatment.

Before closing this review of current practices, I would like to touch on the subjects of suicide and euthanasia. Some patients choose to and are successful in committing suicide by themselves; others seek the assistance of their health professionals. According to Wanzer et al. (1989), the frequency of such assistance is unknown but certainly not rare, even though it is a crime in many states. Furthermore, these researchers consider it ethical for the physician not to attempt resuscitation in the case of such a suicide if the patient is indeed beyond all help and not merely suffering from a treatable depression of the sort common in the terminally ill.

Euthanasia, or the performance of a medical procedure that causes someone's death directly and intentionally, is also a crime in this country. The Dutch, however, have developed criteria whereby euthanasia is medically and ethically acceptable (Wanzer et al., 1989), and the pros and cons of this issue are currently being debated here (e.g., Angell, 1988; Van Bommel, 1986). Although the majority of physicians in the

United States presumably do not agree with the Dutch position, a 1988 Roper poll asking the public whether a physician should be lawfully able to end the life of a terminally ill patient at the patient's request yielded 55% affirmative responses, with only 10% of respondents being undecided (Wanzer et al., 1989).

I will now pull together the themes and discordancies in current practice. Although the use of heroic measures is very much in evidence, it is clear that our society has charted a course between the Scylla of trying to save everyone and the Charybdis of selective treatment by giving patients or, if need be, their proxies the right to make treatment decisions. The functions of health professionals are to diagnose, to prognosticate, and to counsel. The first two functions are considerably unreliable, and health professionals engage in the third with varying consistency and competency. Fear and sadness and possibly greater incompetency cloud the decisions of patients and, for that matter, their proxies. Despite all of these complications, there is a growing consensus that terminally ill patients need not have their deaths prolonged if they (or their proxies if need be) make what appears to be a rational decision to suspend heroic treatment in favor of ordinary care. Controversy persists, however, as to the boundary between heroic and ordinary measures.

Psychosocial Considerations

As indicated by the summary earlier, current practices at the psychological level of the thoughts, feelings, and actions of the individual participants in treatment decisions and the social level of their interactions together bear little similarity to the semblance of order and clarity imparted by legal considerations. Greater effort needs to be expended at the psychosocial level, lest tragedies continue to abound. My way of contributing to this effort is to pose for consideration the meaning of life and death for the patient, the family, the health professional, and society in general. Although research findings are included in this speculative effort, my main intent is to provoke thought in the reader.

The Meaning of Life and Death to the Patient

To date, the major research themes regarding seriously or chronically ill patients have involved compliance to treatment regimens and psychological adjustment to disorders. Factors influencing treatment compliance include (a) coping styles, (b) personality variables, (c) education regarding the treatment, (d) variants in the treatment regimen, and (e) interactions of these factors (e.g., Brantley, Mosley, Bruce, McKnight,

& Jones, 1990; Christensen, Smith, Turner, Holman, & Gregory, 1990; Cummings, Becker, Kirscht, & Levin, 1981; Felton & Revenson, 1984; Finn & Alcorn, 1986; Kaplan De-Nour & Czaczkes, 1972). The same factors have been implicated in the patient's psychological adjustment to the disorder (e.g., Christensen et al., 1990; Devins et al., 1982; Evans et al., 1985; Felton & Revenson, 1984; Kaplan De-Nour & Czaczkes, 1976; Poll & Kaplan De-Nour, 1980). These research approaches have not concerned the patient's decision of whether to undergo the heroic treatment, nor have they considered the psychological significance for the patient of confronting issues of life and death. Such studies are not relevant here because they assume the value of the treatment and the importance of adjusting to its effects.

There is also a literature on preparing the terminally ill patient to die, which emphasizes having an "appropriate" or "good" death (Augustine & Kalish, 1975; Wallston, Burger, Smith, & Baugher, 1988). The dying patient has to contend with anxiety concerning abandonment and separation from loved ones, feelings of being punished, body image concerns, dependency wishes, and lowered self-esteem (e.g., Gray, 1989). In this regard, the concept of appropriate death has emphasized emotional control, an acceptance of non being, empathy for those left behind, an effort for control, and a sense of the meaningfulness of the death process (e.g., Bass, 1985; Gray, 1989; Greenham & Lohmann, 1982; Janofsky & Stuecher, 1983; Kalish, 1972). Appropriate death concepts have developed along with the hospice movement to promote a more humane dying process than is generally available in hospitals (e.g., Franco, 1985; Foster & Paradis, 1985; Frederick & Frederick, 1985; Reynolds & Kalish, 1974).

Research on hospice-based psychosocial or palliative care is in its infancy (Dush, 1988), and available literature tends to be anecdotal. Nonetheless, evaluations of particular hospice settings have been attempted (e.g., Brescia, Sadof, & Barstow, 1984). Further, conceptual efforts have considered the similarity between hospice philosophy and Judeo–Christian religious beliefs (e.g., Adams, 1989; Augustine & Kalish, 1975; Spero, 1981), and have raised questions that could refine thought and practice (e.g., Carr & Carr, 1985; O'Connor, Burge, King, & Epstein, 1986; Mor & Hiris, 1983; Palgi, 1983; Pine, 1986).

Researchers have studied different approaches to preparing terminally ill patients to die (e.g., Razavi, Delvaux, & Desmarez, 1988; Schulz & Schlarb, 1987). Approaches that have been tried include hypnotic death rehearsal (Levitan, 1985), and reading relevant fiction (Husband & Broadhus, 1984, Moore & Mae, 1987), along with more usual means (e.g., Foster & Paradis, 1985; Gray, 1989).

Studies that have considered how to prepare seriously ill patients to undergo heroic treatment are of greater relevance. Generally, these studies have highlighted the importance of a sense of control, hope, and understanding over helplessness, hopelessness, and ignorance (e.g.,

Shipley, Butt, Horwitz, & Farbry, 1978; Shultheis, Peterson, & Selby, 1987; Taylor, 1979). The findings have suggested that, the more actively the patient participates in medical decisions and their implementation, the less devastating the illness and its treatment will become. What follows elaborates conceptually on this theme.

It is the nature of human beings to recognize and to understand things—in short, to experience meaning—through contrast (e.g., Kelly, 1955; Neisser, 1964). Applied macroscopically to the life cycle, this signifies that health acquires meaning through its contrast with illness, youth through contrast with old age, and life itself through contrast with death. This view has been echoed throughout the ages and, in modern psychology, there is, for example, Erikson's (1950) emphasis on ego integrity versus despair. (This stage takes place late in the life cycle, when the person's powers are failing and he or she begins to look backward rather than forward.) The interpretation of life involved may be Cicero's (1969) capstone in the case of ego integrity, or a tragic end, in the case of despair. Despite a different starting point, existential psychology agrees with Erikson concerning the importance of evaluating one's life and that this interpretive effort is facilitated by contemplating impending death. For the existentialists, however, this contemplation of death need not wait upon failing powers and advancing age. For them, life properly understood is always led in the shadow of death. This juxtaposition can either heighten life's meaning or lead to despair (Frankl, 1960; Kierkegaard, 1954).

Existential psychology provides a useful basis for understanding whether the contemplation of death will enhance or detract from the meaning of life. The important consideration is whether or not the person involved is *courageous* (Tillich, 1952) or, if you will, *hardy* (Kobasa, 1979; Maddi & Kobasa, 1984). Simply put, this is a stance involving the strength to change that which needs to be changed, the serenity to accept that which cannot be changed, and the wisdom to know the difference (to paraphrase the old prayer). If the seeds of hardiness or courageousness are instilled in childhood, then a person is able to develop vigorously through learning by failures as well as successes throughout the life span (Maddi, 1988). This strength to contemplate, to face, and to assimilate setbacks facilitates an appreciation not only of health, youth, and life, but also of illness, old age, and death as integral parts of a grand, natural pattern. In this regard, the developing emphasis in our culture on death education (Pine, 1986) may be an effective start.

But the person who fails to learn hardiness or courage in childhood will not be able to contemplate, to face, or to assimilate failures, and this inability will jeopardize vigorous personal development. This weakness in regard to setbacks will lead to embracing conventional views in which health, youth, and life are regarded as wonderful and in which illness, old age, and death are so terrifying that they must be denied (Becker, 1973; Maddi, 1988). Analyses of extant fiction in which response to dying is depicted as stoical for males and tearful for females suggest that our society is still conventional in its views of death.

This context of differing psychological styles will facilitate our considerations of the meaning of life and death to the patient. Faced with serious or even terminal illness, the hardy or courageous patient will not tend to be caught unaware or deny the situation, although this does not imply passive capitulation. Indeed, such a patient would strive mightily to stay alive, having long since achieved true appreciation of how effectively life may be used. Nor would the hardy patient become excessively dependent on health professionals or family, struggling instead to make his or her own decisions. As observed by Siegel (1986, 1989) and others (Simonton et al., 1978), this attitude appears to prolong life despite serious illness. Remember Norman Cousins (1979), who checked out of the hospital and ridded himself of a supposedly incurable disease with his "laughing cure." In general, the hardy patient would make every sensible use of heroic measures, fighting against the damage to quality of life that might ensue. Indeed, such a patient would be using his or her mind as a heroic measure. If every effort failed, however, the hardy patient would truly accept impending death, preparing himself or herself and others for it and conducting this preparatory effort with courage too. In considering such a stance, we are reminded of T. S. Elliot's (1952, p. 129) marvelous observation in the *Four Quartets*, "in my end is my beginning."

In contrast, the nonhardy patient, faced with serious or even terminal illness, will pass through stages similar to those identified by Kübler-Ross (1969). The first reaction will be denial, accompanied by a sense of isolation from others. This is an understandable reaction on the part of someone who believes that he or she will live forever. The next stage is anger, which is a kind of externalization of blame, as if there were culprits to be found on whom to blame one's serious illness. It is as if the patient, having led a conventionally acceptable life, did not expect such a punishment as illness or death. The bargaining stage that follows is a good indication of the conventionality of nonhardy patients. They may have spent so much time amassing the socially acceptable signs of power and accomplishment that they somehow think that they can negotiate themselves out of death. The ensuing stage of depression is predictable, as the realization that denial, anger, and bargaining have failed to make a difference is forced on the patient. If the illness is terminal, this depression shades into a final acceptance that may be more capitulation than courageousness. Such nonhardy patients die a self-preoccupied, unproductive death. Of them too, it can be said "in my end is my beginning," but the meaning is entirely different.

Although serious or terminal illness perhaps provides a more dramatic context than everyday life, people face death as they have lived. A focus on courage or hardiness will help us to understand individual differences in reaction to serious or terminal illness and the use of heroic measures.

The Meaning of Life and Death to the Family

The severe illness or dying of a person is a major disruption to the family unit of which he or she is a part. Themes of grieving emerging from research include guilt, a desire for closeness with the dying person, depression, lowered self-esteem, and—if the dying is prolonged—a wish for relief from constant demands, recurrent anger and resentment, and a desire for an end to the pain, even if this end is death (e.g., Demi, 1984; Mack & Berman, 1988; Moss & Moss, 1989; Razavi, Delvaux, Farvacques, & Rabaye, 1988). In these complex, often contradictory reactions, the ramifications are not only psychological and social, but also economic and legal (e.g., Furman, 1984; Martin, Martin, & Pierce, 1984).

There is now a growing emphasis on helping the families of dying persons to grieve anticipatorily, to accept the impending death, and to reconstitute a new family pattern after the death (e.g., Bendor, 1989; Geyman, 1983; Lavoie, Vezina, & Dompierre, 1985; Rognlie, 1989). Various intervention approaches have been tried to facilitate the family members' contribution to an appropriate death, including support groups formed of people anticipating the death of a family member (e.g., Lavoie et al., 1985; Longman, Lindstrom, & Clark, 1989; Rognlie, 1989), family therapy that includes the dying member (Acworth & Bruggen, 1985), art therapy (Junge, 1985), and more conventional counseling (e.g., Speck, 1985). Much of this work has occurred in a hospice setting. In general, these interventions can help families to accept the impending death, extend support to the dying person and be more stable in general. They are not especially relevant, however, to decisions about prolonging life by heroic measures.

Research reports are beginning to focus on individual differences in reactions of families and family members to an impending death. For example, Gilbert (1989) reported that in 27 married couples confronted with fetal or infant death there were both themes of cooperation and of conflict. Davies (1988) reported that in families with higher cohesion, more joint activities, and greater religious or moral emphasis, the siblings of dying children had fewer behavior problems. As to differential responses of particular family members, factors having an effect include gender, type of illness being adjusted to, closeness of relationship to the dying person, and perceptions of the unavoidability of the death (e.g., Greif & Porembski, 1988, Kirschling, 1989; Kubitz, Thornton, & Robertson, 1989).

Some studies also suggest that the personality of the family member influences his or her grieving process. For example, the lower a family member's sense of purpose in life, the greater the likelihood that he or she will experience more anger at the perceived injustice in the death of a relative (Pfost, Stevens, & Wessels, 1989) and that anticipatory grieving will be less effective (Stevens, Pfost, & Wessels, 1987). These studies suggest individual differences in level of courage or hardiness. Also indicating the relevance of existential formulations is the developing emphasis on the possibility of growth through grieving for another (e.g., Johnson, 1985; Moss & Moss, 1989).

Hardy or courageous persons face not only the problems and setbacks confronting them as individuals, but also those that are of a relational nature. Consequently, the hardy person will have worked out differences with family members long before serious or terminal illness strikes. Thus, the patient's illness and its treatment will be unlikely to arouse pent up emotions, old ambivalences, and painful guilt in family members, if they are hardy. Unburdened by unresolved issues from the past and able to confront setbacks, the hardy family member will be truly available to counsel, care for, and otherwise aid the patient and other relatives. Although such a family member will undoubtedly try to help the patient to survive (having long since decided that the relationship is important), the main thing will be to find the best solution for the ailing person, whatever that may be.

Nonhardy people tend to avoid coping with relational problems and setbacks. Consequently, they build up unresolved issues with family members and have a ready reservoir of anger, guilt, and righteous indignation that awaits the first sign of imperfection. Such people are poorly equipped to help a family member who becomes seriously or terminally ill and must make decisions regarding heroic treatments. Their attempts to counsel, care for, and otherwise aid the patient are colored by selfish considerations often masquerading as just the opposite.

The actions and attitudes of nonhardy family members can have unpredictable consequences. Their anger or envy may subtly push a patient who might otherwise be able to recover toward death, or their guilt might lead to vain efforts to fend off a death that the patient might find relief from. For example, a cardiac surgeon told me of his discussion with a patient concerning a heroic operation that had a high probability of success if done when still elective, but a low probability of success when done on an emergency basis. While fully competent, the patient refused the elective operation. Later, his condition became critical, and he was no longer competent to make a decision. Although it seemed clear to the surgeon that the patient had chosen to die rather than have the operation, his family members exercised their proxy and insisted on the emergency, low probability procedure. When the patient died on the operating table, the surgeon felt outrage and said, "I didn't get into medicine to kill people," and bemoaned the guilt that must have led the family members to countermand the patient's decision. These family members were most likely more concerned with demonstrating that they had done all they could to save their relative than they were with respecting his wishes.

As I observed earlier, the family functions in times of crisis in a similar, if exaggerated, form of its everyday operations. Considerations of hardiness or courageousness are useful in understanding family differences in reaction to the serious or terminal illness of one of its members.

The Meaning of Life and Death to the Health Professional

Much of the recent theory and research concerning care of the seriously or terminally ill has emphasized hospice settings. This literature emphasizes appropriate death for the patient, anticipatory grief for the survivors, and morale maintenance for the staff (e.g., Lister & Ward, 1985; Smith & Varoglu, 1985; Weisman, 1988). With regard to the health care staff, stress and the ability to cope have received attention in physicians (e.g., Patterson, 1989), nurses (e.g., Cooper & Mitchell, 1990; Gray–Taft & Anderson, 1986; Peace & Vincent, 1988), occupational and physical therapists (Lardaro, 1988; Martin & Berchulc, 1987), paramedics (e.g., Palmer, 1983), rehabilitation counselors (e.g., Allen & Miller, 1988), and volunteers (e.g., Amenta & Weiner, 1981; Garfield & Jenkins, 1981) in both hospice and hospital settings. In general, anxiety, sadness, demoralization, frustration, and anger are common reactions of health care staff members.

Some comparisons of health care staff reactions in hospice and hospital settings are now available. For example, Cooper and Mitchell (1990) reported that hospital nurses have lower job satisfaction than hospice nurses, but that hospice nurses have more anxiety and psychosomatic complaints. Peace and Vincent (1988) found no difference in death anxiety in hospice and nonhospice nurses despite the former's greater training in palliative care. The pattern of findings in these studies may reveal individual differences in personality as suggested by Amenta and Weiner's (1981) report that death anxiety was highly related to general anxiety in hospice workers. Furthermore, if findings continue to suggest that hospice workers have high levels of anxiety despite greater training in dealing with death, then we may be observing the effect of an emphasis on palliative care and acceptance of death unbalanced by a struggle for a cure (e.g., O'Connor et al., 1986).

In an event, both hospice and more conventional approaches are receiving a severe challenge from AIDS (e.g., Andersen & MacElveen-Hoehn, 1988; Murphy & Perry, 1988). AIDS is fueling a renewed effort to design settings for care of the seriously and terminally ill and to provide more psychological training and support for health care staff (e.g., Etten & Kosberg, 1989; McCorkle, 1982; Razavi, et al., 1988; Weiner, 1986; Wilson, 1988). To some extent, the training is an attempt to be differentiated enough to recognize individual differences as they may influence reactions to and coping with the dying patient and the grieving family.

There is little emphasis yet in the literature on health care staff on the problem of helping patients and their families with decisions concerning heroic measures and life prolongation. In the hope that conceptual themes may provoke research and practice in the direction of such decisions, let me offer some suggestions. One reason that health professionals enter their chosen fields is to protect health and life and to ward off illness and death. In this sense, the patient with a serious or terminal disease may seem a threat (Jonsen, Cooke, & Koenig, 1986). But the situation is by no means this simple. After all, no one has more intimate knowledge of illness and dying than the health professional, who is continually called on to diagnose, to prognosticate, to prescribe, to intervene, and to counsel. Thus, the task of the health professional equally involves illness, old age, and death, as well as health, youth, and life. All of these conditions together constitute the meaning and calling of the health professions.

Hardy or courageous health professionals will be as open and sensitive to illness, old age, and death as to health, youth, and life. Consequently, they will be ready and willing to perform the functions of diagnosis, prognosis, and counseling of the seriously ill or dying patient. These health professionals will not be hampered by the absence of relevant training in school or by the pressures of a busy schedule. In these functions, they will balance their commitment to health and life with an acceptance of the inevitability of illness and death. Because they will appreciate the value of these juxtapositions, they will be responsible, compassionate, wise counselors, who are able to guide the patients and accept their ultimate decisions. A model of this functioning is provided by Siegel's (1986, 1989) recent approach to his cancer patients.

In contrast, nonhardy health professionals will find it difficult to cope with illness, old age, and death, having rejected their relevance to the overall meaning of life and their work. When forced to diagnose, to prognosticate, and to counsel seriously ill or dying patients, such health professionals will be clumsy, distracted, aloof, cold, and impatient. They will prefer the technical to the psychosocial features of their work. Results of the current upswing of research on quality of life in patients with serious or terminal diseases suggest that many health professionals are finding their counseling function quite difficult. For example, a general consensus exists (Clark & Fallowfield, 1986; Storstein, 1988) that questionnaires completed by patients are more effective guides to their quality of life than are the interpretations made by health professionals. More specifically, health professionals tend to miss psychological problems in their patients (Clark & Fallowfield, 1986) and underestimate their quality of life (Kohn & Menon, 1988). In discussing the results of their interview study, Kohn and Menon (1988) made a poignant summary:

> We found that both the elderly and health care professionals talk
> about life prolongation, but not with one another; that they consider
> some of the same factors as they think about the life prolongation
> decision; and that most of them believe physicians should be respon-

sible for initiating discussion. However, the physician or health care professional who wishes to avoid crisis situations also is reluctant to broach the issue for fear of unnecessarily alarming or compromising the defense mechanisms of the patient. The patient remains patient—waiting—with fears of dependency, memories of previous life threatening experiences, and deep sensitivity for suffering—for the physician to initiate the discussion.

Such findings suggest that many health professionals, themselves, have not come to terms with the failures and fallibilities inherent in the human being and, hence, are remiss in their counseling function.

The Meaning of Life and Death in American Society

In earlier parts of this chapter, the major psychosocial, moral, and economic issues posed for our society by prolonging life have been detailed. The remainder of this chapter will include a synthesis of these issues into overall trends and some final conceptual suggestions.

In a society like ours, the emphasis is on preserving life as an incontrovertible good and ensuring a dignified death when there is no longer any choice. Furthermore, our society facilitates individual freedom of choice while protecting the common good. Although one could argue that we do not pursue these goals with the same alacrity for all persons, it is not surprising that, in our emerging practices concerning heroic measures and life prolongation, we have tended to vest in patients or their proxies the power to make treatment decisions. This combines the emphases on individual freedom of choice, preservation of life, and the right to a dignified death. The trend in our society toward ethical bases for suspending heroic measures in terminal conditions probably reflects not only the value of a dignified death (when quality of life is suffering greatly), but also the protection of the common good (because heroic measures are usually scarce and costly).

The enactment of policies and laws regulating medical practices are in the hands of elected officials and judges. These individuals will act differently depending on whether or not they are hardy or courageous. If they are hardy, they will accurately perceive the directions in medical policy that will fulfill the values of our society. This may involve resisting pressures from special interest groups and attempting to educate the public. In contrast, if officials and judges are nonhardy, they will fail to exercise leadership, catering to the strongest interest groups and the least thoughtful elements in the public, lest they be perceived as unusual or unreliable. In this, they will be venting their own fears, unresolved issues, and guilt, and the path to a comprehensively meaningful social policy may be lost.

The Role of the Psychologist

We have come a long way in considering the problems of life prolongation by heroic measures, various treatment options, and relevant psychosocial considerations. Now I will consider more specifically how the
psychologist can help.

Broaching the Question of Living or Dying With the Patient

As we have seen, the health professional has been given the counseling
role in the patient's treatment decision when heroic measures and serious or terminal illnesses are involved. We have also seen that this role
is uncomfortable for many physicians, who have not received much
psychological training and tend to define themselves in terms of their
technology. The psychologist is a logical professional for whom to turn
for the counseling role.

Working with physicians, patients, and family members, psychologists can facilitate communication. In broaching the questions of pain,
curtailment of functioning, cost, uncertain outcome, and the like that
surround the use of heroic measures to prolong life, the psychologist
can detect and help with the myriad reactions likely from patients and
family members. Perhaps even the physician can benefit in this difficult
situation from discussions with the psychologist.

The psychologist by no means should overlook the distinct possibility that, with encouragement, the patient may actually be able to
improve his or her psychosocial quality of life through the confrontation
of death. In this regard, I am reminded of a woman with advanced breast
cancer and her executive husband, the two of whom I counseled. As
they spent time together during her illness to make the decisions that
it required, she progressed from depression, and he from distancing, to
a vital relationship and intimacy that neither had known since youth.
The progression was from remembering the cherished past, to confronting unresolved relational problems in the present, to planning an immediate future that incorporated certain things the couple had put off.
In talking about one future plan, a trip around the world, the husband
said, "We're not even sure she'll make it to the trip, but the experiences
we had in the planning are worth every minute of it." Their relationship
had vastly improved although she was dying.

Helping With Quality of Life Issues

When the treatment decision is to prolong life through heroic measures,
this course of action may produce unforeseen or insufficiently appre-
ciated curtailments of quality of life. The psychologist can also be of

great help in this situation, offering the compassion and encouragement that will sustain patients in their conviction or helping them to resist further treatments. This assistance might also be extended to family members, overwhelmed by the patient's suffering, so that they can simultaneously gain strength themselves and be more capable of helping their relative.

The pain, outrage, dependency, and pathos of a patient whose quality of life has been impaired by heroic measures can also be difficult for other health professionals to bear. Indeed, a study (Wachter, Cooke, Hopewell, & Luce, 1988) concerning AIDS patients showed that the more experience medical residents had with the treatment of this terminal disease, the less willing they were to counsel and to prescribe the heroic measures that prolong life, but fail to obviate a range of increasingly debilitating symptoms. The psychologist may well have an important role to play in helping physicians and nurses to cope with their own intense or distancing reactions to the patient suffering in the wake of heroic treatment.

Enlisting the Mind as a Heroic Measure

Perhaps the most important role for the psychologist is to enlist the mind itself as a heroic treatment. As indicated earlier, extraordinary claims have been made by some physicians about the power of the mind to prolong life and to cure disease (e.g., Siegel, 1986, 1989; Simonton, et al., 1978). Psychological research also indicates that the hardiness mentioned earlier is an effective buffer against illness (e.g., Kobasa, Maddi, & Courington, 1981; Kobasa, Maddi, & Kahn, 1982; Kobasa, Maddi, Puccetti, & Zola, 1986).

When the patient wishes to fight debilitation and death, it is appropriate for the psychologist to help make this a mighty effort. Of equal importance, the psychologist can dissuade the patient from giving up too easily and encourage tenacity for life. There are currently several approaches to enlisting the mind as a heroic measure. Simonton et al. (1978) advocated visualization and thought patterns that aggressively combat the disease and depict vigorous health. Siegel (1986, 1989) convened individual and group counseling sessions emphasizing analysis of dreams and drawings in a supportive environment for his seriously ill patients. In addition, I have developed and validated a hardiness training course, for groups or individuals, that is based on the existential use of imagination, emotions, and actions to cope with dire circumstances in a manner that builds courage (Maddi, 1987).

The skeptic may find it difficult to entertain the thought that the mind might be enlisted in curing serious or even terminal diseases. The mind and the body are in such close interaction, however, that it is conceivable that intervening at the mental level might have beneficial bodily ramifications. Too many dramatic anecdotes of mentally induced cures are available for us to leave this stone unturned and call ourselves good scientists. If a patient's efforts to use the mind as a heroic measure fail, then it is time for the psychologist to help in preparation for a dignified death.

The Psychologist's Stance

What theoretical assumptions and practical techniques can the psychologist adopt in counseling patients facing treatment decisions that concern questions of life and death? In a sense, the psychologist is faced with an area in which theoretically consistent approaches fall away, and he or she does what is necessary. Certainly, a psychoanalytically inclined psychologist would not want to embark on a full-fledged analysis of the transference with a dying patient facing heroic measures. Nor is cognitive behaviorism likely to be of value, because it would tend to arrange schedules of reinforcement aimed at detaching the patient from the punishment of his or her physical and mental states by presenting more rewarding but distracting activities. A patient who is striving to make treatment decisions and to find the meaning inherent in catastrophic states does not need this.

Fear and depression are very understandable emotions in seriously ill or dying patients. The antidote to these negative states, which can also help patients to construct effective treatment decisions, is straightforward, reflective, and responsible consideration of the resources that are available in the attempt to regain health, the implications of failure in this attempt, and the needed grace to reach difficult conclusions on the basis of this input. Because it lends the necessary ingredient of courage or hardiness to these efforts, and because it is a natural basis for considerations of life and death, the existential approach would seem of great value and, I suggest, should be used more frequently.

Psychological Implications of Radical Life Prolongation

Let me end these remarks by supposing that at some time in the future, medical technology will be successful in radically prolonging the life span. Presumably, this would happen through a combination of effective heroic measures and a slowing of the aging process. I have already alluded to the economic and social problems that might ensue in such a scenario. So I will focus for a final moment on the psychological implications for individual personality or lifestyle.

If the existential position is accurate, courage or hardiness, and the strength of character and vivid appreciation of life that it imparts, is dependent on the contrast between health versus illness, youth versus old age, and—ultimately—life versus death. If illness, old age, and death recede, through the success of radical life prolongation, to remote, easily disregarded abstractions, then we risk trivializing personality and lifestyle in the process. We might love, work, think, and create less well, in unending banality. Clearly, this deteriorated quality of life would be an unfortunate side effect.

This alarming scenario is certainly why many thinkers, from the ancients to those of our own time, have warned that the natural order as expressed in the cycle of life and death should not be disturbed. If the cycle is altered, however, perhaps the previously mentioned economic disasters that might ensue would provide a sufficient basis for suffering so that banality of character would be avoided. But if the economic problem were solved, what would we do then? Would we be doomed to endless psychological indifference and indolence? Although I cannot be certain, perhaps there is a way of avoiding this deterioration. In the purely psychosocial realm, bases for risk and failure would still remain. People would still want those whom they love and admire to love and admire them back. There would still be the risks of parenthood, especially as the psychosocial possibilities for children expanded through radical life prolongation. There would still be the problems of poverty, discrimination, and improper power to be solved. In all this, there would be opportunities to experience the "small deaths" (Maddi, 1970) of reversals, losses, and humiliations that could hopefully be a springboard to depth of character. But without ample courage or hardiness with which to recognize these more subtle deaths for what they are and learn from them, I am afraid there is great psychosocial risk to humankind.

References

Acworth, A., & Bruggen, P. (1985). Family therapy when one member is on the death bed. *Journal of Family Therapy, 7*, 379–385.

Adams, J. L. (1989). Palliative care in the light of early Christian concepts. *Journal of Palliative Care, 5*, 5–8.

Allen, H. A., & Miller, D. M. (1988). Client death: A national survey of the experience of certified rehabilitation counselors. *Rehabilitation Counseling Bulletin, 32*, 58–64.

Amenta, M. M., & Weiner, A. W. (1981). Death anxiety and general anxiety in hospice workers. *Psychosocial Reports, 49*, 962–963.

Andersen, H. & MacElveen-Hoehn, P. (1988). Gay clients with AIDS: New challenges for hospice programs. *Hospice Journal, 4*, 37–54.

Angell, M. (1982). The quality of mercy. *New England Journal of Medicine, 306*, 98–99.

Angell, M. (1988). Euthanasia. *New England Journal of Medicine, 319*, 1348–1350.

Augustine, M. J., & Kalish, R. A. (1975). Religion, transcendence and appropriate death. *Journal of Transpersonal Psychology, 7*, 1–13.

Bass, D. M. (1985). The hospice ideology and success of hospice care. *Research on Aging 7*, 307–327.

Becker, E. (1973). *The denial of death*. New York: Free Press.

Bendor, S. J. (1989). Preventing psychosocial impairment in siblings of terminally ill children. *Hospice Journal, 5*, 153–163.

Brantley, P. J., Mosley, T. H., Jr., Bruce, B. K., McKnight, G. T., & Jones, G. N. (1990). Efficacy of behavior management and patient education on vascular access cleansing compliance in hemodialysis patients. *Health Psychology, 9*, 103–113.

Brescia, F. J., Sadof, M., & Barstow, J. (1984). Retrospective analysis of a home care hospice program. *Omega, 15*, 37–44.

Bulkin, J., & Lukashak, H. (1988). Rx for dying: The case for hospice. *New England Journal of Medicine, 318*, 376–378.

Callahan, D. (1986). Adequate health care and an aging society: Are they morally incompatible? *Daedalus, 115*, 247–267.

Callahan, D. (1987). *Setting limits*. New York: Simon & Schuster.

Carr, C. A., & Carr, D. M. (1985). Situations involving children: A challenge for the hospice movement. *Hospice Journal, 1*, 63–77.

Christensen, A. J., Smith, T. W., Turner, C. W., Holman, J. M., Jr., & Gregory, M. C. (1990). Type of hemodialysis and preference for behavioral involvement: Interactive effects of adherence in end-stage renal disease. *Health Psychology, 9*, 225–236.

Cicero, M. T. (1969). *De Senectute, Ciceron: Collection des Universités de France*. Paris, France Société d'Editions "Les Belles Lettres," p. 85.

Clark, A., & Fallowfield, L. J. (1986). Quality of life measurements with malignant disease: A review. *Journal of the Royal Society of Medicine, 79*, 165–169.

Coni, N. K. (in press). New medicine and old people. In F. C. Ludwig (Ed.), *The scientific exploration of aging: Its scope, its implications, and its limits*.

Cooper, C. L., & Mitchell, S. J. (1990). Nursing the critically ill and dying. *Human Relations, 43*, 297–311.

Cousins, N. (1979). *Anatomy of an illness as perceived by the patient*. New York: Norton.

Cummings, K. M., Becker, M. H., Kirscht, J. P., & Levin, N. W. (1981). Intervention strategies to improve compliance with medical regimens by ambulatory hemodialysis patients. *Journal of Behavioral Medicine, 4*, 111–127.

Davies, B. (1988). The family environment in bereaved families and its relationship to surviving sibling behavior. *Children's Health Care, 17*, 22–31.

Demi, A. S. (1984). Death of a spouse. In R. A. Kalish (Ed.), *Midlife loss: Coping strategies*. London: Sage.

Devins, G. M., Binik, Y. M., Gorman, P., Dattel, M., McCloskey, B., Oscar, G., & Briggs, J. (1982). Perceived self efficacy, outcome expectancies, and negative mood states in end-stage renal disease. *Journal of Abnormal Psychology, 7*, 241–244.

Dush, D. M. (1988). Trends in hospice research and psychosocial palliative care. *Hospice Journal, 4*, 13–28.

Eliot, T. S. (1952). *Four Quarters*. New York: Harcourt, Brace & World.

Erikson, E. H. (1950). *Childhood and society*. New York: Norton.

Etten, M. J., & Kosberg, J. I. (1989). The hospice caregiver assessment: A study of a case management tool for professional assistance. *Gerontologist, 29*, 128–131.

Evans, R. W., Manninon, D. L., Garrison, L. P., Jr., Hart, L. G., Blagg, C. R., Gutman, R. A., Hull, A. R., & Lowrie, E. G. (1985). The quality of life of patients with end-stage renal disease. *New England Journal of Medicine, 312*, 553–559.

Felton, B. J., & Revenson, T. A. (1984). Coping with chronic illness: A study of illness controllability and the influence of coping strategies on psychological adjustment. *Journal of Consulting and Clinical Psychology, 52*, 343–353.

Finn, P. E., & Alcorn, J. D. (1986). Noncompliance to hemodialysis dietary regimens: Literature review and treatment recommendations. *Rehabilitation Psychology, 31*, 67–78.

Foster, L. W., & Paradis, L. F. (1985). Hospice and death education: A resource bibliography. *Hospice Journal, 2*, 3–81.

Franco, V. W. (1985). The hospice: Humane care for the dying. *Journal of Religion and Health, 24*, 79–89.

Frederick, J. F., & Frederick, N. J. (1985). The hospice experience: Possible effects in altering the biochemistry of bereavement. *Hospice Journal, 3*, 81–90.

Frankl, V. (1960). *The doctor and the soul*. New York: Knopf.

Fried, C. (1976). Terminating life support: Out of the closet! *New England Journal of Medicine, 245*, 390–391.

Furman, E. (1984). Helping children cope with dying. *Journal of Child Psychotherapy, 2*, 151–157.

Garfield, C. A., & Jenkins, G. J. (1981). Stress and coping of volunteers counseling the dying and bereaved. *Omega, 12*, 1–13.

Geyman, J. P. (1983). Dying and death of a family member. *Journal of Family Practice, 17*, 125–134.

Gilbert, K. R. (1989). Interactive grief and coping in the marital dyad. *Death Studies, 6*, 605–626.

Gray, E. (1989). The emotional and play needs of the dying child. *Issues in Comprehensive Pediatric Nursing, 12*, 207–224.

Gray-Taft, P. A., & Anderson, J. G. (1986). Sources of stress in nursing terminal patients in a hospice. *Omega, 17*, 27–39.

Greenham, D. E., & Lohmann, R. A. (1982). Children facing death: Recurring patterns of adaptation. *Health and Social Work, 7*, 89–94.

Greif, G. L., & Porembski, E. (1988). AIDS and significant others: Findings from a preliminary exploration of needs. *Health and Social Work, 13*, 259–265.

Heinlein, R. A. (1973). *Time enough for love*. New York: Berkeley Books.

Husband, E., & Broadhus, D. A. (1984). Children's books and stories as therapeutic metaphors: An intervention with seriously ill children. *Paedovita, 1*, 17–21.

Janofsky, K. P., & Stuecher, V. H. (1983). Altruism: Reflections on a neglected aspect in death studies. *Omega, 14*, 335–353.

Jonsen, A. R., Cooke, M., & Koenig, B. A. (1986). AIDS and ethics. *Issues in science and Technology*, Winter, 56–65.

Johnson, L. R. (1985). Growth through grief: A program for college students experiencing loss. *Journal of College Student Personnel, 27*, 467–468.

Junge, M. (1985). The book about daddy dying. *Art Therapy, 2*, 4–10.

Kalish, R. A. (1972). Of social values and the dying: A defense of disengagement. *Family Coordinator, 21*, 81–94.

Kalish, R. A. (1974). Four score and ten. *Gerontologist, 14*, 129–135.

Kaplan De-Nour, A., & Czaczkes, J. W. (1972). Personality factors in chronic hemodialysis patients causing noncompliance with medical regimen. *Psychosomatic Medicine, 34*, 333–344.

Kaplan De-Nour, A., & Czaczkes, J. W. (1976). The influence of patient's personality on adjustment to chronic dialysis. *Journal of Nervous and Mental Disease, 162*, 323–333.

Kelly, G. A. (1955). *The psychology of personal constructs* (Vol. 1). New York: Norton.

Kierkegaard, S. (1954). *The sickness unto death.* New York: Doubleday.

Kirschling, J. M. (1989). Analysis of Bugen's model of grief. *Hospice Journal, 1*, 55–75.

Kobasa, S. C. (1979). Stressful life events, personality, and health: An inquiry into hardiness. *Journal of Personality and Social Psychology, 37*, 1–11.

Kobasa, S. C., Maddi, S. R., & Courington, S. (1981). Personality and constitution as mediators in the stress illness relationship. *Journal of Health and Social Behavior, 22*, 368–378.

Kobasa, S. C., Maddi, S. R., & Kahn, S. (1982). Hardiness and health: A prospective study. *Journal of Personality and Social Psychology, 42*, 168–177.

Kobasa, S. C., Maddi, S. R., Puccetti, M. C., & Zola, M. A. (1986). Relative effectiveness of hardiness, exercise, and social support as resources against illness. *Journal of Psychosomatic Research, 29*, 525–533.

Kohn, M., & Menon, G. (1988). Life prolongation: Views of elderly outpatients and health care professionals. *Journal of the American Geriatrics Society, 36*, 840–844.

Kubitz, N., Thornton, G., & Robertson, D. V. (1989). Expectations about grief and evaluation of the griever. *Death Studies, 13*, 39–47.

Kübler-Ross, E. (1969). *On death and dying.* New York: Macmillan.

Lardaro, T. A. (1988). Till death do us part: Reactions of therapists to the deaths of elderly patients in psychotherapy. *Clinical Gerontologist, 7*, 173–176.

Larson, E., & Spring, E. (1987, March). Life-defying acts. *Christianity Today*, pp. 17–22.

Lavoie, F., Vezina, A., & Dompierre, J. (1985). Recession de programmes de prevention favorisant e'adaptation an deces du (de la) conjoint (e). *Revue Quebecoise de Psychologie, 6*, 52–67.

Levitan, A. A. (1985). Hypnotic death rehearsal. *American Journal of Clinical Hypnosis, 27*, 211–215.

Lister, L., & Ward, D. (1985). Youth hospice training. *Death Studies, 9*, 353–363.

Longman, A. J., Lindstrom, B., & Clark, M. (1989). Preliminary evaluation of bereavement experiences in a hospice program. *Hospice Journal, 5*, 25–37.

Ludwig, F. C. (in press). Scientific exploration of aging, its scope and its limits. In F. C. Ludwig (Ed.), *The scientific exploration of aging: Its scope, its implications, and its limits.*

Mack, S. A., & Berman, L. C. (1988). A group for parents of children with fatal genetic illnesses. *American Journal of Orthopsychiatry, 58*, 397–404.

Maddi, S. R. (1970). The search for meaning. In M. Page (Ed.), *Nebraska symposium on motivation* (pp. 137–186). Lincoln, University of Nebraska Press.

Maddi, S. R. (1987). Hardiness training at Illinois Bell Telephone. In J. Opatz (Ed.), *Health promotion evaluation* (pp. 101–115). Stevens Point, WI: National Wellness Institute.

Maddi, S. R. (1988). On the problem of accepting facticity and pursuing possibility. In S. B. Messer, L. A. Sass, & R. L. Woolfolk (Eds.), *Hermeneutics and psychological theory: Interpretive perspectives on personality, psycho-therapy, and psychopathology.* New Brunswick, NJ: Rutgers University Press.

Maddi, S. R., & Kobasa, S. C. (1984). *The hardy executive: Health under stress.* Homewood, IL: Dow Jones-Irwin.

Martin, D., Martin, M., & Pierce, L. (1984). The dying child: Understanding developmental processes for parents and therapists. *Journal of Child and Adolescent Psychotherapy, 2,* 107–110.

Martin, K. B., & Berchulc, C. M. (1987). The effect of dying and death on therapists. *Physical and Occupational Therapy in Geriatrics, 6,* 81–87.

McCorkle, R. (1982). Death education for advanced nursing practice. *Death Education, 5,* 347–361.

Moore, T. E., & Mae, R. (1987). Who dies and who cries: Death and bereavement in children's literature. *Journal of Communication, 37,* 52–64.

Mor, V., & Hiris, J. (1983). Determinants of site of death among hospice cancer patients. *Journal of Health and Social Behavior, 24,* 375–385.

Moss, M. S., & Moss, S. Z. (1989). The death of a parent. In R. A. Kalish (Ed.), *Midlife loss: Coping strategies* (pp. 89–114). London: Sage.

Murphy, P., & Perry, K. (1988). Hidden grievers. *Death Studies, 12,* 451–462.

Neisser, U. (1964). Visual search. *Scientific American, 210,* 94–102.

O'Connor, J. A., Burge, F. I., King, B., & Epstein, J. (1986). Does care exclude care in palliative care? *Journal of Palliative Care, 2,* 9–15.

Palgi, P. (1983). Reflections on some creative modes of confrontation with the phenomenon of death. *International Journal of Social Psychiatry, 29,* 29–37.

Palmer, C. E. (1983). A note about paramedics' strategies for dealing with death and dying. *Journal of Occupational Psychology, 56,* 83–86.

Patterson, P. R. (1989). The pediatrician coping with the dying child. *Loss, Grief and Care, 3,* 191–198.

Payne, R., & Foley, K. M. (1987). Cancer pain. *Medical Clinic of North America, 71,* 153–352.

Peace, H. G., & Vincent, P. A. (1988). Death anxiety: Does education make a difference? *Death Studies, 12,* 337–344.

Pelletier, K. (1977). *Mind as healer, mind as slayer.* New York: Delacorte.

Pfost, K. S., Stevens, M. J., & Wessels, A. B. (1989). Relationship of purpose in life to grief experiences in response to the death of a significant other. *Death Studies, 13,* 371–378.

Pine, V. R. (1986). The age of maturity for death education: A socio-historical portrait of the era 1976–1985. *Death Studies, 10,* 209–231.

Poll, I. B., & Kaplan De-Nour, A. (1980). Locus of control and adjustment to chronic hemodialysis. *Psychological Medicine, 10,* 153–157.

Razavi, D., Delvaux, N., Farvacques, C., & Rabaye, E. (1988). Immediate effectiveness of brief psychological training for health professionals dealing with terminally ill cancer patients: A controlled study. *Social Science and Medicine, 27,* 369–375.

Razavi, D., Delvaux, N., & Desmarez, C. (1988). L'impact psychosocial de la maladie et de la mort de l'infant-conceptions actuelles. *Annales Medico-Psychologiques, 146,* 523–549.

Reynolds, D. K., & Kalish, R. A. (1974). Work roles in death-related occupations. *Journal of Vocational Behavior, 4,* 223–235.

Redleaf, D. L., Schmitt, S. B., & Thompson, W. C. (1979). The California Natural Death Act: An empirical study of physicians' practices. *Stanford Law Review, 31*, 913–945.

Rognlie, C. (1989). Perceived short- and long-term effects of bereavement support group participation at the Hospice of Petaluma. *Hospice Journal, 5*, 39–53.

Schulz, R., & Schlarb, J. (1987). Two decades of research on dying: What do we know about the patient? *Omega, 18*, 299–317.

Shipley, R. H., Butt, J. H., Horwitz, B., & Farbry, J. E. (1978). Preparation for a stressful medical procedure: Effect of amount of stimulus preexposure and coping style. *Journal of Consulting and Clinical Psychology, 46*, 499–507.

Shultheis, K., Peterson, L., & Selby, V. (1987). Preparation for stressful medical procedures and person x treatment interactions. *Clinical Psychology Review, 7*, 329–352.

Siegel, B. S. (1986). *Love, medicine, miracles.* New York: Harper & Row.

Siegel, B. S. (1989). *Peace, love, and healing.* New York: Harper & Row.

Simonton, O. C., Mathews-Simonton, S., & Creighton, J. (1978). *Getting well again.* Los Angeles: J. P. Tarcher.

Smith, S. P., & Varoglu, G. (1985). Hospice: A supportive working environment of nurses. *Journal of Palliative Care, 1*, 16–23.

Speck, P. (1985). Counseling on death and dying. *British Journal of Guidance and Counseling, 13*, 89–97.

Spero, M. H. (1981). Confronting death and the concept of life review: The Talmudic approach. *Omega, 12*, 37–43.

Stevens, M. J., Pfost, K. S., & Wessels, A. B. (1987). The relationship of purpose in life to coping strategies and time since the death of a significant other. *Journal of Counseling and Development, 65*, 424–426.

Storstein, L. (1988). How would changes in life-style be measured in cardiovascular disease? *American Heart Journal, 114*, 210–212.

Taylor, S. E. (1979). Hospital patient behavior: Reactance, helplessness, or control? *Journal of Social Issues, 35*, 156–184.

Thomasma, D. C. (1986). Quality of life judgments, treatment decisions, and medical ethics in geriatric medicine and social policy. *Clinics in Geriatric Medicine, 2*, 17–27.

Tillich, P. (1952). *The courage to be.* New Haven, CT: Yale University Press.

Toulmin, S. (1988). The recovery of practical philosophy. *American Scholar, 121*, 337–352.

Van Bommel, H. (1986). *Choices for people who have a terminal illness, their families, and their care-givers.* Toronto: NC Press.

Wachter, R. M., Cooke, M., Hopewell, P. C., & Luce, J. M. (1988). Attitudes of medical residents regarding intensive care for patients with the acquired immunodeficiency syndrome. *Archives of Internal Medicine, 148*, 149–152.

Wallston, K. A., Burger, C., Smith, R. A., & Baugher, R. J. (1988). Comparing the quality of death for hospice and non-hospice cancer patients. *Medical Care, 26*, 177–182.

Wanzer, S. H., Adelstein, S. J., Crawford, R. E., Federman, D. D., Hook, E. D., Moertel, C. G., Safar, P., Stone, A., Tansig, H. B., & van Eys, J. (1985). *The physician and the hopelessly ill patient.* New York: Society for the Right to Die.

Wanzer, S. H., Federman, D. D., Adelstein, S. J., Cassel, C. K., Cassen, E. H., Crawford, R. E., Hook, E. W., Lo, B., Moertel, C. G., Safar, P., Stone, A., & van Eys, J.

(1989). The physician's responsibility toward hopelessly ill patients: A second look. *New England Journal of Medicine, 320*, 844–849.

Weiner, A. (1986). Living with dying: A model for helping nursing home residents and staff deal with death. *Activities, Adaptation and Aging, 8*, 133–141.

Weisman, A. D. (1988). Appropriate death and the hospice program. *Hospice Journal, 4*, 65–77.

Wetle, T., Cwikel, J., & Levkoff, S. E. (1988). Geriatric medical decisions: Factors influencing allocation of scarce resources and the decision to withhold treatment. *The Gerontologist, 28*, 336–343.

Williams, G. (1989, May). Resurrection for sale. *Longevity*, pp. 23–27.

Wilson, D. C. (1988). The ultimate loss: The dying child. *Loss, Grief and Care, 2*, 125–130.

SANDRA M. LEVY

HUMANIZING DEATH: PSYCHOTHERAPY WITH TERMINALLY ILL PATIENTS

S andra M. Levy is associate professor of psychiatry and medicine at the University of Pittsburgh and director of the Division of Bio-behavioral Oncology at the Pittsburgh Cancer Institute, University of Pittsburgh School of Medicine. Before joining the faculty at Pittsburgh, she was chief of the Behavioral Medicine Branch at the National Cancer Institute, Bethesda, Maryland. While at the National Cancer Institute, she held a faculty appointment in psychiatry at the Johns Hopkins University School of Medicine. Levy was awarded the PhD in clinical psychology from Indiana University at Bloomington in 1975. She received the Distinguished Doctoral Dissertation Award from the American Psychological Association (Division 12) for her doctoral research on schizophrenia.

Levy's major interest over the last several years has been in examining the role that behavior plays as a biological response modifier relevant to disease end points, both cancer risk and progression, as well as infectious sequelae in essentially healthy populations. She has been particularly interested in studying aspects of the immune system and the effects of central nervous system input on various types of lymphocytes, relevant to tumor control or spread. More generally, as a behavioral scientist, she has written extensively about behavior as it contributes to cancer control.

Levy is the author of *Behavior and Cancer: Life-style and Psychosocial Factors in the Initiation and Progression of Cancer*. She has also edited *Biological Mediators of Behavior and Disease: Neoplasia* (1982) and *Cancer, Nutrition, and Eating Behavior* (with T. Burish and B. Meyerowitz, 1985). She is codirector of an NIMH-supported, postdoctoral training program in behavioral immunology and has received a number of federal and private research grants to support her program of research in this area. Levy has also published numerous articles and chapters related to behavior and its role in the prevention and treatment of cancer. She is a consulting editor for the *Journal of Human Stress, Annals of Behavioral Medicine*, and *Journal of Professional Psychology* and is an elected member of the Academy of Behavioral Medicine Research.

SANDRA M. LEVY

HUMANIZING DEATH: PSYCHOTHERAPY WITH TERMINALLY ILL PATIENTS

Introduction

One of the earliest written forms of the "living will," published in 1969 and distributed by the Euthanasia Educational Council, begins: "Death is as much a reality as birth, growth, maturity and old age—it is the only certainty of life" (Behnke & Bok, 1975). Since the case of Karen Ann Quinlan came to the public's attention, the issues surrounding the conditions in which people approach death have gained prominence through the mass media and have been a focus for discussion among health care professionals, ethicists, and laypersons alike.

In this chapter, I will address some of the bioethical issues surrounding the right to die embedded in the common law right of personal autonomy. Within the medical, legal, and ethical context, I will then consider the role of the psychologist in the therapeutic treatment of the dying and of their families. Finally, a summary of issues will be followed by a consideration of research and professional opportunities for psychologists working with the dying in the biomedical arena.[1]

---

[1]Because of limitations of space in this chapter, I will not consider the rather large collection of psychological literature on the perceptions of death and dying, death anxiety, attitudes toward death, and the like. Rather, this chapter will have a distinctly clinical, therapeutic focus, with a major emphasis on the psychologist as part of the health care delivery team in a medical or hospice setting. Also, because of space constraints, the focus will be primarily on adult, rather than pediatric, patients.

The following is a caveat regarding my personal perspective: Cancer has been the realm of my experience, both in terms of research and in terms of clinical focus. In fact, most of the literature in the area of death and dying is concerned with malignancy, despite the obvious fact that people die from other diseases (cardiovascular diseases kill more Americans than cancer does). Thus, although a major focus in this chapter is on death from cancer, the actual process of dying involves a common pathophysiological pathway of vital system failure (Younger et al., 1985), where many, if not most, issues generalize from one *cause* of death to another. My concern here is with the final trajectory and with the role that the psychologist might play in humanizing the process of death.

Dying in America: Trends and Countertrends

Geyman (1983) discussed a number of underlying issues that have generated problems related to death and dying in this country. For example, many physicians commonly rely on *curative* care, even when the patient's disease or condition can no longer be altered. Additional experimental or potentially curative protocols are often administered, risking iatrogenic morbidity at high financial and emotional cost to the patient and family. A related problem is the inadequate preparation for death on the part of the patients, because in many cases patients have not considered the treatment (or nontreatment) options for themselves and have not left explicit directives for their physicians and family members—that is, they have not, in a real sense, maintained control over their own care in its final stages—inappropriate *curative* rather than *carative* protocols are undertaken.

In fact, the rise in medical specialization and subspecialization coupled with advanced diagnostic and therapeutic technology has produced a medical care environment in which the machinery of curative care is frequently in direct conflict with what those who are dying actually need. "[M]echanical maintenance without medical purpose" (Geyman, 1983, p. 126) is often more frightening than the actual fact of dying for many patients. As a consequence, a number of countertrends have begun to emerge in the terminal patient care setting, reflecting a *consumer movement* that gives dying patients and their families greater rights in determining the conditions and timing of death.

The first clear countertrend was the development of the hospice movement, which was given impetus by the establishment of St. Christopher's Hospice in London in the late 1960s. Patient autonomy and the right to die in as comfortable a manner as possible are key principles to hospice care. The hospice philosophy, which spread to this country, stresses individualized nursing and medical care, with the major goal of reducing discomfort in the patients while fostering the participation of family members in the patient's care. Hospices have developed in this country that are both in-patient facilities and "hospices without walls," the latter with around-the-clock staff, allowing the patient to die, in relative comfort, in his or her own home.

The second countertrend has been a growing wave of popular support for the concept of a "living will." (I will consider at greater length such wills in the next section.) Living wills are signed and witnessed documents directing the attending physician regarding the extent of extraordinary care the patient wishes to receive. In effect, the growing legal recognition of such directives vests in the patient the power to exercise autonomy over the process of his or her own dying through such explicit instructions to their physicians.

A third and final, explicit countertrend accompanying the development of technology that allows the almost in perpetuum maintenance of patients in vegetative states is the so-called no-code orders placed in patient charts. Such patients are not to be resuscitated (usually in the case of cardiopulmonary failure) under certain, carefully prescribed conditions (Meisel, Grenvik, Pinkus, & Snyder, 1986; Ruark, Raffin, & the Stanford University Medical Center Committee on Ethics, 1988). This countertrend reflects growing acceptance within medical circles that sustained, vegetative life without hope is potentially inhumane and even cruel. As we shall see below, the criteria for no code are simple and rather straightforward; applying them in individual cases usually is not.

Time To Quit: Bioethical Issues

Emphasis on patient autonomy and patients' rights to control the progress of their own medical care is a relatively recent trend in our society and in the biomedical community. In recent years, there have been a number of studies conducted and articles written on issues concerning the withdrawal of life support (Bedell & Delbanco, 1984; Cohen, 1982; Crispell & Gomez, 1987; Emanuel, 1988; Finucane, Shumway, Powers & D'Alessandri, 1988; Haug, 1978; Johnson and Justin, 1988; Lo & Jonsen, 1980; Meisel et al., 1986; Pinkus, 1984; Ruark et al., 1988; Shmerling, Bedell, Lilienfeld, & Delbanco, 1988; Stephens, 1986; Wanzer et al., 1984; Wanzer et al., 1989; Younger et al., 1985; Zimmerman et al., 1986), including the seminal report prepared by the President's Commission for the Study of Ethical Problems in Medicine and Biomedical and Behavioral Research, "Deciding to Forego Life-Sustaining Treatment" (1983).

Crispell and Gomez (1987) defined terminal illness as "a state of disease characterized by progressive, irreversible deterioration, with impairment of function and survival limited in time" (p. 74). The ability of the medical profession to prolong the dying process has created the current, confusing situation for all concerned: The patient, his or her family, and the medical care team itself. As Crispell and Gomez pointed out, the situation is particularly difficult in large, university teaching hospitals. Such institutions, referred to as *tertiary* care centers, are usually hospitals of "last resort" for many patients, many of whom are in fact terminal and have been referred by community physicians who can no longer manage their care. At training facilities, interns and residents, who are on the front line of care for such patients, order innumerable tests and curative treatments in order to provide every medical opportunity for patients under their care. Crispell and Gomez suggested that over the next decade, Congress will be making very critical decisions regarding the use of the "health dollar." Most people agree that the government should not be deciding who is to live and who is to die, and they agree that this issue should be resolved by those most concerned—the medical profession and the public, both informed by ethical debate. Crispell and Gomez warned about the "slippery slope" to euthanasia "by omission, if cost containment becomes the major force in formulating policy on the proper care of the dying" (p. 74).

Here, I will consider the levels of medical care for patients, including the withdrawal of life support, with a focus on issues surrounding cardiopulmonary resuscitation (CPR). Inextricably linked with these issues are the principles of autonomy and privacy of patients, levels of patient competence to make decisions, and the question of surrogates as decision makers. I will also consider the questions of assisted suicide and euthanasia, which have become much more publicly debated in medical circles in recent years.

Levels of Medical Care

Wanzer et al. (1984) described four levels of care for patients that can be collapsed into two major categories: (a) basic life support, which essentially includes general medical care (including antibiotics, drugs, surgery, and artificial hydration and nutrition) and general nursing care, with efforts to make the patient comfortable (pain relief and hydration and nutrition as dictated by the patient's thirst and hunger); and (b) advanced life support, which includes emergency resuscitation and intensive care procedures. I would like to point out that patients requiring only basic life support are usually clearly in the terminal phase of an irreversible disease. For these individuals, routine monitoring procedures (e.g., temperature and pulse monitoring) as well as diagnostic measures and the use of antibiotics may be ended. In fact, all procedures not aimed at patient comfort should be discouraged.

Withdrawing Life Support

The final common pathway of terminal illness almost invariably involves loss of cardiopulmonary function. The Uniform Determination of Death Act, which was developed in collaboration with the American Bar Association, the American Medical Association, and the National Conference of Commissioners Uniform State Laws, states that an individual who has sustained either (a) irreversible cessation of circulatory and respiratory functions or (b) irreversible cessation of all functions of the entire brain, including the brain stem, is dead. There is the "in between" state where brain function, for all human practical purposes, has ceased, but the individual continues to exist in a vegetative state. Occasionally, patients such as Karen Ann Quinlan remain suspended between living and dying, unassisted by respirator, for lengthy periods of time. In the latter case, the individual is not technically dead, but the vegetative coma is usually irreversible.

My focus in this chapter will be on the first definition of death and on forgoing heroic measures to sustain cardiopulmonary function. I will address the latter area in a more limited way, when considering the withholding of basic life support. (The interested reader is referred to the President's Commission for the Study of Ethical Problems in Medicine and Biomedical and Behavioral Research, 1983, for a further discussion of the nature and implications of the nearly brain dead, persistent vegetative state.)

One countertrend to modern technological advances in medicine briefly discussed earlier is the placement of no-code orders in terminally ill patients charts (Meisel et al., 1986; Ruark et al., 1988). Generally three criteria should be met in applying the no-code order: "1) the patient should be irreversibly and terminally ill, so that resuscitation would not change the inevitable outcome (the basis for this judgment should be explicitly documented); 2) the no-code order should be discussed with the patient and family, and their desires should be documented in the medical record; and 3) the order must be written" (Geyman, 1983, p. 126).

Psychologically, not initiating heroic life support measures, such as CPR, is more palatable than withdrawing support measures that have already been initiated. However, the same principles apply. Ideally, a discussion and understanding will have taken place between the patient and care givers during the preterminal phase, at which time the patient's intention in this regard has been made clear. If this process has been carried out, and if the patient is still competent during the terminal phase (or if incompetent, a surrogate has been named), then decisions regarding the withdrawal or noninitiation of intensive care measures can be made with some certainty.

Ruark et al. (1988) made the following suggestions: Reasonable judgment should be exercised regarding the likelihood of benefit from further treatment; the patient's competence must be assessed and professionally evaluated if there is any doubt in this regard (by a psychologist or other mental health professional); unanimity regarding disposition should be sought from all the members of the health care team; the patient's wishes must be vigorously sought (through consultation with the still competent patient, or if the patient is no longer competent, through a surrogate or a living will left by the patient and through personal knowledge of the patient's wishes by the physician (Ruark et al., 1988, p. 29).

Ruark et al. discussed the handling of such decisions with families of patients who are no longer entirely competent (which will be most patients at the end of their lives). They suggested not rushing the decision, but they also suggested giving temporal guidelines in order to help the family adapt within a time frame that has been provided by the care team.

> For example, the doctor might say to the adult children of a man who had been on a ventilator with respiratory and renal failure for two weeks, "If we see no signs that your father has improved over the next 72 hours, then we believe you should consider withdrawing life support. We believe your father is suffering and has essentially no chance to regain any reasonable quality of life, and to withdraw life support would allow him a more peaceful and dignified death." (1988, p. 29)

Because cardiopulmonary failure is the most common pathway to death, almost every person who dies is a potential candidate for CPR. In fact, with the increasing number of "rescue squads" and community training programs for lay people, even those who die at home are no longer immune to the benefits and burdens of CPR. This is the only medical intervention that can be performed by a nonphysician without a physician's order. In fact, a physician's order is required only if CPR is to be withheld, even if the patient is attended to at his or her own home!

CPR raises many ethical questions. A patient in cardiopulmonary failure presents a medical emergency to the health care team, generally galvanizing the medical staff into emergency action. Unless physicians have ascertained beforehand the patient's wishes in this regard, quick action must be taken before severe organ damage, including irreversible brain damage, occurs. Most patients do not realize the aggressive, invasive, and sometimes brutal nature of the procedure or the possibility of experiencing additional iatrogenic damage from severe blows to the sternal region and so on. Bones are commonly broken during the procedure, particularly in the frail elderly, who already have compromised brittle bones and cartilage.

A recent study by Bedell, Delbanco, Cook, and Epstein (1983) showed that only 14% of all patients who received CPR over a one-year period survived to leave the hospital. Only 19% of all patients discussed the procedure with their physicians, and in only 33% of the cases was the family consulted about resuscitation. Similar findings have emerged in more recent studies (Bedell & Delbanco, 1984; Younger et al., 1985). Bedell and Delbanco (1984) also found that when they subsequently interviewed 24 competent patients who survived CPR, in order to compare their actual attitudes about resuscitation with their physicians' opinions about their attitudes, they found only a weak correlation between the physician's opinion about the patient's wishes and the preference expressed by the patient. Shmerling et al. (1988) carried out a survey study of 22 male and 53 female, competent, ambulatory patients regarding their wishes with respect to CPR. They found that only 7% of those interviewed had an accurate understanding of what CPR meant. The study showed that 87% thought discussion about CPR should take place routinely, but only 3% had previously discussed this issue with their physicians. Most felt that such discussions should take place during periods of relative health, and that patients' views should be part of the medical record.

Many physicians clearly do not broach the subject of life sustaining procedures with their patients, and, as Wanzer et al. (1989) discussed, medical schools do not yet train their young physicians to deal skillfully with such crucial issues. In a study that was carried out by Finucane et al. (1988), the authors conducted a clinical trial with elderly outpatients, randomly subjecting half to a condition in which physicians, during an outpatient visit, would initiate a discussion of life support procedures under conditions of extreme or incapacitating illness. The study found that some emotional reactivity was elicited in patients when confronted unexpectedly with the topic; one patient out of a sample size of 74 became visibly upset. "Nevertheless, all patients who received the intervention and completed the study were pleased that their doctor had asked" (p. 322). There were real methodological limits to this study, including most importantly the possibility of a biased sample. Doctors participating in the study excluded all patients who could not, in their judgment, "meaningfully participate in the discussion," or if there was any likelihood of "significant emotional harm." Nevertheless, the results suggest that the topic of limits to terminal care could be broached in a vulnerable population, still competent to consider the issues and make reasonable decisions in partnership with their care givers.

The withdrawal of basic life support, such as withdrawal of nutrition supplied through feeding tubes, is still rather controversial, although legally, the question of withdrawal of nutrition and hydration from incompetent patients has been treated in the same way as has withdrawal of advanced life support (Ruark et al., 1988). No one is comfortable with the notion of a loved one "starving to death," and, legal sanctions aside, guilt will remain in family members if the issues are not dealt with and resolved. (I will return to the role of the psychologist in this regard.) Ruark et al. (1988) pointed out that the key to resolving the ethical problems in this area lies in clarifying the patient's interests.

Again, if the patient is competent, that is, has *decision-making capacity* (a term that Wanzer et al., 1989, preferred to *competent*, because the latter is a legal determination that can only be made by the courts, and the former is a descriptive term for what is ethically required in the situation), then a decision can be reached regarding the proper course to take during terminal care. The competent patient has final authority over his or her care on the basis of the courts' recognition of the common law right to autonomy (to be left alone to make one's own choices) as well as the patient's constitutional right to privacy (to be protected from unwanted invasive medical treatment). However, if the patient is not competent, other means must be found to arrive at a just decision in the patient's interest. Wanzer et al. (1984) described the following four categories of incompetent patients: (a) patients with brain death, who are considered medically and legally dead and for whom no further treatment is required; (b) patients in a persistent vegetative state in which it is morally justifiable to withhold antibiotics and artificial nutrition and hydration, allowing the patient to die; (c) severely and irreversibly demented patients, for whom treatment that serves mainly to prolong dying may be withheld if the patient's previous wishes are known (if not known, then the most humane course must be pursued, including the provision of comfort only); and (d) elderly patients with permanent mild impairment of competence (the "pleasantly senile"), for whom comfort and emergency care are provided only sparingly in the light of prospects for improvement and of the patient's or surrogate's wishes.

The whole question of surrogates for the patient is a complex one. First, the attending physician has the responsibility to decide on the competence of the patient. Clearly, patients falling into the above categories are permanently incompetent, but other conditions such as dementia, depression, mental retardation, delirium, psychosis, and so on, reduce, but do not necessarily permanently eliminate, capacity for choice. Surrogates for patients who are judged to lack decision-making capacity, ideally, should have known the patient recently and well, and be able to speak with confidence regarding the now incompetent patient's wishes. If the patient has not designated a surrogate, then the attending physician is responsible for finding one. Generally, a close family member or friend will be selected. If the patient has none, then a member of the health care team, in consultation with a hospital ethics committee, may serve that role: "In case of intractable conflict among family members and/or close friends over who ought to serve as surrogate, or if there is no one to serve, judicial appointment of a surrogate must be sought" (Meisel et al., 1986, p. 242).

The attending physician is not compelled to accept the patient's choice of surrogate, and there are a variety of reasons why a surrogate's decision will not be honored. For example, if the attending physician cannot comply for strong reasons of conscience, or if he or she has a good reason to believe that the surrogate's decision would be contrary to the wishes of the patient, or if the surrogate himself or herself lacks decision-making capacity, his or her views will not be followed by the attending physician responsible for the case.

Gaps in the System

Despite all of the reasons to the contrary, the fact is that few patients currently execute living wills, and very few appoint surrogates to act in their stead during terminal illness. "There is a large gap between what the courts now allow with respect to withdrawal of treatment and what physicians actually do. All too frequently, physicians are reluctant to withdraw aggressive treatment from helplessly ill patients, despite clear legal precedents" (Wanzer, et al., 1989, p. 845).

Moreover, as I discussed earlier, very few physicians currently initiate discussions with their patients regarding their wishes during terminal care when the patients are competent and have the energy to consider such options in a rational manner. The issue of cognitive set colored by current conditions could also be considered here. The possibility exists that intentions will shift from the perspective of a relatively well individual to a different perspective assumed under entirely different and life-threatening conditions. This complicating psychological factor has not, to my knowledge, been considered in any of the legal and bioethical discussions of living wills and surrogate knowledge, but the reader would do well to ponder the implications in this regard. A related and complicating factor is the problem of determining what constitutes an outdated surrogate appointment or written directive and how often, or how recently, such arrangements need to be reaffirmed.

Hastening Death

In the most recent statement regarding medical responsibility toward the hopelessly ill (Wanzer et al., 1989), the heretofore taboo topics of assisted suicide and euthanasia were considered. With respect to physician-assisted suicide, I asked the question whether it is ever justifiable, and one is left with the clear impression that it not only is, but that it is frequently undertaken. The frequency of physician-assisted suicide is unknown because, although no physician has yet been jailed for such assistance, it is still illegal in many states to help someone take his or her life. I noted that if there is no treatable component to a patient's depression, and the patient's pain or suffering is refractory to treatment, then the wish for suicide may be rational. Wanzer et al. (1989) concluded that assisted suicide should be considered a "separate alternative" in such cases. For psychologists, the ethical rules that govern our profession may not apply in such cases. Normally, when a patient under our care threatens suicide, we are obliged to alert authorities and prevent self-destruction. However, in the case of terminally ill patients, the rules break down. Again, the question of assisted suicide is being addressed more openly by all professionals that care for the terminally ill.

Euthanasia requires the physician to perform a medical procedure that causes death directly. This too, is carried out in this country, probably not infrequently, but statistics are unknown because it is illegal and the physician is subject to prosecution. However, recently euthanasia has been discussed more publicly in the United States, and the public response has been increasingly favorable. Results from a Roper poll of 1,982 adults carried out in 1988, asking whether a physician should be lawfully able to end the life of a terminally ill patient at the patient's request, showed that 58% of respondents said *yes*, 27% said *no*, and 10% were undecided. Some laypersons and physicians fear that active voluntary euthanasia could lead to involuntary euthanasia and then to murder (the "slippery slope" hypothesis).

Nevertheless, as Wanzer et al. (1989) concluded, the medical profession and the public will undoubtedly continue to debate the role of euthanasia in the years to come, so that "people dying of an incurable painful disease should be allowed (and in this case, assisted) to end their lives before the disease runs its course" (Wanzer et al., 1989, p. 844).

Psychological Needs of Dying Patients and of Their Families

The discussion of care for the terminally ill, when considering the technological possibility of extended "life" maintenance, coupled with the financial and emotional stress experienced by patients and families, at a time when the focus is on the patients' (and by extension, surrogates') rights ultimately to decide about the termination of care, provides some insight into the psychological complexities and needs of all involved. I will now turn to consider the role of the psychologist in this setting.

Psychosocial stress and mental health needs that arise from impending death can certainly be considered both from the vantage point of the patient who is terminally ill and from the vantage point of close family members who frequently suffer as much, and sometimes more, than the patient. An early study of psychiatric symptomatology among seriously ill cancer patients (Craig & Abeloff, 1974), that used the Symptom Distress Checklist (SCL-90) as a psychiatric screening instrument, indicated that more than half of the 30 patients studied showed moderate to high levels of depression, and 30% had elevated levels of anxiety. Surprisingly, nearly one quarter of the patients had overall symptom patterns virtually identical with those seen in patients admitted to an emergency psychiatric service. The study was methodologically limited because of a small sample size and a heterogeneous group of patients who were unmatched for treatment conditions. Self-report was corroborated by one of the authors, an oncologist, who "categorized all patients in terms of perceived global emotional distress at the time of administration of the SCL-90" (Craig & Abeloff, 1974, p. 1325). Even though one might question the criterion validity of such an external corroboration, the findings of substantial pathology, or at least high clinical distress levels, are consistent with other studies (Goldberg, 1981; Katon, 1982) that have been carried out on other seriously ill populations.

Katon (1982) pointed out that despite the high prevalence and incidence of depression in hospitalized, seriously ill patients, primary care physicians frequently do not recognize serious psychiatric disorders. In a study by Moffic and Paykel (1975), the total rate of depression for seriously ill medical inpatients was found to be 28.3%, yet only 4% of the 153 patients were recognized by the medical staff as being depressed. Similarly, Knights and Folstein (1977) reported a 35% false–negative diagnostic rate by staff physicians in their study of hospitalized patients. Although these studies were carried out in the 1970s, the situation has not changed appreciably in the current decade.

Organic Contributors

Depression, of course, often presents itself as a somatic complaint, and, for patients who are already seriously physically ill, it can exacerbate the experience and expression of somatic distress. It is frequently difficult to disentangle the psychic from the somatic contributors to depression. For example, it is not always clear whether the concomitant conditions of depression and illness result from central nervous system monoamine changes triggered by the medical disease or whether depression ensues in response to the patient's perception of the advanced nature of the disease process. The diagnosis of a major depressive episode classically relies on the presence of somatic symptoms (e.g., appetite loss, sleep disturbance, and fatigue). In all likelihood, particularly in advanced disease patients who have generalized systemic disorder that is due to major organ failure, both primary affective disorder and mood disorder that is secondary to the disease or its treatment (or both) underlie the presentation of clinical depression (Plumb & Holland, 1981).

In advanced cancer, as well as in other serious medical conditions, a variety of organic factors may play a causal role in depression, as well as in anxiety states, dementia, and delirium. Metabolic encephalopathies are among the most frequent neurological conditions compromising the sensorium and manifested as depression. Hypercalcemia, concomitant with a number of cancers, including advanced breast cancer with bone involvement, is associated with psychiatric symptoms, including depression. Additionally, a variety of ectopically produced hormones (including adrenocorticotrophic hormone, which is secreted by lung tumors) are responsible for changes in mental status in some patients (Bukberg, Penman, & Holland, 1984; Katon, 1982; Peteet, 1979). Brain tumors are often responsible for mental status changes, and occult brain metastases should always be suspected in advanced malignancy when a change in what had been a stable mental status occurs. Personality changes and other mental symptoms have been reported in such patients (Ken, Schapira, & Roth, 1969; Malamud, 1967).

Nutritional status impairment and drug-induced changes are also important contributors to depression and other mental disorders in patients with advanced diseases. For example, steroids may produce a variety of psychiatric changes, including psychosis, depression, or even euphoria. Central nervous system depressants will often produce mental states resembling depression, and a variety of treatments, including irradiation therapy or palliation may well produce symptoms of depression or other mental dysfunction (Goldberg, 1981; Kathol & Petty, 1981). Finally, for patients experiencing severe pain that is organically based, the distress-related contribution to existing depression is very hard to diagnose. Frequently, when appropriate analgesics are administered, the depressive symptomatology will also resolve (Goldberg, 1981; Katon, 1982).

Psychosocial Contributors

Before discussing the sources of negative mood and distress in dying patients, it is important to consider that most patients, even those who are aware of their terminal condition, remain resilient, courageous, and even hopeful into the end stage of disease. In fact, hope dies hard. As death approaches, the object of hope may shift. Initially, the patient hopes for recovery, but when the disease progresses, his or her perspective shifts, and he or she hopes to live until spring (until the graduation, the wedding, etc). Later, hope may become invested in family members who will survive and in a peaceful death for himself or herself. If the individual is religious, he or she may hope for eternal life and eventual reuniting with family (Stedeford, 1979, p. 11).

Nevertheless, feelings of alienation or abandonment by friends, family, employers, and even the physician are not uncommon in patients and generate distress and depression in them. Friends and family frequently withdraw for a variety of reasons, ranging from feelings of inadequacy and guilt to fears of contamination from the disease. Communication patterns during terminal illness are often complicated by past family dynamics in which unresolved tensions and conflicts aggravate the already tense situation surrounding withdrawal-of-treatment decisions that need to be made by the patient or his or her family.

As the disease progresses, the patient also faces abandonment from the physician. Loss of interest and "therapeutic zeal" is frequently perceptible to the patient and family. An underlying sense of failure on the part of the physician may reinforce his or her belief that there is nothing left to do for the patient, and decreasing visits during hospital rounds could be viewed by patients as abandonment by the medical care giver.

Loss of control is inevitable to varying degrees in all forms of illness, and most clearly, during advanced and terminal illness in which once independent and autonomous individuals become increasingly helpless as the disease progresses. The importance of this factor varies depending on the personality of the individual as well as the age of the patient. For example, adolescents who developmentally are at a state at which independence and autonomy are hard won milestones may be particularly resistant to forced dependency. Reactions to the latter may be displayed in "acting out" behavior such as noncompliance with essential therapeutics.

Finally, physical loss, including the loss of physical integrity, can lead to mourning and depression, as well as to problems of mobility and self-care. As patients enter the last predeath "common pathway," such loss is inevitable and can create feelings of helplessness, if not sensitively addressed by care takers and therapists. It is important to consider that patient withdrawal from others in the last stage of their illness may not be due to depression, but rather may be attributed to natural separation processes that occur at the end of life.

Suicide is also a major risk factor in patients with chronic, advanced medical conditions, including a reported 400% increased in incidence of suicide in dialysis patients compared with community controls (Abram, 1978). Goldberg (1981) suggested that every patient with advanced medical illness and depression should undergo inquiry into suicidal ideation. He suggested a gradual series of probes such as "I wonder if you're becoming very discouraged? Do you find yourself having crying spells? What sort of thoughts go through your mind at those times? Have you thought that rather than going on like this, life may not be worth living? Have you actually thought of what you might do to end your life?" (Goldberg, 1981, p. 376). When suicidal ideation is uncovered, appropriate referrals can then be made for treatment of the underlying depression. Katon (1982) concluded that screening and adequate treatment for even moderately severe depression can be achieved and that, when depression is successfully managed, somatic complaints also may be improved.

The main burden of support frequently falls on family members, particularly on the spouse or significant other, and frequently the health care provider loses sight of the fact that such individuals are under a great deal of strain—emotional and, frequently, financial in nature. In addition, role shifts typically accompany the dying of a significant family member, and the whole family as a unit suffers. Frequently, when such internal reorganization occurs, the ongoing sense of family itself is threatened. Geyman (1983) pointed out that this is especially true in a small nuclear family, which is more vulnerable to these stresses and is potentially less functional than an extended family.

Psychological Support for Dying Patients and Their Families

Clearly, the terminal situation is bioethically and biologically complex and patients and their families frequently experience role conflict and other interpersonal sources of distress. For the patient, depression and other psychological disturbances are frequently exacerbated by systemic organic contributors to cognitive dysfunction and overall poor quality of life. It is important now to consider aspects of psychological support for patients and their close family members.

Weisman (1986) developed three concepts related to terminal disease that have therapeutic meaning. These concepts include what he referred to as safe conduct, anticipatory grief, and an appropriate death. In a sometimes lyrical piece, he addressed some of the central therapeutic concepts that I will discuss below, but they are worth describing here in Weisman's terms as an entrée to the topic.

By *safe conduct*, Weisman meant the provision of decent care, including palliation or relief from distressing symptoms, which becomes more crucial the closer a patient comes to the end of his or her life. But more positively, Weisman also meant "intuitive assistance," supporting the very sick patient through progressively disappointing reverses during the process of dying and the termination of life.

Anticipatory grief, as the term is commonly understood, helps to prepare the survivors for the inevitable loss to come. For Weisman, the main aim of anticipatory grief is to initiate bereavement, not just lessen the intensity of grief to a more manageable degree. Anticipatory grief does not shelter the mourner from a profound sense of loss, but "eases the accommodation to actual death, without wholly blunting the shock" (p. 28). Attention to family members' grief by health care professionals, and particularly by psychologists on the care team, can facilitate the preparatory adjustment so essential to their own mental health.

Finally, Weisman discussed his concept of an *appropriate death*—death that is timely, desirable, and desired. He viewed an appropriate death as simply the outcome of good psychosocial management, a manifestation of the safe conduct referred to earlier. That is, the prerequisite of an appropriate death is the management of pain and suffering. Beyond pain management, however, an appropriate death also includes other forms of psychosocial relief, including social bonding, adequate psychosocial support from significant others, and good medical care.

I will return later to the consideration of places for care for such patients, but will consider here psychotherapeutic approaches to the patient and family, including assistance with decisions about terminal care and its aftermath, across the stages of end-stage disease. That is, I will discuss the following: appropriate psychological support for patients who have been diagnosed with an incurable and terminal disease but who are in the "preterminal" phase of the process; support for patients and families when the patient is considered in a terminal stage or has only a short period of time to live; and support for families after the patient has died. Along with considerations of psychotherapeutic support across the stages of final illness, I will also consider alternative places of treatment for such patients and their families.

Psychotherapy and Support in Preterminal and in Terminal Care Decisions

Preterminal Care

Psychosocial interventions. The earlier in the terminal process that the patient is referred to a psychologist or other mental health professional, the greater the opportunity to prevent premature deterioration in quality of life and to help the patient and family use coping strategies as the disease takes its course. Moreover, patients have more energy at this point of the process to focus on major issues of concern to them and to their families. At this stage there is a greater likelihood that new adaptive strategies can be learned as a function of treatment. In short, it is here that something akin to psychotherapy (as usually meant by psychotherapists by the term) can actually be implemented. As we saw earlier, however, depression and other psychiatric disorders are frequently overlooked or are tolerated to a greater degree than they need to be ("Wouldn't you be depressed if you had cancer?"). Thus, precisely when the patient and family might benefit most from the intervention of a mental health professional, the care takers who might make the referrals are frequently uninformed about the dysfunction potentially present and about the opportunity to treat successfully the maladaptation, and enhance quality of life at this stage of the patient's life.

Ideally, it is in this phase that family members are also brought into the therapeutic process, because again, the fact of a dying family member introduces stress into the whole family unit. It is also the family that is a main source of potential support for the patient. As Goldberg (1981) pointed out, the therapist should look to the spouse (or another key support person) as an important ally in the treatment process. Whenever possible, spouses should also be brought into the therapy session, and their interaction should be observed in order to facilitate better understanding and communication within the family network. Goldberg also suggested that the "loss of physical intimacy, which often accompanies severe illness, may leave a couple stranded from each other if they are unaccustomed to sharing intimate feelings in other ways" (p. 375).

Supportive therapy for patients can also be provided by means of group therapy. In two early reports of group therapy for dying patients (Franzino, Geren, & Meiman, 1976; Furgeri, 1978), general conclusions suggested that the groups provided significant mutual support for their members in the face of death. In one case (Franzino et al., 1976), the group formed specifically to provide support for patients already terminally ill; in the other case (Furgeri, 1978), the group formed as an ongoing, cohesive group, one of whose members became terminally ill and died during the course of group therapy. The group experience specifically enabled the members to make their needs and wants known because of their shared experience.

Places for treatment. In addition to considering psychotherapeutic needs and other support requirements that a dying patient and his or her family have, it is also important to consider alternative places for such treatments for the varying stages of dying. Because the preterminal patient is treated generally on an outpatient basis, obviously the patient and his or her family can be treated individually, in groups in the therapist's office, or in the hospital setting providing primary biomedical treatment for the patient. In addition, for the still relatively independent, intact preterminal patient, other resident treatment options have developed over the past decade throughout the country.

Two resident group treatment facilities for relatively independent cancer patients have developed and flourished. The Wellness Community, founded in 1982 by Harold Benjamin in Santa Monica, California, now has facilities located in a number of other communities around the country. As a lawyer, Benjamin had many years of prior experience with Synanon, a group treatment program for drug abusers. He observed that Synanon participants became part of a therapeutic community and participated in the program on the premise that people fighting to recover from a malady can psychologically benefit from long-term intimate contract with others facing the same or similar problems and can benefit from continuous exposure to therapeutic groups. From 1976 to 1981,

Benjamin became involved in the Center for the Healing Arts in West Los Angeles, created to train psychologists to treat individuals with life-threatening illnesses. The Center for the Healing Arts led Benjamin to start the first Wellness Community, a resident facility providing a meeting place for cancer patients and counselors and providing psychological support as an adjunct to medical treatment. (For a more extensive discussion of the history and concept of this facility, see Benjamen & Trubo, 1987).

The second resident facility is Commonweal, which was founded by Michael Lerner approximately a decade ago and is located in Bolinas, California. Cancer patients visit the facility for extended workshops aimed at enhancing their quality of life. These resident sessions include training in relaxation, yoga, meditation, and general group support, both spiritual and psychological in nature. Lerner is a dedicated and serious scholar, who has evaluated the field of complementary cancer therapies, among other subjects.

Both Commonweal and The Wellness Community are open to all forms of physical healing, but are conservative in the sense that they view all nonmedical forms of healing as "adjuvant" additions to standard therapy. At any rate, both facilities provide the opportunity for residential, therapeutic communal experiences for seriously ill and terminal patients. Although I am not aware of any systematic evaluation research being carried out within either setting, the patients who choose to participate appear to benefit psychologically from the group support experience.

Aims of therapy. Something akin to psychotherapy is possible at the preterminal stage of disease, nevertheless, therapy with the dying is different in the sense that the probing and uncovering of dynamic conflicts is less appropriate here, and the use of denial and other defense mechanisms, as long as they are adaptive, is not only tolerated, but fostered. The goal is not to change the individual's personality, life-style, or fundamental values, but to build on strengths within the patient and his or her family that can assist adaptive strategies and that are already at least a nascent part of the patient's repertoire of adaptive behaviors.

In a thoughtful article on psychotherapy with the dying patient, Stedeford (1979) defined an adaptive reaction as "one which brings most relief or causes least suffering to the patient himself and also to his family and those patients and staff with whom he is in close contact" (pp. 7–8). Although there is obviously no single way to approach dying patients, Stedeford urged approaching them with an open mind and respect, recognizing that they are frequently more aware of their needs, strengths, and weaknesses than is the therapist. He also urged therapists to help patients rely on coping mechanisms that have allowed them to function in an adaptive way during past crises. For Stedeford, the basic aim of therapy is to establish good rapport with the patient. In some cases, this understanding can then be imparted to a close family member, and the therapist can withdraw, having served as a bridge to the patient's own natural support system.

Defenses are an important element of coping for the dying patient, and the therapist needs to examine carefully whether the defenses being used are adaptive or not before intervening. The most common defense used by terminal patients is denial, and Stedeford elaborated on various forms of this mechanism. In addition to existential denial (the inherent capacity to suppress awareness of the dangers ubiquitous to everyday life), there are *psychological denial* and what Stedeford referred to as *nonattention denial*. Psychological denial, the defense against potentially overwhelming anxiety, is manifested in the patient who intellectually has heard the diagnosis of his or her condition and the attending prognosis but, on another level, has not absorbed the facts. The patient will continue to "ask around" until someone gives an answer regarding his or her condition that he or she can accept as tolerable. Such a behavioral pattern frequently gives the patient time to absorb more gradually the full impact of what has been told to him or her, and no intervention except compassionate support is required. Psychological denial only creates a problem when it interferes with communication or with eventual planning for terminal care.

Stedeford wrote that nonattention denial occurs when the patient has fully grasped the situation, gotten his or her affairs in order, and then sets the situation aside in order to continue to enjoy his or her life to the extent possible. Such denial is only maladaptive when this defense blocks communication or planning.

Geyman (1983) suggested that while a patient is still relatively independent is the time when decisions about terminal care could be gently raised, such as decisions about location of terminal care (e.g., hospice, hospital, or home), about living wills and desires regarding termination of treatment, and about plans for family and business affairs, including a will. Geyman provided a model approach to these issues by suggesting that the care giver (including the psychologist as a member of the team) might say: "There may come a time when you become too ill to communicate with us about your medical care; are there any specific instructions you might want us to follow at such a time?" (1983, p. 129). With recurrence of disease and with the failure of multiple therapies, usually the patient gradually recognizes that he or she is in fact dying. This dawning of awareness may allow the patient to become more open to discussion of issues such as the timely establishment of no-code orders.

Terminal Care

Supportive interventions. Dying patients have at minimum four basic requirements (Geyman, 1983): independence (as much as possible), dignity, acceptance by others, and relief from symptoms (primarily pain, nausea, elimination dysfunction, nutritional deficits, and sleeplessness). Symptoms of depression are frequently present during patients' terminal phase of disease and are likely to be generated by the disease process itself, as well as by possible psychosocial factors (e.g., isolation) that exacerbate the condition. Family dynamics remain an issue and a frequent source of depression and distress for patients, even during the terminal phase of illness. In fact, families that are troubled tend to become more so under conditions of such extreme stress. As Stedeford (1979) pointed out, terminal illness strains any marriage, but particularly the ones in which there are underlying and unresolved problems. Whatever the underlying causes of depression, antidepressants should be considered for terminally ill patients experiencing serious depressive symptoms. The use of tricyclic antidepressants for depression associated with advanced cancer, for example, has proven especially useful in reducing sleeplessness, crying spells, and social withdrawal (Katon, 1982).

In addition to pharmacological interventions at the terminal phase of care, there are still aspects of the patient's behavior that can be the focus for improving the quality of life that remains. For example, fear of loss of control, as discussed earlier, can be a major issue at this time. However, patients can still exercise some control over their environmental and treatment. They can experience a sense of control by continuing to be involved in family decisions; by learning behavioral methods, such as systematic relaxation and selfhypnosis to decrease side effects of drugs as well as of the disease itself; and by making small decisions, such as which vein to select for venipuncture. The psychologist, as part of the therapy team, can assist in this regard by identifying environmental factors that can be controlled by the patient, even for those confined to a bed in a hospital room or in a hospice. Quality of life can be improved by such careful attention of modifiable aspects of the patient's life, when coupled with an understanding of the patient's need in this regard.

Places to die. A major decision that needs to be made by the patient, family, and physician is where the patient will be cared for during the dying process. Options include a hospital, a nursing home, a hospice, or at home, the latter often facilitated by a hospice or by the availability of other personnel for home visits that provide patient and family support. The question of locale for dying is ultimately a matter of family and patient preference, but options should be considered and discussed with the patient's physician or with other health care professionals. Most Americans turn to the hospital for dying, and most current medical and nursing literature focuses on improving hospital care for the dying patient. Yet, as suggested earlier, hospitals, which emphasize cure or rehabilitation, may hinder the provision of appropriate care for the dying (Dupee, 1982).

Early studies (Krant, 1972; Martinson, 1976; Nielsen, 1972; and Rose, 1976) suggested that terminally ill patients cared for in their homes experienced more dignity and comfort, and their families had less difficulty adjusting to the impending death than did patients cared for in the hospital. More recently, Putnam, McDonald, Miller, Dugan, and Lougue (1980) conducted structured interviews with 44 patients and family pairs to determine where patients and family members wished themselves or their ill family member to die. Approximately 50% of the respondents indicated a preference for home care, but there was only a 27% paired agreement within the sample. Paired agreement was higher (approximately 50%) when a hypothetical situation was presented to both respondents describing the availability of ideal home care support from the community.

Whether the patient dies in the hospital, home, or in a "hospice with walls" (as opposed to hospice care in his or her own home), his or her needs for humane care and psychological support, as well as the needs of the primary family members, remain the same. As a key member of the care team, the psychologist clearly has a particular opportunity to support the dying patient and family members in making decisions, clarifying conflicts, and improving quality of life for all touched by the dying process.

Follow-Up Care

Wherever the patient dies, because of the increase in prevalence of morbidity and even mortality in surviving family members (Helsing & Szklo, 1981), it is very important for the therapist to see the surviving family members, particularly the spouse, for follow-up visits after the death. Just as oncologists and other physicians frequently see the family a few weeks after the death of the patient for a "postmortem" session regarding the death in order to answer lingering questions and to review the course of the terminal illness with the family, there should also be a "psychological postmortem" with a member of the mental health team.

Geyman (1983) suggested that on the first follow-up visit, the family support system and the grieving process should be discussed, as well as possible lingering guilt over any termination-of-life decisions made by family members. In the second visit, discussion areas may include the impact of the death on other family members and the possibility of future resumption of intimate relationships on the part of the surviving spouse. Counseling during this period frequently involves emotional ventilation and support of the family members in working through the grief period to the extent that the survivors become actively engaged with the next stage of their life. As Geyman pointed out, for the average adult, this process takes between 18 and 24 months. He suggested inquiring into details of the death or recollecting about the lost family member to facilitate the process of catharsis.

Postscript: Implications for the Therapist

Psychotherapists bring to the therapeutic process both their cognitive abilities and their emotional empathy, which have been developed through long years of training and practice (Lewis, 1979; Ralph, 1980). In turn, therapists continue to develop professionally and personally from their ongoing experiences with patients, as well as with others in their personal lives. Situations in which the therapist feels helpless to alter any final outcome, and those that confront the therapist with his or her own death, may precipitate intense reactions and have profound consequences for the therapist's own life. In a thoughtful piece written by Lewis (1982), the author described the conduct of therapy with four acquaintances who were dying. In describing the process of therapy, he noted that, in the end, each friend seemed either to have accepted death or to have resigned himself or herself to it. For those whose dying took several months, there seemed also to be an element of relief as they approached the end. Lewis stressed, however, that this final stage of resignation (and even relief) should not be interpreted as a final stage in an orderly sequence of stages, as depicted by Kübler-Ross (1969) and others. The sole commonality was resignation and acceptance, or even welcome of death in the end.

After their deaths, he analyzed the impact of the experience on his own defensiveness during therapy (occasionally forgetting an appointment or withdrawing from his wife), as well as the impact of the experience on his own life. He suggested that the experience encouraged him to look at the ways that his own total life-style could be seen as a way of avoiding thoughts and concerns about death. Lewis quoted Walker Percy (1980), who referred to this "everydayness" in the following way: "Not once had he been present for his life. So his life had passed like a dream. Is it possible for people to miss their lives in the same way one misses a plane? And how is it that death, the nearness of death, can restore a missed life?" (quoted in Lewis, 1982, p. 264).

In Lewis' reflections on the meaning of his friends dying and his reactions to their death, he believes that he has become a more sensitive therapist, particularly with individuals who seek his help who are "successful" for all practical purposes, but nevertheless filled with dread and despair about their lives. He also believes he is better able to respond to individuals who wish to speak of suicide and convey his response in a more sensitive way.

Whenever a psychologist treats a dying patient, the experience itself presents the potential for profound learning in regard to the therapist's own life, both as a professional and as a person. Because everyone dies, moreover, perhaps the dividend is greatest for the care giver.

Research and Professional Challenges

It should be clear from this chapter that there are numerous research issues that are worthy of pursuit regarding psychotherapy with the terminally ill. Very little good research has been carried out in terms of careful, systematic assessment of cognitive, mood, and behavioral morbidity in the terminally ill. Rarely, if ever, have prospective studies been conducted that examine mental health morbidity in carefully defined patient groups and that distinguish between biological and psychosocial sources of dysfunction. Certainly, careful assessment and a descriptive understanding of the clinical phenomena provide the foundation for systematic treatment planning, whether this planning is carried out within a clinical trial, within a research framework, or whether intervention is planned within a clinical setting to ameliorate patient suffering.

Beyond assessment, it appears to me that the greatest challenge and excitement in this area concerns the mental health and biological effects of psychosocial interventions. Many questions remain unanswered. Although there have been a number of studies that have examined the mental health effects of intervention strategies in the terminally ill (Cain, Kohorn, Quinlan, Latimer, & Schwartz, 1986; Epstein, 1982; Franzino et al., 1976; Furgeri, 1978; Gordon et al., 1980; Stedeford, 1979), many of the therapies remain unspecified, and in all likelihood, unreplicable. Individualized "counseling" and "psychological support" have been carried out in an unsystematic and unspecified manner, and much of the literature in this area is anecdotal and clinical in nature. Studies using carefully defined and replicable protocols carried out with "clean" samples (i.e., with patients matched for disease, stage, and treatment characteristics) are still quite rare.

Important dependent variables include not only functional capacity and quality of life, variously defined, in both preterminal and terminal patients under medical care, but also might include the psychosocial morbidity that is common in families with preterminal and terminal patients, the latter disrupting the fabric of the family as a system.

Professional opportunities are also more than obvious from the discussion in the first two sections of this chapter. The mental health professional has the opportunity to play an essential role in the team caring for the terminal patient. As noted in the section on bioethics, despite the fact that some states recognize the living will and the right of the patient or surrogate to suspend life-sustaining treatment, there are still gaps in the system. In many cases, (perhaps most), the actual decision-making process is an arduous one, fraught with anxiety, anger, and despair on all sides—physicians and families alike. The mental health professional can function as an essential bridge between the patient and his or her needs and the sometimes competing needs of the system within which dying takes place.

I firmly believe that the role of the psychologist in the medical setting, particularly the tertiary care setting where terminally ill patients and their families are seen, presents an opportunity for significant professional contribution toward comprehensive patient care. Assessment and treatment issues generated within this setting also offer a research challenge for the behavioral scientist with potential contributions to knowledge on the frontiers of medicine. Finally, systematically documenting the psychological consequences of prolonged dying, for both care givers and families of terminally ill patients, provides an opportunity for psychologists to play an important role in shaping health care policy in this country as we approach the twenty-first century.

References

Abram, H. S. (1978). Repetitive dialysis. In T. P. Hackett & N. H. Cassem (Eds.), *Massachusetts General Hospital handbook of general hospital psychiatry* (pp. 342–364). St. Louis, C. V. Mosby Company.

Bedell, M. D., & Delbanco, T. L. (1984). Choices about cardiopulmonary resuscitation in the hospital. *The New England Journal of Medicine, 310*, 1089–1092.

Bedell, S. E., Delbanco, T. L., Cook, E. F., & Epstein, F. H. (1983). Survival after cardiopulmonary resuscitation in the hospital. *The New England Journal of Medicine, 309*, 496–576.

Behnke, J., & Bok, S. (1975). *The dilemmas of euthanasia* (p. 152). Garden City, NY: Doubleday and Company.

Benjamin, H. H., & Trubo, R. (1987). *From victim to victor*. Los Angeles: Jeremy P. Tarcher Inc.

Bukberg, J., Penman, D., & Holland, J. (1984). Depression in hospitalized cancer patients. *Psychosomatic Medicine, 46*, 199–212.

Cain, E. N., Kohorn, E. I., Quinlan, D. M., Latimer, K., & Schwartz, P. (1986). Psychosocial benefits of a cancer support group. *Cancer, 57*, 183–189.

Cohen, C. B. (1982). Interdisciplinary consultation on the care of the critically ill and dying: The role of one hospital ethics committee. *Critical Care Medicine, 10*, 776–784.

Craig, T. J., & Abeloff, M. D. (1974). Psychiatric symptomatology among hospitalized cancer patients. *American Journal of Psychiatry, 131*, 1323–1327.

Crispell, K. R., & Gomez, C. F. (1987). Proper care for the dying: A critical public issue. *Journal of Medical Ethics, 13*, 74–80.

Dupee, R. M. (1982). Hospice: Compassionate, comprehensive approach to terminal care. *Terminal Care, 72*, 239–246.

Emanuel, E. J. (1988). A review of the ethical and legal aspects of terminating medical care. *The American Journal of Medicine, 84*, 291–302.

Epstein, R. S. (1982). Outpatient psychotherapy in conjunction with a home care nurse. *Bulletin of the Menniger Clinic 4*(5), 445–457.

Finucane, T. E., Shumway, J. M., Powers, R. L., & D'Alessandri, R. M. (1988). Planning with elderly outpatients for contingencies of severe illness. *Journal of General Internal Medicine, 3*, 322–325.

Franzino, M. A., Geren, J. J., & Meiman, G. L. (1976). Group discussion among the terminally ill. *International Journal of Group Psychotherapy, 26*(1), 43–48.

Furgeri, L. B. (1978). The celebration of death in group process. *Clinical Social Work Journal, 6*, 90–99.

Geyman, J. P. (1983). Problems in family practice. Dying and death of a family member. *The Journal of Family Practice, 17*, 125–134.

Goldberg, R. J. (1981). Management of depression in the patient with advanced cancer. *Journal of the American Medical Association, 245* (pp. 373–376).

Gordon, W. A., Friedenbergs, I., Diller, L., Hibbard, M., Wolf, C., Levine, L., Lipkins, R., Ezrachi, O., & Lucido, D. (1980). Efficacy of psychosocial intervention with cancer patients. *Journal of Consulting and Clinical Psychology, 48*, 743–759.

Haug, M. (1978). Aging and the right to terminate medical treatment. *Journal of Gerontology, 33*, 586–591.

Helsing, K. J., & Szklo, M. (1981). Mortality after bereavement. *American Journal of Epidemiology, 114*, 41–52.

Johnson, R. A., & Justin, R. G. (1988). Documenting patients' end-of-life decisions. *Nurse Practitioner, 13*(6), 41–52.

Katon, W. (1982). Depression; somatic symptoms and medical disorders in primary care. *Comprehensive psychiatry, 23*, 274–287.

Kathol, R. G., & Petty, F. (1981). Relationship of depression to medical illness. *Journal of Affective Disorders, 3*, 111–121.

Ken, T. A., Schapira, K., & Roth, M. (1969). The relationship between premature death and affective disorders. *British Journal of Psychiatry, 115*, 1277–1282.

Knights, E. B., & Folstein, M. F. (1977). Unsuspected emotional and cognitive disturbance in medical inpatients. *Annals of Internal Medicine, 87*, 274–287.

Krant, M. J. (1972). The organized care of the dying patient. *Hospital Practice, 7*, 101–108.

Kübler-Ross, E. (1969). *On death and dying.* New York: Macmillan.

Lewis, J. M. (1979). The inward eye: Monitoring the process of psychotherapy. *Journal of Continuing Education in Psychiatry, 40*, 17–26.

Lewis, J. M. (1982). Dying with friends. Implications for the psychotherapist. *The American Journal of Psychiatry, 139*, 261–266.

Lo, B., & Jonsen, A. R. (1980). Clinical decisions to limit treatment. *Annals of Internal Medicine, 93*, 764–768.

Malamud, N. (1967). Psychiatric disorder with intracranial tumors of the limbic system. *Archives of Neurology, 17*, 113–128.

Martinson, I. M. (1976). Why don't we let them die at home? *RN, 39*, 58–65.

Meisel, A., Grenvik, A., Pinkus, R. L., & Snyder, J. V. (1986). Hospital guidelines for deciding about life-sustaining treatment: Dealing with health "limbo." *Critical Care Medicine, 14*, 239–246.

Moffic, H. S., & Paykel, E. S. (1975). Depression in medical inpatients. *British Journal of Psychiatry, 126*, 346–353.

Nielsen, S. (1972). Home visiting for patients receiving special care. *Nurse Clinics of North America, 7*, 383–387.

Percy, W. (1980). *The second coming.* New York: Farrar, Straus, & Giroux.

Peteet, J. R. (1979). Depression in cancer patients. An approach to differential diagnosis and treatment. *Journal of the American Medical Association, 241*, 1487–1489.

Pinkus, R. L. (1984). Families, brain death, and traditional medical excellence. *Journal of Neurosurgery, 60*, 1192–1194.

Plumb, M., & Holland, J. (1981). Comparative studies of psychological function in patients with advanced cancer II: Interviewer-rated current and past psychological symptoms. *Psychosomatic Medicine, 43*, 243–254.

President's Commission for the Study of Ethical Problems in Medicine and Biomedical and Behavioral Research. (1983). *Deciding to forego life-sustaining treatment*. New York: Concern for dying: An Educational Council.

Putnam, A. T., McDonald, M. M., Miller, M. M., Dugan, S., & Lougue, G. L. (1980). Home as a place to die. *American Journal of Nursing*, 1451–1453.

Ralph, N. B. (1980). Learning psychotherapy: A developmental perspective. *Psychiatry, 43*, 243–250.

Rose, M. A. (1976). Problems families face in home care. *American Journal of Nursing, 76*, 416–418.

Ruark, J. E., Raffin, T. A., & the Stanford University Medical Center Committee on Ethics. (1988). Initiating and withdrawing life support. *The New England Journal of Medicine, 318*, 25–29.

Shmerling, R. H., Bedell, S. E., Lilienfeld, A., & Delbanco, T. L. (1988). Discussing cardiopulmonary resuscitation: A study of elderly outpatients. *Journal of Internal Medicine, 3*, 317–321.

Stedeford, A. (1979). Psychotherapy of the dying patient. *British Journal of Psychiatry, 135*, 7–14.

Stephens, R. L. (1986). 'Do not resuscitate' orders. *Journal of the American Medical Association, 255*, 240–241.

Wanzer, S. H., Adelstein, S. J. Cranford, R. E., Federman, D. D., Hook, E. D., Moertel, C. G., Safar, P., Stone, A., Taussig, H. B., & Eys, J. (1984). The physician's responsibility toward hopelessly ill patients. *The New England Journal of Medicine, 310*, 955–959.

Wanzer, S. H., Adelstein, S. J., Cranford, R. E., Federman, D. D., Hook, E., D., Moertel, C. G., Safar, P., Stone, A., Taussig, H. B., Eys, J. (1989). The physician's responsibility toward hopelessly ill patients. A second look. *The New England Journal of Medicine, 320*, 844–849.

Weisman, A. (1986). Terminality and interminable psychoanalysis: An incomplete report. *Psychotherapy and Psychosomatics, 45*, 23–32.

Younger, S. J., Lewandowski, W., McClish, D. K., Junknialis, B. W., Coulton, C., & Bartlett, E. T. (1985). "Do not resuscitate" orders. Incidence and implications in a medical intensive care unit. *Journal of the American Medical Association, 253*, 54–57.

Zimmerman, J. E., Knaus, W. A., Sharpe, S. M., Anderson, A. S., Draper, E. A., & Wanger, D. P. (1986). The use and implications of do not resuscitate orders in intensive care units. *Journal of the American Medical Association, 255*, 351–356.

EARN CONTINUING EDUCATION CREDITS THROUGH HOME STUDY PROGRAMS BASED ON THE APA MASTER LECTURES

The Master Lectures, presented each year at the APA Convention, can be used to earn Category I Continuing Education (CE) Credits through the successful completion of a test developed to accompany most volumes of this series. The following Home Study Programs are available:

1990—"PSYCHOLOGICAL PERSPECTIVES ON HUMAN DIVERSITY IN AMERICA"

1989—"PSYCHOLOGICAL ASPECTS OF SERIOUS ILLNESS"

1988—"THE ADULT YEARS: CONTINUITY AND CHANGE"

1987—"NEUROPSYCHOLOGY AND BRAIN FUNCTION"

1986—"CATACLYSMS, CRISES, AND CATASTROPHES: PSYCHOLOGY IN ACTION"

1985—"PSYCHOLOGY AND WORK: PRODUCTIVITY, CHANGE, AND EMPLOYMENT"

1984—"PSYCHOLOGY AND LEARNING"

For more information about the Home Study Programs, detach and mail the form below (please print, type, or use pre-printed label), or telephone 202/955-7719, 9 a.m.–5 p.m. EST/EDT.

- ✂

Please send me more information about APA's Home Study Programs for Continuing Education Credit.

Name: _____

Address: _____

_____

_____
   (City)   (State)   (Zip code)

Daytime phone: _____ / _____
            Area Code

Mail this form to the following address:

Continuing Education Home Study Programs
American Psychological Association
1200 17th Street, N.W.
Washington, DC 20036
202/955-7719